■ ■ ■ READING *PROJECT*

CONTEMPORARY NORTH AMERICAN POETRY SERIES Series editors Alan Golding, Lynn Keller, and Adelaide Morris

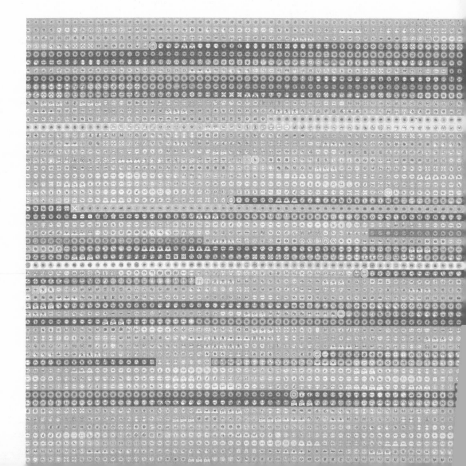

READING *PROJECT*

A COLLABORATIVE ANALYSIS
OF WILLIAM POUNDSTONE'S

Project for
Tachistoscope
{Bottomless Pit}

JESSICA PRESSMAN, MARK C. MARINO, AND JEREMY DOUGLASS

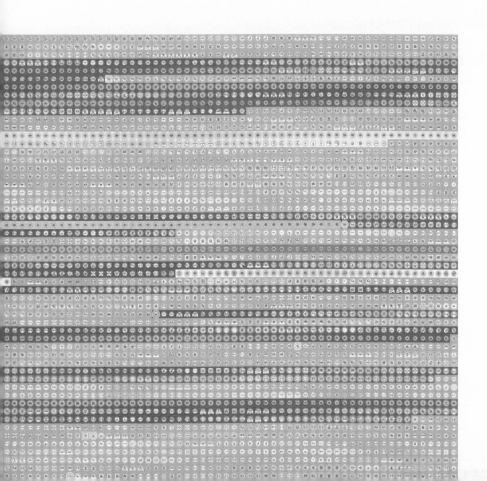

University of Iowa Press, Iowa City 52242
Copyright © 2015 by the University of Iowa Press
www.uiowapress.org
Printed in the United States of America

DESIGN BY TERESA W. WINGFIELD

The University of Iowa Press is a member of Green Press
Initiative and is committed to preserving natural resources.

Printed on acid-free paper

LIBRARY OF CONGRESS CATALOGING-IN-PUBLICATION DATA

Reading Project : a Collaborative Analysis of William Poundstone's
Project for Tachistoscope {Bottomless Pit} / Jessica Pressman,
Mark C. Marino, Jeremy Douglass.
     pages   cm
  ISBN 978-1-60938-345-9 (PBK), ISBN 978-1-60938-346-6 (EBK)
    1. Poundstone, William.   2. Hypertext literature—History
and criticism.   3. Literature and technology.   I. Pressman,
Jessica.   II. Marino, Mark C. III. Douglass, Jeremy.
  PS3566.08136Z84   2015
  818'.54—dc23   2014034890

■ ■ ■ To all the collaborators who made this book possible, especially our loving families

CONTENTS

ACKNOWLEDGMENTS

OUR GREATEST DEBT is to Adelaide "Dee" Morris, who heard our ELO conference presentation back in 2010 and pulled us aside to suggest that we turn our approach into a book. With grace and acuity, she shepherded the concept through to this book, along with her fellow editors Alan Golding and Lynn Keller. We are deeply (bottomless pit grateful) to Dee for her vision, support, and unsurpassed good nature. Dee, Alan, and Lynn are the best kind of series editors. They believed and supported this book at each level, turn, and glitch. We thank them and all of the staff at the University of Iowa Press for turning our reading project into *Reading* Project.

This would have been a very different book if we had read some other work of digital literature. We extend our sincerest thanks to William Poundstone; first, for his fascinating, intoxicating, and highly-addictive literary work, and, second, for sharing its source files with us. Further thanks to Philip Dorin, Keith Gustafson, Tom Klein who helped with the analysis of the code.

Although it did not support the writing of this book, our ACLS Collaborative Research Fellowship did support our development of a platform to promote work like ours, collaborative scholarly inquiry of complex, digital works like *Project*. We are grateful to ACLS for taking a chance on our collaboration. We also extend sincere thanks to Lucas Miller, Craig Dietrich, and Erik Loyer for their expertise in helping us to design a new collaborative space online using Scalar.

We are fortunate to have mentors who taught us, inspired us, and supported us from our grad school days to today. We love them and savor the opportunity to thank them here: Kate Hayles, Alan Liu, Lev Manovich, and Rita Raley.

Finally, there are not enough words to thank those partners who labored with us as we labored to write this book. Thank you to our partners—Brad Lupien, Barbara Marino, and Holly Rushing—for their unflagging support, generosity, and patience.

INTRODUCTION

WILLIAM POUNDSTONE'S *Project for Tachistoscope {Bottomless Pit}* (2005) is a beautiful and challenging work of electronic literature that presents a high-speed, one-word-at-a-time text animation accompanied by frenetic visual and aural effects.[1] The text tells the tale of "the Pit," a mysterious abyss of unknown depth that grows and shifts unexpectedly, reshaping and destabilizing the community surrounding it. Complementing the instability of the narrative, the tale is presented through a digital poetic that is dazzling and disorienting. The complex interplay of content and form produces a work that dramatizes a crucial moment in the evolution of reading and writing practices: ours. Like the people living around the Pit in the diegetic narrative, readers of the work are confronted with the realization that the world as we know it is changing beneath our feet. In this piece that revolves around the challenges of interpretation, that shifting ground is literature, poetics, and the reading practices we bring to bear on them.

This book is about reading *Project*, but it also is a project about reading.[2] It presents interwoven interpretations in three voices, following three very different readers as we embark on an experiment in collaboratively reading *Project* as text, as image, and as software. Our story began as a mystery that led to an adventure. What did *Project* mean, and how did it make meaning? How would our different approaches address such questions, and what discoveries would we make together that we could never make separately? In each chapter we document the process as our readings were developed, complicated, reversed, and synthesized. After presenting that journey, we use our conclusion to reflect on what this process taught us about multimodal literature, collaborative interpretation, and reading in this digital era.

A TALE TOLD THROUGH A TACHISTOSCOPE

The title of *Project for Tachistoscope {Bottomless Pit}* identifies a poetic "project" that—like sheet music or a medical slide—is an offering "for" a particular instrument; the project requires that instrument in order to fulfill its purpose and be performed. That instrument (or

FIGURE 0.1: *Project* start screen with seven entryscreen icons. (Screenshot by authors; with the permission of William Poundstone.)

family of instruments) is a "tachistoscope," first developed in the nineteenth century for cognitive and optical research. The form of the title suggests two different ways of approaching Poundstone's work. On the one hand, it is the story of a Bottomless Pit: a tale told in text, image, and sound. On the other hand, the story is a "project" developed for and alongside a specific reading machine: a piece of custom-written code that operates as a software "tachistoscope." Together the story and scope form one work, *Project*. In *Reading* Project, we approach this work by examining the allegorical narrative about the Bottomless Pit as a meditation on the medium that delivers it, exploring what it has to say about reading machines and the writerly and readerly projects they support.

Programmed in Flash and published online, *Project* produces a different combination of text, image, and sound each time it runs. Some of these differences are immediately obvious, while others we only discovered gradually as we pursued our collaborative methods. The nature of *Project*'s variability is difficult to ascertain in part because *Project* teases you, its reader, into approaching it within a particular set of conceptual frameworks. It does this framing through a set of short expository paratexts, which we call "the entryscreens." When *Project* first loads, but before the narrative animation begins, the reader encounters an interactive menu that features a large start button. Pointing at this button causes a circle of seven icons to swoop in and encircle "START." These icons vie for the reader's attention and literally frame the entrance to the main text.

Clicking these icons leads to seven different static entryscreens, containing paragraphs of text that situate the work in historical, cultural, and poetic contexts. The screen "Aporia," for example, alerts readers that *Project* will employ the technique of "semantic priming" by flashing hidden words at subliminal speeds. It and other entryscreens sketch historical connections between three main topics: early work in concrete poetry, a notorious hoax in subliminal advertising, and priming techniques in cognitive psychology. The entryscreens focus the reader's attention on *Project*'s relationship to avant-garde poetry and media history. At the same time, they serve to enact one of the work's primary aesthetic strategies: they direct and distract the reader, foregrounding the question of how concrete poetry and subliminal messages work in *Project* while obscuring many other tropes and symbols operating within the layers of text, image, sound, and code.

To begin the narrative, the reader presses start, launching the animation and unleashing the fast-paced, flashing, and unceasing stream of words that form the central narrative of *Project*: "Sinkholes / and / unstable / soil / characteristic / of / the / karstland."[3] The text streams for over nine minutes; then it repeats, endlessly. Each word appears alone atop a simple visual icon, producing a series of "imagetext" combinations.[4] These imagetexts appear atop a background image of a vortex, a circle of blue that pulses, expanding outward and then contracting as it shifts across a spectrum of colors. Accompanying this visual display is a dynamically generated audio component: a rhythmic droning intermittently interrupted by bursts of pipe organ, chimes, and high-pitched synthesizers. These aural effects create an ambiance that slips between mesmerizing and panic-inducing, driving the reading pace and coloring the reader's engagement with the text. The result is a dynamic, multimodal performance that is distinctly digital in ways that challenge our print-based reading practices and expectations.

Project is at once compelling and challenging, enticing and elusive. Its fast-flashing aesthetic is seemingly incompatible with the slow, sustained contemplation of close reading and other traditional methods of literary analysis. Indeed, *Project* resists any attempt by the reader to control its pace. Its interface offers no options to pause, slow, or rewind the animation. Yet its orchestration of words, images, design, music, and movement captures our attention. *Project* pushes you to sit back and absorb the stream of flashing content. It stuns you into passive receptivity while simultaneously compelling you to draw near the screen and actively construct coherence out of the fragmented and fleeting impressions left by its imagetexts. These enigmatic imagetexts narrate a community's efforts to explain another enigma. In the tale, readers of all sorts—geologists, tourists, and neighbors alike—peer deep into the famed "Bottomless Pit" and attempt to measure it, map it, and make sense of it. The Pit thus becomes emblematic of the work itself. The Pit and *Project* both compel a variety of hermeneutic and technological readings to explain what they mean and why their meaning matters.

Our own efforts to approach the Pit and make meaning from *Project* prompted us to collaborate on a joint analytical reading of *Project's* project—hence our title, *Reading* Project. Drawing upon recent innovations in analytic methods inspired by the proliferation of digital reading and writing tools and techniques, we approach *Project* as an opportunity to work through questions of how literary analysis changes and why it continues to matter in the digital age.

THE METHOD OF OUR BOOK

This book is an experiment in braiding together three intersecting approaches to analyze a single work of digital literature. Together, we close read on-screen content, analyze computer source code, and create (and reflect on) media visualizations. This is a collaboration, not just in writing, but in collectively thinking *through* a literary work in dialogue with one another. By bringing our individual perspectives and critical methodologies to bear, we learned from each other how to read in new ways both this work in particular and also literature in general. As with any literary scholar or critic, each of us had preferred techniques that led us to assume a role in the group (although these boundaries began to blur over time). Jessica approaches a literary work in a traditional style of literary history and hermeneutics, close reading the aesthetics of on-screen poetics and examining that content within larger contexts of literary and media history. Using the methodologies of Critical Code Studies, Mark explores the unseen layers and environs that produce the on-screen performance, namely the source code, the files and assets, and the software platform, Flash. Drawing on techniques from cultural analytics and information visualization, Jeremy creates visualizations that transform the experiential effects of the digital work and produce new ways of viewing the piece.

The one constant that cut across our explorations was that individual methods led our collaborative reading to new ways of seeing the work, which, in turn, meant a process of continually shifting perspective. Metaphorically, these shifts in perspective constantly moved us between different degrees of "zooming in" and "zooming out." For example, when Mark discovered a source code file that contained all of the story text and all of the subliminal words, we could suddenly read the story slowly and carefully, as we would a work of print literature. With this discovery, we zoomed in. When Jeremy created a montage image, assembling thousands of periodic screenshots from the flashing animation into a large grid, we could suddenly see patterns in individual elements across the entire work. We zoomed out. When Jessica examined the history of patents and accounts of the use of machines called "tachistoscopes," we came to see how *Project* performs an artistic version of media archaeology. With that realization, we zoomed out to perceive new contexts that led us to zoom in again, but differently. Each new discovery changed our approach to reading *Project*.

In this book we have tried to retain the sense of wonder and discovery that was part of our interpretative process. Rather than moving from point to point, from thesis to support, this book moves by calling forth questions and braiding responses into the fold. For us, weaving together hybrid reading practices means proposing an idea, investigating it, and then, with our collaborative partners, repositioning that idea and building upon it. Our interpretations evolved through an ongoing process of proposition, investigation, and revision; the structure of the book performs that process.

Each chapter opens with a vignette that evokes the chapter's motivation. Individual sections then develop out of the arguments and interpretations presented in previous sections before building toward conclusions and new questions.

- "Chapter 1: Project" details the individual elements that produce *Project*'s on-screen aesthetic. Describing the experience of engaging *Project*'s nine-and-a-half minute animation, this first chapter plots out the perimeter of the conceptual area that we excavate around *Project*'s eponymous Bottomless Pit. We show how the choreographed performance of these on-screen elements produces a visual priming that informs the reader's perception of the work. A discovery in the code then forces us to challenge and reverse this interpretation. We argue that this work about gazing into a bottomless pit is an allegory for reading in the digital age.
- "Chapter 2: Tachistoscope" examines *Project*'s digital remediation of

a class of "reading" machines that originated in the nineteenth-century: the tachistoscope. This leads us to a comparative exploration of *Project*'s Flash software as an analogous scopic (or tachistoscopic) tool. The chapter introduces the book's larger focus on reading machines and media archaeology, upon which we rely as we begin our own machine-enabled reading practices.

• "Chapter 3: Bottomless Pit" plumbs the depths and explores the shifting rim of the Pit that is *Project*'s central trope. We investigate the functioning of conceptual subliminal pits, spaces of liminality produced by Flash's layers and tweens, as well as the connections between psychoanalysis and subliminal advertising. As we try to measure and map various pits— whether in the text, on the screen, or hidden in the metaphors of Flash's interface—we discover that the work undermines the very epistemologies used in this effort.

• "Chapter 4: Subliminal Spam" pursues the elusive subliminal text in *Project* and the ways that this text complicates and complements the larger, and more legible, story of the Bottomless Pit. A central discovery in *Project*'s code prompts us to reconsider our understanding of how *Project* uses subliminal text and reroutes our overall interpretation of the tale and the work.

• Our conclusion ties together our braided threads, reflects on larger lessons learned, and introduces the next stage of our collaboration: our construction of a web-based portal that supports scholarly collaboration of digital objects.

In the scholarly communities that we call home, engagement with the digital is proving transformative. Literary criticism is changing with the literature we read and with the reading machines through which we encounter it. But, models showing how to build interpretative analysis from digital tools and methods remain scarce. We intend for this book to intervene in current discourse about the digital humanities by demonstrating how digital reading practices can produce interpretative analysis that is both decidedly new and also an extension of traditional humanistic practices.

Our *Reading* Project shows how digital poetics compel different critical approaches, particularly methods that are themselves computationally inspired and informed. Traditional practices of textual close reading can be enhanced and renovated using a computer, not only as a device for browsing and parsing, but also as a partner in reenvisioning the object of study and as a means of engaging human partners in collaborative reading. We present this book—our experiment in collaborative critical computational analysis—as both a deep and specific engagement with Poundstone's *Project for Tachistoscope {Bottomless Pit}* and as a general example of how humanities computing can inspire literary analysis.

■ ■ ■ READING *PROJECT*

■ ■ ■ Jessica Encounters a Beautiful View

I was sitting in my office, chatting with two colleagues, when the e-mail arrived. Half-listening to the conversation around me, I opened the attachment and watched the image spread across my screen.

"Oh my goodness!" I exclaimed. "It's beautiful!" The words escaped me and interrupted my colleagues' discussion.

"What is it?"

I turned the screen toward them and watched their eyes scan the rows of horizontal squares, each containing miniature bursts of text, color, and design.

"It visualizes nine minutes of animation from *Project for Tachisto-scope*—a work of electronic literature that I'm writing about. I've been analyzing that work for months, reading it over and over, but I've never seen it like this!"

A moment of silence passed.

One finally asked, his voice registering sincere interest, "What does it mean? How do you read it?"

The other scoffed, "It's just a pretty picture. You can't read it."

I let out a small sigh, turned my attention back to the screen, and replied, "Depends on what you mean by 'read.'"

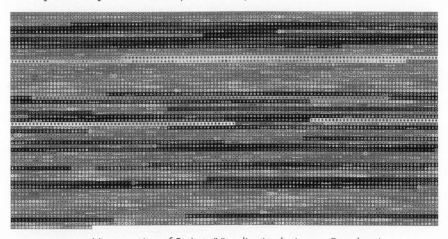

FIGURE 1.1: Montage view of *Project*. (Visualization by Jeremy Douglass.)

Project tells the story of an enigmatic abyss, the Bottomless Pit. The narrative begins, "Sinkholes and unstable soil characteristic of the karstland around Bluefields long plagued construction of the Beale Pike between Breezewood and Roanoke Park." This first line indicates the style of Poundstone's text: it is dense and compact but also simple and compelling. *Project* presents a labyrinthine narrative, complete with metacritical inquiry into semiotics and epistemology, which emerges around the Pit and is condensed into a deceptively simple short story. The narrative contains less than three thousand words. When transcribed, it reads as prose, but it is presented one word at a time as rhythmic poetry that flows steadily to a musically enhanced pace as its streams via a nonstop animation. The text's tendency toward condensation demands careful parsing, but its fast-flashing formal presentation disallows such activity. This tension generates *Project*'s poetic.

The story begins with a mundane situation that transitions quickly into the fantastic. It appears construction efforts to build a road have proceeded without problem or delay until disaster strikes. "The 59th day began unseasonably warm and cloudless," but workers soon "felt the ground rocking beneath their feet. Those who could run to safety did. Behind them a great chasm opened in the earth." This gaping hole swallows "73 workers and nearly four million dollars of government equipment." This sinkhole immediately becomes more than a death-trap and a financial nightmare; it becomes an enigma to be read, measured, and explained. Beginning in the tone of an engineer's report, these early sentences detail geological elements in the environment, such as the "finely compacted kaolin silica and gabbro." But the text slips from an accounting of a pit that doomed the construction project to a description of the Pit, a proper noun, signifying its status as both symbolic entity and autonomous subject. The Pit is the central character in *Project*'s narrative, and the story pivots around different people of diverse approaches, professions, and perspectives attempting to explain and interpret it.

"The Pit's early history is sketchy," we are told, but its history is at least partially documented. In the nineteenth century, "a sign painter inventor libertine and atheist" named Chandler Moody "collected all that had been written about the Pit." His archive becomes the basis of the New Lebanon Historical Society, which is housed in "the first substantial dwelling built in the area." This archive is the central location and organizing feature of the community that develops around the Pit, one which will later be lost when most of the New Lebanon Historical Society's collection is devoured by the Pit. This detail prompts the reader to question the foundations of the metanarrative, for if the records were lost, how can this history be known? The narrative subsequently twists from historical report into ontological exploration. The more the Pit grows, the more of its own history it consumes. As a result, readers both within and beyond the diegesis attempt to excavate the Pit's history and interpret it. The narrative about a geological entity takes an epistemological turn, turning the Pit into a challenge that forces us to reflect on how we see, read, and know.

"Daring men have attempted to attain great depths in the Pit," so as to explain it. Kellogg the astronomer was one such man. He "was the first to describe many famed phenomena of the Pit," including a situation wherein "weather permitting a viewer standing at the Pit's rim at sunrise or sunset may see weird shadows cast on a bank of fog miles away haloed by a prismatic effect of light producing a famous illusion of Our Lady." As the work takes a turn toward the *phenomenal* (from the Greek, "thing appearing to view"), efforts to see into the Pit also foreground philosophical questions about *how* we see. "Visibility in the Pit is a complex matter," we are told, and this complexity becomes part of the Pit's allure and part of *Project*'s purpose; for, as we explore in later chapters, *Project* focuses attention on the mechanisms and machines involved in seeing and in reading.

The Pit delivers either opportunities or misfortunes (and sometimes both) to those who encounter it. Its ledges provide shelter to feral cats, but it also devours the homes of humans built too close to its edges. The Pit's presence props up the economy—locals seek creative means of profiting from it, whether by selling Pit fragments at roadside stands or offering to throw unwanted objects into it "for a fee"—but it also devastates the real estate market, transforming nearby Carbondale into a shantytown of collapsing buildings. Yet, while the Pit tears down buildings, it also inspires new construction. The narrative ends by detailing a particularly ambitious commercial venture: "A 3,000-room Indian casino was once planned for the Bottomless Pit's south rim." But, "Financing fell apart when it was discovered that an engineer had been tampering with survey markers in order to conceal progressive subsidence."

We can understand these survey markers as tools for geographic inscription; by outlining the area, they turn a physical pit into something to quantify and sell.

The narrative's final sentences describe the casino project in ways that turn the story about the Pit into an allegory of reading in our digital age. The tale concludes, "Large cracks parallel to the Pit's rim have appeared in the ground where construction was to have begun and this pattern of ground deformation has preceded past subsidence events." The sentence's complexities exemplify *Project*'s writing style and also hint at the philosophical questions that permeate the work. The sentence identifies natural signs ("large cracks") existing alongside the man-made (and man-altered) survey markers. Both types of signs can and should be read, for they present a pattern. The sentence uses a past perfect infinitive ("was to have begun") that denotes unfulfilled conditions—the intended construction of a casino—and qualifies the description of the ground and its cracked surface. These cracks are not only visible; they are also semiotic and symbolic. They record a historical happening, designate an unfulfilled plan, and represent the need to read into the Pit. The next sentence continues to register our reliance on historical artifacts: "The Pit has swallowed part of the safety rail system encircling the Pit's perimeter." Part of the safety rail remains, and it is from that visible remnant that one can begin to reconstruct history.

Project presents and promotes excavatory reading practices. Its narrative centers around the actions of individuals who actively read (and read into) the Bottomless Pit and who also leave traces for others (including you, dear reader) to discover and explain. Such excavatory reading is important, the work suggests, because "In recent years the Pit has both widened and gotten alarmingly deeper." On that ominous note, the tale of the Bottomless Pit ends. The work concludes by signaling the proliferation of change, by noting the growing instability of surfaces, and by suggesting that we need to direct our attention to these transformations. We claim throughout this book that learning to read the Pit—and, thereby, learning to read *Project*—is about learning to read our changing contemporary media landscape. *Project* invites such metacritical analysis, but it is also very much a work of its own time that exemplifies a particular moment in electronic literary history.

CONTEXT: SITUATING *PROJECT* IN THE FIELD OF ELECTRONIC LITERATURE (JESSICA)

Project dates from the early years of the new millennium, and its aesthetic is exemplary of a strain of work popular during that moment in the history of electronic literature. Before the adoption of interactive animation authorware (such as Director and Flash) in the late 1990s, which transformed the field of electronic literature by introducing highly visual, time-based, and kinetic poetics, hypertext was king. Hypertext literature was text-based and presented nonlinear reading paths through a link-and-node structure of connecting "lexias,"[1] and, as a result, it was characterized by poetics of exploration, disorientation, and exhaustion. As electronic literature entered an era of sophisticated visuals and interface design, novel-length hypertexts were displaced by short animations. The new, highly visual and even cinematic aesthetic flourished in such online journals as *Poemsthatgo.com* (edited by Megan Sapnar and Ingrid Ankerson, which published new issues quarterly from 2000–2004), whose title describes the aesthetic of the literature it presented. Exemplary of this type of work is Young-Hae Chang Heavy Industries (YHCHI),[2] a critically acclaimed artistic duo who use Flash to present a flashing aesthetic of image, text, and sound—epitomized by its one-word-at-a-time delivery—that produces a minimalist and yet sophisticated aesthetic effect. Like YHCHI's work, Poundstone's *Project* is compact and poetic in ways that offer multiple entry points for readers seeking connections across diverse artistic genealogies, from literature to film to graphic design. As I have elsewhere argued, such speeding, unstoppable work both invites and challenges close reading.[3]

The introduction of Flash, and other similar animation software, produced a pivotal moment in the history of electronic literature. In her schematic history of the field, N. Katherine Hayles identifies this moment as the division between two "generations" of electronic literature. Hayles explains,

> First generation works, often written in Storyspace or Hypercard, are largely or exclusively text-based with navigation systems mostly confined to moving from one block of text to another. Second generation works, authored in a wide variety of software including Director, Flash, Shockwave and xml, are

fully multimedia, employ a rich variety of interfaces, and have sophisticated navigation systems.[4]

As with any narrative of media history, linear succession was neither clear nor decisive but, rather, recursive and remediative.[5] Yet, the importance of this shift in electronic literary aesthetics is important to note, both for understanding digital literature and for recognizing how *Project* is exemplary of a signal moment in the history of electronic literature and its emergent poetics.

Though *Project* reflects this period in electronic literary history, it is also unique, both artistically and because of its artist. *Project*'s importance to the field is signified by its inclusion in the *Electronic Literature Collection*, volume 1, an online digital anthology published by the Electronic Literature Organization that curates and archives important works of born-digital literature.[6] Unlike other writers included in the *ELC*, William Poundstone is the author of fourteen print books of nonfiction and has been twice nominated for the Pulitzer Prize. His books range in scope and focus, but all share an interest in unearthing and explaining the central facets, figures, and complex theories of our technoculture. His print oeuvre traces the intersections of computing, cognition, and capitalism: *The Recursive Universe: Cosmic Complexity and the Limits of Scientific Knowledge* (1984), *Prisoner's Dilemma: John von Neumann, Game Theory, and the Puzzle of the Bomb* (1992), *How Would You Move Mount Fuji?: Microsoft's Cult of the Puzzle—How the World's Smartest Companies Select the Most Creative Thinkers* (2003), *Priceless: The Myth of Fair Value (and How to Take Advantage of It)* (2010). Poundstone's books explore and expose: *Big Secrets: The Uncensored Truth About All Sorts of Stuff You Are Never Supposed to Know* (1983), *Bigger Secrets: More Than 125 Things They Prayed You'd Never Find Out* (1986), *Fortune's Formula: The Untold Story of the Scientific Betting System That Beat the Casinos and Wall Street* (2005). These thematic interests carry over into *Project*, as does Poundstone's formal method of storytelling in which he develops a fixation point for his reader's attention and then draws a complex constellation around it. To see how he translates historical storytelling into digital literature, we dive into *Project* and examine the first screens that the reader encounters: the prefatory entryscreens.

FIGURE 1.2: Title screen of *Project*. (Screenshot by authors; with the permission of William Poundstone.)

Project for
Tachistoscope
{Bottomless Pit}

2005

WILLIAM POUNDSTONE

DIVING IN: THE ENTRYSCREENS (JESSICA)

Project begins with a title screen that then dissolves into a start screen. The word "START" appears in large, trim, sans serif, white capitalized letters at the center of the screen. The word remains static as a pulsing circular ball expands and contracts around it. Composed of a lighter blue than the background, the circle cycles through a range of colors and creates the effect of a vortex at the center of the screen. The vortex focuses attention on the noun-verb "START" and invites the reader to click on it with their mouse pointer. Doing so activates the main animation and begins the flashing story of the Bottomless Pit.[7]

However, before the reader's pointer can reach the word, its movement triggers something unexpected. A ring of seven icons swoops in from the outskirts of the screen to encircle the word "START." Whenever the reader's mouse hovers near "START," the icons appear, like summoned attendants to the entry portal. The icons are summoned by an event specified by the source code, and the reader cannot begin the work without encountering this circle. These icons further demand attention because they are punctuated by a succession of fluorescent colors and moving stimuli that make the images impossible to ignore. The circle of icons contain titles that overlay the image and that reference the larger cultural histories and discursive circles in which the work operates. With titles such as "Concrete Poetry & Subliminal Advertising," "Aporia," and "System Requirements," these icons orient the reader to approach the work within specific poetic, cultural, and technological

FIGURE 1.3: The interactive entryscreen of *Project*, with START leading to the main piece and links to seven paratexts arranged in a circle. (Screenshot by authors; with the permission of William Poundstone.)

contexts. From the start, *Project* draws attention to the many ways interpretation may be framed by reading technologies, whether through advertising delivery mechanisms or through the system requirements for the work itself.

Clicking on any one of the seven icons that encircle "START" opens a new screen—what we call an "entryscreen." These single, static screens are filled with text laid out in paragraph form. Each provides a specific historic or technical context for approaching the work. These entryscreens are "paratexts," echoing Gerard Genette, for they are neither separate nor superfluous.[8] A reader could choose to skip the screens and dive right into the story of the Bottomless Pit, but each screen provides meaningful content. They serve to explain, frame, or anchor the main text and its design poetics. For example, the entryscreen titled "Aporia" presents *Project* as sharing "the spirit" of the Oulipo and other constraint-based artistic experiments, including "a number of exercises in randomly distorting semantic content while preserving elements of structure—among them the telephone game, exquisite cadaver, and the Oulipian N+7 algorithm." Such experiments are often identified as predecessors of born-digital computational poetry because they emphasize the process of generating texts, not just the final product.[9] In effect, such experimental poetries share an understanding that a poem can be a process or algorithm as well as the result of them. By referencing such poetic exercises in its prefatory screens, *Project*'s paratexts situate this digital work within a longer genealogy of procedural poetics.

The title of the entryscreen "Concrete Poetry & Subliminal Advertising" references a different form of experimental poetry—concrete poetry—and offers the following provocative claim: "Subliminal advertising is coeval with concrete poetry." The relationship between these two genres is central to *Project*. After all, the imagery used throughout *Project*—from the icons on its paratextual entryscreens to the image-texts of its main narrative—is drawn from advertising and consumer culture. Each entryscreen features an icon as its background so that the text of the aforementioned entryscreen "Concrete Poetry & Subliminal Advertising" is presented upon a small white silhouette of Brazil, a birthplace of concrete poetry. Clicking that icon opens a static expository screen whose background is a large, white single-prop airplane. The incongruous image is better understood in the context of the relationship between subliminal messaging and concrete poetry. For Brazilian poet Décio Pignatari's foundational work of concrete poetry, "beba coca cola," transforms the words "coca cola" into "coca" (cocaine). This work was published alongside the seminal manifesto "Pilot Plan for Concrete Poetry" (1958).[10] This sloganeering commodity-turned-illegal-drug provides a context for Poundstone's single-prop airplane icon, which symbolically imports concrete poetry into the U.S. in a fashion that evokes media panic over Brazilian drug trafficking. The airplane icon also puns on the word "pilot" invoked in the title of that famous manifesto. As the paratextual entryscreens suggest, Poundstone's vision of the coevolving concepts of subliminal advertising and concrete poetry is central to *Project*, even if it is not the primary focus.

That history contextualizes the work's own subliminal text—text that flashes faster than the text of the main narrative and thus interrupts the primary narrative stream by appearing in between its visible words. In an authorial statement introducing *Project* in the *Electronic Literature Collection*, Poundstone claims, "The piece is, as far as I know, the first to use subliminal effects in a work of electronic literature."[11] This statement draws attention to the very thing his poetic elides. Using Flash authorware, Poundstone displays words so fast the reader cannot grasp them; then, through statements like this one and also through his paratextual entryscreens, he focuses attention on the presence of this subliminal text. The result is a palpable tension between what is hidden and seen, surface and depth, and Poundstone goes out of his way to introduce this context before the narrative even begins.

He does so explicitly on the entryscreen "Subliminal Con." The text on this screen introduces a pivotal backstory for *Project*, one that cements the constellation composed of computational poetics, advertising, and visual poetry. The entryscreen tells the following apocryphal tale from American cultural history:

> In September 1957 ad man James M. Vicary announced that he had used a
> device called a tachistoscope to flash spilt-second ads during movies. The
> ads, too fleeting to be perceived consciously, worked. One that said 'Drink
> Coca-Cola' increased sales 18.1 percent. A similar ad for popcorn boosted
> sales 57.5 percent.

The entryscreens provide a brief history of the fallout from Vicary's subliminal stunt, which Vicary later declaimed as "a gimmick." We explore Vicary's experiment in chapter 4, where we consider it as both an important cultural event and a media-based artistic experiment, but now we want to explain that the purpose of these introductory screens is to direct the reader's attention toward certain aspects of the work and away from others. In so doing, they function much like visual priming mechanisms, which serve to influence perception and prove central to *Project*'s poetics. Poundstone's framing ends when the reader clicks "START," as the circle of icons are swept off beyond the pale of the screen, replaced by an onslaught of fast-flashing content.

THE VISUAL LAYERS (JEREMY)

Just as the Pit is the central character in the narrative, so too is it the primary design feature of *Project*'s interface aesthetic. From the moment the work begins, a pit-like vortex of concentric circles pulses at the center of the screen. As the work plays, it remains—sometimes modulating in color, but always present. The vortex evokes a sense of depth in the flat interface and simultaneously acts like a bull's-eye; it fixates the reader's attention on the location at center-screen where words appear. In this way *Project* presents a visual pit on-screen upon which and within which it flashes the tale of the Bottomless Pit. The connection between these two pits is crucial. The convergence of aesthetic and narrative depth informs the reader's perception of the work as "having depths" that may be excavated; thus, in order to perform analysis of the work, we first need to identify the various elements—or, to use the depth metaphor of the work, the layers—that comprise its on-screen aesthetic. This chapter lays the foundation for further analysis by striving to carefully consider the layers of visual elements employed on-screen to produce *Project*'s aesthetic. We do so using two approaches. First, we analyze from a distance: we diagram the abstract system of the work operating at full speed. Next, we move up close: we carefully unpack a specific frozen moment as captured in a screenshot—a single frame.

Conceptually, we can describe visual layering in *Project* by using a depth metaphor that proceeds from bottom-to-top or from back-to-front, such that elements that are closer to the viewer may act to conceal ones that are further away. *Project*'s screen is composed of six main layers, all of which will change in content but not in order, and nearly all of which are aligned to the center of the screen: [12]

1. The Background layer, containing background color
2. The Rim layer, containing shifting radial graphics
3. The Icon layer, containing a white clip art image
4. The Text layer, containing either a story word or subliminal word
5. The Image layer, containing a small colorful subliminal-graphic
6. The Exit layer, containing a pulsing red EXIT mark in the lower-left corner

The background (layer 1) is always present; its primary state is blue, though it oscillates, often, between different shades. This background color may become black or even shift to shades of pink. The rim (layer 2) appears upon a cerulean background. The rim consists of many circles shifting between multicolored gradients that give the impression of flatness or depth, even alternating between these states right before our eyes. The rim produces a smaller circle at center-screen, a scope of sorts that serves to focus the reader's attention. The rim also frames within it the combinations of text and image, the imagetexts, that present *Project*'s narrative content and serve to comprise layers 3, 4, and 5.[13] The first of these is the icon layer (layer 3), which displays a constantly changing figure: an airplane, a dagger, a martini glass, a house, a bomb. Each icon is rendered in a simple abstract style; it is the same style that the reader first encounters on the entryscreens. The icons are white, flat shapes that appear at center-screen, and they offer a stark visual contrast to the gradiated colors of the rim and background layers. These images are icons in the semiotic sense; they present both an illustration and a figurative meaning. Specifically, they are symbols taken from the visual languages of maps, of international signage, and of advertising. They are also cultural commodities from consumer capitalism, and they operate at a conscious and an unconscious level, for we can read and recognize them without context or explanation. Atop these icons appear words (layer 4) that flash one at a time in an ongoing stream. The story words appear in black, while the faster-flashing, subliminal words are most noticeable when they appear in white. Sometimes these subliminal words are made invisible by a lack of contrast with the color of their surroundings; other times, they are obscured by a small colorful image (layer 5), such as a floral pattern or a cartoon face. These images sit atop the text layer and occlude the words behind it. The effect is a momentary but unmistakable palimpsest, a visualization of layered depth on-screen. The final element to note is the EXIT sign (layer 6), a word in red capitals which rhythmically appears and vanishes in the lower right corner of the screen.[14] This word is also an icon in the particular sense that it affords a software action; clicking it takes the reader out to the start screen. It is also, at the same time, a symbol—not just the word exit, but a recognizable image of a standard building exit sign, and its appearance suggests the idea of *Project* as an architectural space.

We have described these layers as if each may be considered separately, yet they interact in complex ways in space and time, pushing the limits of their legibility. Not all layers are visible at all times; layers appear, disappear, and change at different speeds and with different rhythms. Layers also may overlap in space, combining, occluding one another (when appearing above) or concealing through lack of contrast (when appearing below). Pictures may combine with icons, or may occlude words; icons may be obscured by story words or may instead conceal subliminal text. Each moment of *Project* presents us with a new composition. Whether we watch these moments dance by at great speed or we instead contemplate one as a still image, the compositional logic remains the same. However, by closely considering one instant of *Project* in which all layers are present, we can better understand the interactions of elements and how they combine to produce a cumulative expression.

For our close reading I have selected a screenshot of one moment in one run of *Project*. This screenshot is captured ephemera; it is quite possible that this image may not again appear in precisely this way during any subsequent viewings of the work. As instants in *Project* go, it also captures an uncommon occurrence—a moment in which all six visual layers are simultaneously visible. Here, the word "psychologists" appears on-screen, framed by a biohazard icon and partially occluded by a small circular image of blossoms, with the red Exit in the corner.

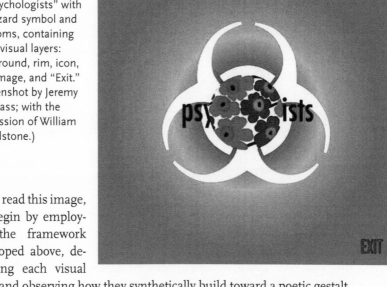

FIGURE 1.4: Screenshot of "psychologists" with biohazard symbol and blossoms, containing all six visual layers: background, rim, icon, text, image, and "Exit." (Screenshot by Jeremy Douglass; with the permission of William Poundstone.)

To read this image, we begin by employing the framework developed above, describing each visual layer and observing how they synthetically build toward a poetic gestalt. The background (layer 1) presents a typical variation of sky blue, and the rim (2) also appears in its usual shade of teal-blue. The biohazard icon (3) is centered on-screen, and its central segment (the negative circle at the center of the symbol) is both framed by the rim and, in turn, frames the image (5), which is a circle of brightly colored blossoms. The text (4) is sandwiched between icon and image, with the word nearly occluded by the image. Its beginning and end poke out, revealing letters that appear about two and a half minutes into the sequence, in the line "Government psy____ists have noted the self-validating elements of these stories." Whether this word designates psychologists, psychiatrists, psychotherapists, or some other group is unclear at this moment and in this particular iteration of the text (although multiple viewings will reveal that the word is in fact "psychologists").[15]

The word invokes professionals who attempt to read and explain the unconscious, yet this word is blocked, interrupted, and challenged by the image layer. The screen thus expresses a main trope in the work: the parallel between the Bottomless Pit and the pit of human perception and cognition. This parallel is pursued and presented formally in this screenshot, for the appearance of the word designates the need for and impossibility of interpretation. The word is hidden yet legible and thus invites reading across the gaping hole designated by flowers placed upon a biohazard sign. In this way, the screen invokes a Freudian psychoanalytic effort to read the gaps, absences, and occlusions—to make legible the latent meanings. As this screen suggests, albeit briefly and even subconsciously, psychological experience is an important dimension of *Project*. The final layer (6), the Exit sign, is also captured in this screenshot, and, in the context of the interpretation just presented, it serves to suggest a desire to evade analysis and escape the analyst's couch. Or, in light of the presence of the biohazard symbol, we might understand this screen to be suggesting the hazards of such readings of the psyche.

The screenshot has an unoriginal, "found" quality to it, in that it appears to be assembled from preexisting anonymous ingredients such as icons, generic fonts, and stock images. Its aesthetic of remix and ready-mades turns attention to the selection and arrangement of the elements and layers used on-screen. For example, the image of the blossoms (layer 5) is no mere anonymous scrap of texture. It is a sample from the center of the "Unikko" pattern, an iconic piece of Scandinavian design that is both an object of art and a mass-market commodity.[16] The blossoms of the unikko—or poppy—are a source of opiates, and since antiquity poppy blossoms have served as a symbol of both sleep and death. The relevance of death and sleep (particularly dreams) to psychology and psychoanalysis is undeniable, and laying the poppies above the text "psy____ists" serves to both disrupt and exemplify the mysterious, stimulating questions about how the psyche works and how we perceive what we do.

The image is an emblem; it exemplifies a concept that exceeds and escapes the meaning of the original word it replaces.[17] Moreover, this combinatorial emblem is a momentary gestalt of individual elements from the six layers. Each element appears on the screen in its own time; all cohere for an instant; then, things change, and the emblem loses coherence and is gone, soon to be replaced by another. It is not enough to say that these layers create a combination of connotations, for this emblem *is* a unique visual sign whose layers evoke their own complex signifying logic. Combined in this way, the word and images illustrate a paradox of containment: the images appear inside the word (between "psy" on the left and "ists" on the right) while simultaneously surrounding the word (which is sandwiched between the poppies layer before it and the biohazard behind). Within and without, simultaneously terrifying and stupefying, dangerous sedative and delightful commodity, the word "psychiatrists" is thus reworked by *Project* into an emblem that is read in its stead. ("Government psy⬡ists have noted . . .") Recognizing this fact shows how *Project*'s on-screen poetics represent and promote an understanding that perception is always in the process of being interrupted and recontextualized.

Understanding how this interruption happens in *Project* requires doing more than reading into the visual layers of the work's interface design. Having considered how visual depth is presented on-screen, we are now poised to explore the technical depths of the software that produces it. As Mark shows below, this software also employs a metaphor of layers to describe and enable its operations.

FLASH: HOW IT WORKS (MARK)

So far we have used the metaphor of "layers" to describe *Project*'s palimpsestic and emblematic on-screen aesthetics. Through close inspection, we identified six layers that produce the interface design, but exploration of the Flash file that produces *Project* reveals that these six layers are, in fact, generated by forty-nine separate layers in the source code. So, while we see six layers on-screen, what we see when we open *Project*'s .fla source file in the Flash authoring environment is quite different. Nonetheless, there remains a guiding principle and recurring metaphor shared by *Project*'s interface design and Flash's graphical user interface (GUI): the layer. Flash employs layers as one of a set of operational metaphors in its GUI. Indeed, to author a file in Flash is to engage with a constellation of spatial and temporal metaphors for creating and manipulating code. These authoring metaphors mediate the work's creation and also resonate with *Project*'s narrative and aesthetics. For these reasons, we engage with them in order to understand the role that code authoring plays in *Project* and its resulting poetics.

Layers are just one of the many metaphors Flash uses to communicate with its users and to convert the abstractions of its programming environment into more familiar terms. The interface simulates a drafting table or light box—concrete physical elements in the working environment of visual artists. The software affords users the option to drag cutout shapes around in space rather than having to specify those shapes and their movements mathematically. However, Flash is also built on spatial and temporal metaphors adapted from film and theater. For example, Flash employs the conceptual term "frame" (as in a frame in a film) to refer to a single segment of the digital animation; "timeline" describes the visual representation of a series of frames (similar to a film strip); "stage" designates the area that will appear on-screen when the program is run; "keyframes" are the beginning and ending points of the animation; and "tween" describes the animated transitions and transformations that fill the frames *in between* two keyframes.

When building an animation in Flash, the programmer views the authorware screen from a point-of-view positioned above "the stage" and looks downward onto its interface. This visual metaphor is a convention used in many popular image authoring programs (such as Photoshop or Gimp). The Flash manual compares its layers to "transparent sheets of acetate stacked on top of each other." However, because Flash is time-based, the authoring environment also provides a cinematic timeline view that displays a stack of layers, each made of a strip of frames which extend the duration of the piece.

This timeline view presents time horizontally, and it arranges layers of different content vertically. Continuing the film editing metaphor, time segments are organized as a progression of frames that move forward in time from left to right. Marks on the timeline (grey or purple rectangles spanning one or more frames) indicate when content will be presented in the animation, either as image via the screen or as sound via speakers.[18] The timeline is divided into frames, and a frame with a black dot indicates a keyframe—that is, a location on the timeline where new information has been placed. Grey frames that extend after each keyframe represent how long that information will be delivered, whether displayed on the screen or played over the speakers. An arrow symbol that stretches between keyframes over purple cells denotes a tween— that is, a place where the program is creating an animation effect.

Layers present both a depth metaphor for arranging visual assets and an organizational structure for arranging content. Simply, content placed on lower layers in the stack will be displayed beneath or behind any content placed on higher layers. Conventionally, designers also use different vertical layers to separate content types (such as code, audio, and visual elements), although a layer may combine elements of all three. Since the timeline mimics a filmstrip, the relationship between the visual content on the layers and the way it will be displayed on the screen is more immediately apparent than in the case of the sound or

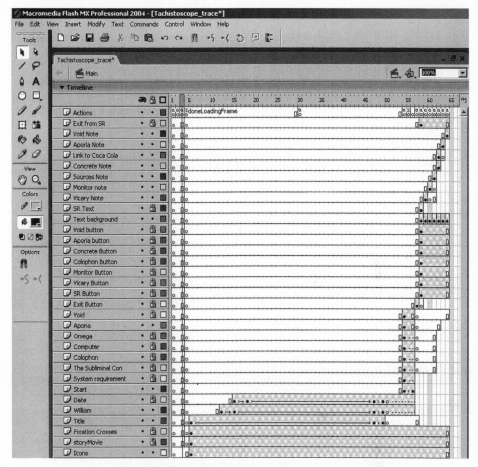

FIGURE 1.5: Flash authoring environment view of *Project* source code with timeline (left-to-right) and layers (top-to-bottom). (Screenshot by Mark Marino; with the permission of William Poundstone.)

code content. This layered system of viewing and building produces a depth metaphor, and it is tempting to extend this metaphor—connecting *Project*'s on-screen aesthetic to its programming environment and beyond—to the reading of its source files and codes. The result would be a vertical axis in which screen output is the top layer and the code is somewhere deep underneath. But we should proceed carefully here. Matthew Kirschenbaum and others have rightly warned against approaching code through such depth-based metaphorical paradigms as "looking under the hood."[19] As Wendy Chun suggests, pursuing the code in such a manner presents the search for an inner essence that is an ideological enterprise, a kind of projection.[20] Our interest in code here, however, is not pursued out of a misguided belief that it represents some deeper, original truth. We seek to read *Project*'s code in order to understand its relationship to the on-screen poetics it produces. The code is "underneath" the visual metaphors of the integrated development environment (IDE) only inasmuch as it is represented by and produces that development environment. However, these graphical representations are part of the code of the piece as well.

Project employs depth metaphors from its interface design to its narrative content to its code. Thus, a media-specific analysis of the work needs to take into consideration that which connects its content, form, and platform: the metaphor of depth. From the diegetic pit to the pulsing vortex on-screen to Flash's "layers" of programming elements, this work uses depth as a central trope. Flash uses depth as its operational metaphor, and it produces an on-screen animation—like *Project*'s narrative about a bottomless pit—through the arrangement of "layers." Thus, not only can we consider a Flash file to be a pit of layers, but *Project*'s on-screen appearance and narrative tropes demand that we do. However, just as in Poundstone's story about a pit that produces sinkholes, the topology of metaphors that constitute Flash also prove unstable ground on which to tread.

Although metaphors, such as layers and frames, have become standard (and hence transparent) in film, photo, and illustration editing software of all kinds, such metaphors are deceptive and unreliable in Flash. For example, if we follow the cinematic metaphor, we see that each frame on the stage represents the appearance of the screen for a segment of time. This description sounds like the concept of "frame" as found in a film reel; however, the analogy to film breaks down in significant ways. Unlike film, images in Flash are not indexical signs; the images are data objects. Nor are these images delimited to the frame because they are sets of data that can be manipulated, dragged, and dropped in ways that connect them to multiple frames. Also, a designer can pause the progression of the timeline indefinitely, stretching one frame to any length of time. Another important distinction from film is that the program refers to the space within any individual frame as a "stage" as opposed to a screen, a linguistic decision that shifts the frame of reference from film to theater. Thus the metaphors used to present and interpret the interface shift between a performance space and a series of snapshots.

Still, depth can be deceptive. An artist working in Flash can arrange the appearance of the screen by positioning objects on the stage along an x- and y-axis. However, in order to arrange objects along the z-axis, with depth, an artist will typically create an arrangement of layers. What remains invisible to users who have come to internalize these metaphors is the slippage from one conceptual framework to another. For example, the terms "higher" and "above" map one spatial relationship in the authoring interface (layers closer to the top edge of the screen) onto another spatial relationship in the animated output (superimposed layers appearing "in front of" or "behind" others). Depth is built into both the operational metaphor of the system and its use. However, through the use of code, programmers can move objects inserted through any of the layers to different positions on the z-axis. This point is important because it reminds us how the conceptual underpinnings of the authorware are, for the most part, more of a convenient set of user interface metaphors than an actual set of technical limitations. In other words, programming in Flash is not just about code, data, and technology. It is about metaphors.[21]

The force of these metaphors is that they turn the act of programming into an act of symbolic manipulation: algorithms represented as analogies. Like the Bottomless Pit described in Poundstone's Flash-based work, the Flash authorware operates through a collection of metaphors and symbolic structures that serve to obscure hidden operations and present an interface that masquerades as a physical space. For example, the vertical depth of Flash's layers is purely metaphorical—a depth without thickness. The fact that these operational metaphors resonate with the poetic metaphors presented in *Project* is neither an accident nor an extraneous point. It is this very deceptive nature that gives these metaphors particular importance for analyzing *Project*. Indeed, Flash's operational metaphors of depth and layering present another kind of bottomless pit. Most importantly, they invite consideration of the connection between literary form and programming format.

In this chapter we offered an overview of the work's story and situated it in the field of electronic literature. We dived into entryscreens, read the visual layers of the work's imagetexts, and explored the metaphors of the Flash authoring environment. We now move to build upon this foundation by considering the other central technology that informs *Project*'s poetic and is invoked in its title: the tachistoscope.

CHAPTER TWO

TACHISTOSCOPE

■ ■ ■ Mark Seeks the One True Tachistoscope

MARK: Can you tell me more about how *Project* works like a tachistoscope?

JESSICA: No.

MARK: Why not?

JESSICA: Because there is no such thing as "a tachistoscope."

MARK: Um, I think we're in trouble then.

JESSICA: No, we're not. It's actually quite intriguing. Tachistoscopes are media that mediate, but they can take different technological forms and perform different functions. They may use sliding paper or mirrors or text-projection; they have been used in laboratories, classrooms, and, most famously, in subliminal advertising. There is no one thing that is "a tachistoscope." But that doesn't mean there's not a media history out there for us to explore.

MARK: But we can't simply ask, "How does this work of e-lit function like a tachistoscope?"

JESSICA: We could, but it might not mean much.

MARK: Oh.

JESSICA: It might make more sense to ask, "Which tachistoscopes does *Project* resemble, and why?"

I remember this exchange with Jessica distinctly. It was early on in our collaboration, and it was a pivotal moment for me because I realized that we could not assume that our task would become easier because we brought three different people, perspectives, and skill sets to untangling a work of digital literature. What became evident in that exchange was that seemingly simple descriptive statements about the work's poetics, which each of us might casually make—such as, "*Project* acts like a tachistoscope"—actually required more rigorous and media-specific definition and that my collaborators would push me to interrogate such easy assumptions. In my previous readings of source code, I often created analogies as a point of entry to analysis. I was hoping to do the same thing here by comparing Poundstone's code to the workings of a tachistoscope. But that just wouldn't work, at least not in any clean and simple way.

Jessica's research into the media history of the tachistoscope had exposed the diverse definitions of "tachistoscope." The machine was used for perception studies, military training, literacy training, psychological priming, and more. This media archaeology of the machine, or the set of technologies that we would come to know as "tachistoscope," changed the way I looked at Poundstone's *Project*. It opened up like an artichoke when steamed.

ARCHAEOLOGY OF THE TACHISTOSCOPE (JESSICA)

Tachistoscopes, whose etymology combines the Greek words for "speed" and "viewing," were developed in the mid-nineteenth century and used into the twentieth century for optical, psychological, and cognitive research. The first tachistoscope placed a seated, staring viewer before a machine that focused her vision on a single location. Staring at that location, the machine then displayed a series of fast, flashing images before the viewer's eyes. This is the tachistoscope's primary mode of operation, and its earliest purpose was to serve laboratory researchers in testing and studying the thresholds of perception and reaction time. Alfred W. Volkmann, a physiologist interested in optics research, introduced the tachistoscope in 1859. He presented the tachistoscope as a tool capable of solving two central problems in current optical laboratory research: (1) how to measure response time to a stimulus when the object is viewed in the dark and when light is required to see it and (2) how to dispense with eye movement in the study of optical reflexes. Tachistoscopes were later adopted into diverse fields of study and adapted to serve different pursuits. This history led Ruth Benschop to conclude, in her seminal article on the tachistoscope, "All the varieties and forms of the tachistoscope can be organized by reference to what it is used *for*."[1] The word "tachistoscope" does not index a mechanical specification, but rather a type of tool employed to produce a particular experience: swift-viewing.

Project's fast-flashing performance adapts the experience of tachistoscopic swift-viewing and focuses attention on the machines involved in reading. The work promotes questions about what counts as reading, what distinguishes recognition from reading, and how reading machines participate in these practices and histories. Excavating the history of the tachistoscope exposes that though the tachistoscope was not originally intended to be a reading machine, this is precisely the purpose to which it was applied in the twentieth-century and, later, in Poundstone's twenty-first century adaptation of it.

Volkmann's tachistoscope inspired numerous adaptations whose variants entered the twentieth-century's research laboratories, classrooms, and leisure spaces, but by 1910, it had become a reading machine. Guy Montrose Whipple's *Manual of Mental and Physical Tests* describes the tachistoscope as a machine for testing reading: "In the main, the tachistoscope has been most used for the experimental investigation of the process of reading, and, accordingly, with an exposure field containing printed texts, isolated words, nonsense syllables, single letters, etc."[2] As the twentieth century progressed, the tachistoscope was more deliberately employed as a training device to foster visual acuity and speed-reading. A 1925 U.S. patent identifies a tachistoscope apparatus for testing "the speed of adjustment of the eyes," which "is very important in some vocations, such as aviation and locomotive engineering, that the eyes of those engaged therein shall be capable of quick and accurate adjustment in changing from near to far objects and from far to near objects."[3] This training-via-testing vision marks a shift in the use of the tachistoscope from an instrument for measurement to one for enhancement.

The tachistoscope was originally designed not to deliver information to a seated viewer but as a device for delivering data to a third-party observer, the researcher performing the experiment. But, as its domain moves from research laboratory to educational sphere, the tachistoscope begins to be employed as a reading machine that can train various types of readers to speed-read. One notable version of the tachistoscopic reading machine in American cultural history is the Renshaw Recognition System, developed by psychologist Samuel Renshaw for use by the United States Army and Navy. It was used to train pilots to quickly, even subliminally, discern and distinguish the signs identifying approaching planes as friend or foe (or IFF). Renshaw's 1946 patent for his tachistoscope apparatus acknowledges the evolutionary history of the machine by claiming that "the present invention" is an "improved tachistoscopic apparatus."[4] Renshaw's "improved" apparatus helped facilitate the adoption of the tachistoscope into educational settings and promoted its use as a training and testing machine.

Thereafter, the tachistoscope comes to be used not only to assess but also to alter the perception and performance of its user. It begins

to serve a direct pedagogical purpose. A 1939 U.S. patent for a tachistoscopic device describes it as an "educational device" for "teach-
ing various sequences of action of the pupil or subject, such as those
known as 'mental maze problems.'"[5] However, in its most popular and
mass-marketed variations, the tachistoscope served as a device to train
speed-reading. In this capacity, the tachistoscope facilitated the shift in
educational discourse toward ever-increasing interest in using technology to train and test readers.

Despite, or perhaps because of, its long and varied history, the tachistoscope had been largely left out of media history. Notable exceptions are the brief but important mentions of the tachistoscope in the
cultural histories put forth by Jonathan Crary and Friedrich Kittler,
both of whom identify the tachistoscope participating in and symbol-
izing signal shifts toward our modern media-laden culture. In his work
on the emergence of modern vision and subjectivity at the turn of the
nineteenth century (when the tachistoscope was invented), Jonathan
Crary describes the tachistoscope as "one of many examples of how,
within the context of technological modernization, faster mechanical speeds are reciprocally related to new bodily forms of stasis."[6] In
other words, the tachistoscope can be seen as representing what Crary
sees as a central paradox of modernity—speeding machines and static
bodies—a situation that we in the twenty-first century experience daily
in our navigation of the World Wide Web without moving more than
our fingertips. Friedrich Kittler also acknowledges the importance of
the tachistoscope in his media-based epistemological history, *Discourse
Networks 1800/1900*. He describes the tachistoscope as designating a
transformation in the history of technologized reading and writing,
wherein writing "is no longer based on an individual capable of imbu-
ing it with coherence through connecting curves and the expressive
pressure of the pen;" instead, tachistoscopic writing "swells in an apparatus that cuts up individuals into test material."[7] Written content—as
well as the individual reader of this content—becomes disconnected,
discrete, digital.[8] The tachistoscope, Crary and Kittler suggest, helps to
usher in the modern digital age. But it is in a recent work of cultural
studies that the tachistoscope really gets its real due.

In *Swift Viewing: The Popular Life of Subliminal Influence*, Charles
Acland describes the tachistoscope as "an underacknowledged and
highly influential apparatus."[9] Acland presents an extended study of

the tachistoscope in the process of examining his main focus: the role of subliminal messaging—or, "the subliminal thesis" as he calls it—in twentieth-century American society. Acland's book provides an indispensable historical context for understanding *Project*, particularly its adaptation of the tachistoscope as a means for presenting subliminal messaging. But there is a glaring and indicative absence in Acland's cultural studies approach; at least, it is glaring to the gaze of a literary critic approaching the tachistoscope via Poundstone's digital literature. Acland neglects to discuss in detail the images and texts displayed on the tachistoscope, and this disinterest in the specific material presentation and poetics of swift-viewing is particularly apparent in Acland's otherwise authoritative documentation of Vicary's subliminal hoax, but it is not unique to this book. Rather, it is characteristic of media studies and media archaeology more generally, wherein a focus on technology often diverts consideration away from the *techne*, from the artistic or affective meaning. Poundstone's *Project* promotes a focus on the tachistoscope *through* digital poetics. It experiments with the kinds of "projects," the kinds of poetics, that a digital tachistoscope can produce. In so doing, Project performs media archaeology *in* art.

"Media archaeology" describes critical efforts to excavate and examine the cultural contexts surrounding individual media technologies and their use. Rather than denote a specific critical method, "media archaeology" excavates and examines the historical specificities of media forms and practices. Forged from the work of Marshall McLuhan, Michel Foucault, and Friedrich Kittler, such practices approach media objects as operating within larger ecologies or environments, which include technologies but also historical, cultural, and political protocols.[10] As a result, such critical excavation supports the consideration and reassessment of media objects and practices as well as the continual rewriting of media history. Wendy Chun writes that media archaeology enables "seemingly forgotten moments in the history of the media we glibly call 'old' to be rediscovered and transformed."[11] *Project* is one such effort: it rediscovers the tachistoscope in ways that encourage excavation and rediscovery of its role in a particular history of reading practices (speed-reading) and poetic effects.

Project's act of media archaeology depends upon its remediation of the tachistoscope into Flash. As Jay David Bolter and Richard Grusin define it, "remediation" is "the representation of one medium in another."[12]

Remediation is a way of understanding media history that supports focusing on media *as* content. The theory of remediation repurposes (or "refashions," to use Bolter and Grusin's language) Marshall McLuhan's dictum that "the medium is the message," and *Project* exemplifies McLuhan's point that "the 'content' of any medium is always another medium"[13] by making the tachistoscope the content of its digital remediation. This repurposing of the older medium into the newer one, as Bolter and Grusin explain, "ensures that the older medium cannot be entirely effaced; the new medium remains dependent on the older one."[14] *Project* performs an artistic act of media archaeology that shows how the tachistoscope is a vital part of the history of digital media and poetics.

ARCHAEOLOGY OF THE AUTHORING TOOL (MARK)

Flash is one of *Project*'s central reading machines, and reading it tells us much about the literary work it presents. Indeed, if *Project*, in its executed form, offers a remediation of the tachistoscope that promotes consideration of it as a reading machine, then the Flash source files offer a way of understanding tachistoscopes as writing machines. To create the tachistoscopic effects of the animated web work, Poundstone had to make key choices about what aspects of these devices to represent and how to simulate them. Would this be a tachistoscope for training speed-reading or for testing comprehension? Would the virtual machine display a series of words, or the same word, or groups of words? Would the device present one text or be a tool for viewing multiple texts? However, no decision was more pivotal than his selection of his artistic tool for producing his tachistoscope, the Flash animation software. This tool demands our attention and deserves a bit of media archaeology of its own.

We might begin by considering how Flash presents a software analogy to the tachistoscope or to the class of technologies that have borne that name. By "software analogy," I mean that the software's functioning and interface bear an analogous relationship to those featured in tachistoscopes. On one hand, both Flash and tachistoscopes engage and exploit the limits of human vision; both technologies are ocular devices for the timed presentation of images, wherein revealing and concealing are tightly entangled. However, where the tachistoscope is often used to bring to the forefront the potential and limitations of human visual perception, Flash capitalizes on these limitations to create the illusion of seamless motion. To put these two tools in relation to one another is to create a kind of dialogic relationship that accentuates their similarities and differences.

During the past two decades, Flash has become one of the most prominent tools for animation design due to its affordances for producing slick animations and its metaphor-driven GUI.[15] Surely, there was a time in the late 1990s when Flash was synonymous with glossy splash pages and dazzling advertisements on the Internet, even as its uses were being explored for animation and games.[16] Flash began as drawing software called SmartSketch (created by FutureWave in 1994), but with the affordances of the Internet and the Java add-ons in browsers such as Netscape, the company converted the program into animation software for the web. Originally called CelAnimator, and then FutureSplash Animator (1996), the program drew praise, especially from graphic designers interested in animation effects, for its ease of use in producing animations.[17] Rereleased by Macromedia as Flash (a portmanteau of its previous name) in 1996, the product quickly rose to prominence and popularity.[18] Flash produced animations ready for online distribution, which distinguished it from Director, the forerunner to Flash in the Macromedia studio, which was aimed more at CD-ROM distribution.

Flash offers two modes of computational creation, either through the graphical interface with its keyframes and layers or through the composition of alphanumeric code using ActionScript. Though they offer relatively equal methods for programming, it is Flash's visual interface that distinguishes this program and did so even in its earlier incarnation as FutureSplash Animator. By enabling users to build without writing code, by virtue of its sophisticated graphical user interface, Flash lowered the barrier to entry for web design. Beginning by offering a set of actions that could be added to objects, Macromedia developed a scripting language based on ECMAScript (also known as Netscape JavaScript). Macromedia released ActionScript as part of Flash 4 in 1999, revised the language with ActionScript 2.0 in 2003, and revised it again with ActionScript 3 in 2006. As described later in this chapter, *Project*'s use of ActionScript 2.0 makes many of the piece's more remarkable visual effects possible. The addition of this scripting language, with its increasing affordances for interactivity, to the intuitive GUI environment made Flash an extremely attractive authoring tool. Indeed, the field of electronic literature illustrates Flash's rise to prominence, for, as Jessica explained in chapter 1, the second generation of electronic literature was largely Flash-based. Flash, and the aesthetic of dynamic animations and novel interfaces it enabled, made a lasting impact on what people have come to expect from the Internet, specifically online games, online animation, and electronic literature. Flash's pervasiveness led Lev Manovich to coin the term "Generation Flash" to describe the cultural moment in which a critical mass of designers and developers used this platform to generate digital content.[19]

But, Flash is a proprietary technology, and this fact has had technical, commercial, and ideological consequences. After it was acquired by Adobe Systems in 2005, Flash became the target of ire from both Internet programmers worried about its security vulnerabilities and also competitor Apple Computers, whose late cofounder and charismatic leader, Steve Jobs, took on Flash as his personal nemesis. In a 2010 post, Jobs decried Flash as buggy software that introduced security vulnerabilities and whose "100% proprietary" nature shutdown innovation and development.[20] These two critiques are entwined, for the paradigm of proprietary software forestalls the development communities who so powerfully contribute to open-source projects and help exterminate software bugs and other security vulnerabilities. However, Jobs may have had other motivations, since Flash offered a platform for developing glossy games and applications without going through an app store such as Apple's. Regardless of his motivations, Jobs's critique of Flash painted the software in hues that never fully faded. With the advent of HTML5 and Apple's initial refusal to run Flash (with the exception of YouTube) on iPads and iPhones, Flash lost its prominence as the definitive platform for creating animation effects on the Internet.

The closed nature of Flash directly impacted our reading of *Project*. Flash's code is a "compiled" language—a programming language whose original source code is converted into a machine-readable form before it is run—and, unlike a web page which can be examined by selecting "view source," compiled code usually lacks many details of the original source. What one sees is often condensed in a fashion that makes it largely inscrutable to humans. While *Project* was originally authored in a human-readable source format (.fla), the software compiles the exported file into bytecode (.swf) for running on the Flash virtual machine. The human-readable text that was originally present in the source code (.fla) is absent from the final compiled form of the work (.swf) that was published and distributed. This absence is a challenge for readers wanting to access the programming code. Much in the same way that literary scholars seek to consult manuscript versions of print-published texts, we sought to consult the code in order to study the work's creation and evolution. The lack of access to the proprietary code provided a challenge similar to what a literary historian finds when confronting the absence of a stage play or a set of galley proofs in an author's archived papers. However, when excavating for the .fla source file, we have some recovery options that are not available to the scholar in search of missing galleys.

Compiling is a one-way process that produces the .swf from the .fla file, and the original source code cannot be fully recovered from the final object. However, it can be reconstructed—in part—through a process called "decompiling." Decompiling is usually productive for recovering the many "assets" of the original, such as the individual image files and sound files. However, the decompiler cannot "discover" the previously existing ActionScript source code because that code has been transformed and translated and is consequently absent. Instead, it infers functionally equivalent code that achieves the same ends, even if this new code lacks the nuances of the original. The decompiler will, for example, supply code that has the same effect as that written by the original programmer, but that replacement code may lack the programmer's style and grace.

People who do not program often assume that code is like arithmetic, with symbols and processes that are expressed in the only way possible. However, programming actually creates artifacts of processes that reflect the selections made by the programmer from the paradigm of possible options in the programming language. In this way, programming has more in common with architecture than arithmetic; it is a constructive process that creates objects that must be able to stand and operate within the constraints of set determinants: a budget, material affordances, natural forces, etc. The original source code bears the imprint and inflection of all of these constraints as well as artifacts from the stages of its creation. For this reason, using a decompiler is not so much excavating or uncovering as it is the creation of a proxy. To read decompiled source (or to read a reconstructed proxy) is an act of machine-assisted imagination, an intervention in the locked-away or hidden processes of proprietary software production and distribution that conceal the means of production from both consumers and competitors.

When we ran a decompiler on *Project*[21] to recover and reconstruct its source code (see selected contents in Appendix E), we expected to find certain things. Namely, we were looking for the narrative text and the words that interrupt the narrative—which we considered "subliminal" words due to the influence of Poundstone's prefatory framing in the entryscreens. We were not sure what the text would look like or where it would be in the .swf, for there are countless ways the visual effect of the interspersed words could have been created. Both sets of words (the words that comprise the story and those that provide the subliminal text) could be contained in one array, or one sequence of the story words could be layered on top of the blinking subliminal words in discrete movie clips. We certainly did not anticipate the structure that our excavation uncovered. It turned out that the story words and the subliminal words are stored in variables as two separate lists. The words of the story are not enclosed in the recreated .fla (and this was not a side effect of using the decompiler); instead, the code contained a call to load the text from an external file named BP.txt.

The BP.txt (presumably Bottomless Pit) file was located alongside the Flash file on any site that hosted *Project* (see contents in Appendix A). The .txt extension stands for "text file," a simple document with minimally formatted alphanumeric characters. That text file contained the complete contents of the story in linear form (without paragraph or line breaks) and also something else: a list of the words that constitute the subliminal text (which we discuss in more detail in chapter 4). We found another element in that file: a final variable "done" which indicates that all text has been loaded and the piece can begin. This brings the total of variables assigned in that file to three: the story words, the subliminal words, and "done." Discovering this separate text file (BP.txt) had a dramatic effect on how we understood *Project*'s formal and technical operations. First, we now had the complete text of the story and in a text-only format. Second, we knew that *Project* operated by displaying the sequence of the story words interspersed with subliminal words drawn from another list, though we did not know in what order the subliminal words were presented.

Given our experience watching the animation, we largely assumed a randomness to the presentation order. With the discovery of this file, we could examine the story and subliminal words as text; we could separate them from the intentionally disruptive multimodal interface design and the rapid, flashing display speed that constitutes *Project*'s poetic.

More significantly, the BP.txt file proved that all of *Project*'s text is actually external to its form. The story text and subliminal text is programmatically separate from the software scope that formally remediates a tachistoscope. This means that when we read the story of the Bottomless Pit, human interactors actually use *Project* as a scope or reading machine to load and view BP.txt. This technical fact, uncovered in the source files, informs a new interpretation of *Project*'s formal performance. We can now suggest the following: *Project* is a scope. On the surface, it appears to be a multimodal animation that plays as a single digital .swf file. However, *Project* is not one file. It is something through which we look in order to see something else. That something else, it turns out, is a separate text file, BP.txt. Essentially, the Flash manifestation of the piece, the embedded .swf or Shockwave-Flash, operates as a medium or tool for viewing text. Think of the Tachistoscope.swf file as a kind of slide projector and the text of the story and subliminal words as the slides. Consequently, the formal design of *Project* could theoretically be repurposed to present other text; all it would take is to change the words in the BP.txt file.[22] Any text can be dropped into that file, so long as it is assigned to the variables that *Project* loads into its movie. This means that the story of the Bottomless Pit is really just one possible text of many that could play through this tool that Poundstone created.

Project, or more properly "Tachistoscope.swf," is technically and programmatically a reading machine. Understanding this technical fact shows how the tale of the Bottomless Pit that *Project* tells and that "Tachistoscope.swf" presents is literally the "project" for the remediated digital tachistoscope. Reading the code of this work of digital literature thus exposes how *Project* remediates the tachistoscope into digital code, creating a scopic reading machine for presenting the story of Bottomless Pit.

THE SEVEN "DISTRACTIONS" (MARK)

Tachistoscopes are tools used to test, train, and condition perception via swift viewing. Many of them possess a core functionality: they display a barely detectable or difficult-to-detect set of signs accompanied by a more easily detected set of signs. Consequently, tachistoscopes are machines that can either facilitate fast reading or disrupt reading via distractions.

Project remediates both aspects of the tachistoscope. At certain moments in the fast-flashing animation, the screen is bombarded by an onslaught of small moving icons. Little plus signs and spheres fly across the screen and interrupt the steady stream of flashing narrative text. In these moments, the soundtrack reverberates with the sound of collisions, unsynchronized rhythms, and clanging sounds that pierce the meditative tone of the soundtrack and aurally register the disruption happening on-screen. These distractions draw the reader's attention away from the pulsing vortex at the center of the stage. When we explore the code (excerpted at length in Appendix D), we see that *Project* produces distractions in order to divert from the main story text at the center of the screen; moreover, we see how the work employs the tachistoscope's functionality to do this in ways that also serve to complicate simplistic binaries distinguishing attention from distraction.

Project's "distractions" are actually a multisensory arrangement of individual elements and display modes—clusters of settings which may change the work. In the code, there are seven "Levels" of distractions, and they are constituted by a combination of a few basic elements: a background color, a color for the main text, a color for the subliminal text, a sound, and an animation (usually authored using the Flash GUI rather than the ActionScript code). Poundstone's term "level" does not refer to a depth metaphor (since these elements are not actually stacked vertically atop each other), nor does it refer to increasing intensity (since higher number levels do not add more distracting elements than lower numbered ones). Instead, these "levels" operate as parallel planes of experiencing the work, theme, and variation of the presentation mode of the system. They are modes of engaging this multimodal work. I call these clusters of effects "distractions" because they primarily serve to disrupt the reader's ability to focus attention on the continuous stream of text flashing at the center of the screen.

The "levels" are called forth in a random order, so a reader might consider them as individual effects (for example, a new sound loop) that are layered on without any intentional order. Consequently, these elements might be perceived as disruptions to the story, "noise" that keeps the reader from comprehending the communicated message.[23] These screen and sonic effects might create a chaotic event, but they are not mere noise. Indeed, these arrangements and sequences of effects actually produce meaning through meaningful juxtapositions. Examining their convergences exposes how *Project* works to control and choreograph the reader's attention. We can pursue such examination by considering the source code that determines their appearance. When we do, we see that these "distractions" serve a central poetic purpose in *Project*: they distract in order to direct attention. They draw attention to themselves; they disrupt, but they are in themselves meaningful elements.

Table 2.1 presents a list of the effects produced in each of the eight "levels." Given that the story text is always black, we can see in the table that level 0 (the default level) will present both story and subliminal texts in black against the pulsating blue gradient circle against a blue background. Within some levels, variations are created through the random selection of colored icons and background colors—as in the example of the randomly chosen background color in level 3. Additional variety is created because not all levels erase all the previous effects. For example, level 0 does not erase the level 4 movie of a collapsing yellow ring. In that way, the code does allow for certain palimpsests that are not described in each individual level but instead can add effects to ones initiated during the previous executed level. Also, not every level includes a sound, but those that do add various additional sounds that create dissonant bursts in the soundtrack.

The code for these sections reveals how much distraction is determined by ActionScript and, thus, how much distraction Poundstone intentionally developed. Consider the following annotated code.[24] These annotations take the form of code comments—text lines prefixed by a double-slash (//), which indicate that they should be ignored by the machine. All comments were written by Poundstone. I added line numbers to the code in order to make it easier to read and explicate.

TABLE 2.1: Table of the seven levels of distraction.

#	Movie	Background	Sound	Description
0	background2_mc persists, all levels. . . . and unloads: level2Effect_mc, level3Effect_mc	Blue	Mainloop (persists on all levels)	*// get rid of purple background but allow orange-yellow if playing* The default level. Visual: Teal ring, pulsing blue background. Aural: Mainloop, pulsing electronic rhythm with cello sawing.
1	level4Effect_mc: inwardGradient . . . and unloads: level3Effect_mc	Blue	My Song26	Visual: Yellow-ish gradient circle shrinks. The additional pictures appear. Aural: Vibrato organ runs.
2	level2Effect_mc: level2Effect	Blue	My Song5	Visual: Pulsing target in orange and yellow. Aural: Manic organ runs followed by more melodious chimes.
3	myFixationCrosses: fixationCrosses . . . unloads: level2Effect_mc	Random		Visual: White crosses, then random white icon flutters in 4 corners. Random background color. Subliminal: text is white (normally black).
4	level4Effect_mc: inwardGradient . . . and unloads: level2Effect_mc	Black	Tweak effect	Visual: Yellow-ish gradient circle shrinks. Aural: Just one high flute note like a single flute tweet or piano key.
5	level3Effect_mc: level3Effect		My Song18	Visual: Pulsating concentric circles of blue white, target. Background unchanged. Aural: Notes descend in octaves, ascend in synthesized, high-pitched vibration.
6	level6Effect_mc: level6Effect	Blue	My Song21	Visual: Orange spheres or red 3-D crosses speed horizontally to the screen edge. Aural: Electronic sounds evoke synthesis or computer-generated audio.
7	myLevel5Effect: level5Effect . . . and unloads: level3Effect_mc	Blue	My Song22	Visual: Ring pulses white to blue; flashes yellow when collapsing and disappears. Aural: Single chord, hard attack on a synthesizer.

```
1.   var index = math.random();
2.   if (index>.75) {
3.         level = 1;
4.         my_extraSound.attachSound("My Song26.mp3");
5.         my_extraSound.start();
6.         // get rid of purple background but allow orange-yellow if playing
7.         centerPoint.attachMovie("inwardGradient", "level4
           Effect_mc", 111);
8.         _level0.centerPoint.level3Effect_mc.unloadMovie();
9.         // set blue background color
10.        myColor.setRGB(0x0099CC);
11.        mySubliminalColor.setRGB(0x000000);
12.        }
```

First, we notice that the code chooses which level will be displayed, and it does so using the "math.random" function to draw from eight evenly apportioned segments (setting level 1 in the range of .75 to .825) (lines 1–4). As a result of equal division, no display effect is likely to be displayed more than any other. We also notice that, if we call only the base level 0 the original display mode, then *Project* spends seven-eighths of the time in distraction mode. In other words, though I'm referring to these other seven levels and their effects as "distractions," the majority of the playthrough of *Project* is composed of story text accompanied by these additional visual and sonic effects; this fact calls into question just how foundational the base level is. In that sense, it is foundational the way a jazz melody is: more often represented in variation than in its original form.

Next in this sequence, the code creates some auditory distraction when it "attaches" the mp3 "My Song26.mp3" to the extraSound object. "My Song26" is a chord played with a vibrato effect on what sounds like a silent movie theater organ (line 5), increasing the eerie feeling of this layer. To the centerPoint object, the code attaches a movie to be played behind the words: "inwardGradient" is the name of the movie in the file's library; "level4Effect_mc" is the name of this particular instance of that movie; and "111" refers to the display depth on the z-axis (line 8). The movie "inwardGradient" displays a yellow circle (with a gradient fill) that collapses in on itself within the duration of approximately one second. Poundstone adds a comment in the code that is worth notice here. He notes that this distraction will "get rid of purple background but allow orange-yellow if playing" (line 6). Here, "purple background" refers to the level3Effect, the pulsating concentric blue circles. The vortex, this iconic element of *Project*, is thus wiped from the screen during this level, proving it to be yet another effect rather than a constant backdrop. Finally the level sets the background color ("myColor") to blue and subliminal word color (mySubliminalColor) to black (lines 10–11).

While "distraction" serves a useful purpose for discussing these clusters of effects, the term is an oversimplification of their role in remediating the tachistoscope. These distractions actually serve a specific purpose: they prime the reader to detect some, though not all, of the subliminal text. Calling them "distractions" imposes a hierarchy of signs (text, subliminal text, and distraction) and mischaracterizes their actual and poetic functioning in the piece. Examining the code, as we will do with the level 3 effects in particular, suggests that one of the distractions—what Poundstone describes, in his code, as "fixation crosses"—serves a very specific purpose. It sets up the viewer for transmissions in the optical periphery and liminal space of consciousness. Specifically, the fixation crosses herald the arrival of the subliminal words and prime the viewer to perceive a partial vision of the piece. Let's see how this works by turning to the code.

Level 3 is marked by a musical snippet of a high-pitched flute, a sonic layer that adds discord rather than harmony to an already noisy soundtrack. The code reads:

```
1.  if (index>.50) {
2.          level = 3;
3.          _levelo.centerPoint.level2Effect_mc.unloadMovie();
4.          var hue = Math.floor(Math.random()*(noOfColors+1));
5.          myColor.setRGB(palette[hue]);
6.          mySubliminalColor.setRGB(0xFFFFFF);
7.          fixation_mc.attachMovie("fixationCrosses",
            "myFixationCrosses", 300);
8.  }
```

In the first two lines of code, the level 3 effect is chosen one-seventh of the time—that is, index has been assigned a randomly chosen number

FIGURE 2.1: The Level 2 movie (pulsing yellow and orange). (Screenshot by Mark Marino; with the permission of William Poundstone.)

commodious

between 0 and 1, and this level will trigger if that number falls between .5 and .625 (index>.50). On line 3, the sequence begins by clearing away the level 2 movie (unloadMovie), which is the pulsing yellow and orange target.

Next, the code chooses a random color, using the "Math.random()" function on the noOfColors or "number of colors." It will assign this color to the background. The most significant change happens next, as the color of the blinking subliminal words is switched from black to white (0xFFFFFF), and then a movie, which Poundstone names "fixationCrosses," plays at depth "300," which represents its placement on the z-axis. This value ensures that the movie is playing in the foreground. The combined effects of level 3 demonstrate the ways in which *Project* directs our attention to some of its elements while obscuring others.

The key animation in this sequence displays the "fixationCrosses," a group of four white crosses that flash across the cardinal locations of NW, NE, SW, and SE. The term "fixation cross" describes a feature of optometric measurement machinery. It is the plus sign in the center of your visual field when your optometrist asks you to peer into a device for measuring eyesight. It is also part of the history of the tachistoscope, for the visual element is used to focus or fixate the subject's vision on a particular spot. However, fixation crosses are not, as their name might suggest, meant to ensure that the viewer continues to perceive them. They are visual markers that assist in directing attention but do not necessarily become themselves the object of fixation. Indeed, fixation crosses are used in many tests of visual perception to steady and position the subject's vision so that peripheral vision can be measured. In other words, it is often what is not displayed at the point of fixation but something else that matters and is the object of study whenever the cross appears. This is important to recognize because fixation crosses serve to index and signify the fact that the viewer's gaze can be influenced, set by some outside, intervening force. This is what *Project* does and shows. By priming and fixating the reader to focus on the white objects on the screen, *Project* seems to be cuing the viewer to perceive the subliminal words that appear in white, but the code reveals something very different happening.

To the general reader, who just reads *Project* on-screen and via a web browser, *Project*'s poetic presents the story one word at a time, interrupted occasionally by faster-flashing, white, subliminal words. However, opening the Flash file that enables this performance and examining the eight different levels reveals something remarkable: the subliminal words are actually constantly displayed in the same order every time. They alternate with the story words, though obviously for a shorter duration of time, but they are *always* flashing. For some evidence of the constant display of words and the order in which they appear, see Appendix C (wherein the stream of output from one playthrough of the story text is presented in chronological order and printed into a text file, just as the words appear on-screen). This list was created by altering the Flash file to output into a separate screen every word displayed. However, a typical viewer of *Project* will not perceive all of these words. Most likely, she will only notice the ones that appear in white, starkly distinguished from the black story text; these white words only occur while the level 3 effect is displaying.

This discovery is significant for a few reasons. First, we find that the subliminal words in *Project* are not merely distractions or momentary visual effects. Rather, they are presented as a continuous and constant thread. These words are woven throughout *Project*'s fabric. However, their persistence is obscured on-screen by something else. As I have demonstrated, when this thread becomes more noticeable to the naked eye—when the subliminal words appear in white letters so that they can be viewed against the colorful background—then, "fixation crosses" appear. Appearing as flashes of white, the crosses cue the eye to discern more whiteness just before the color of the subliminal words is set to turn white. In actuality, the subliminal words are constantly displayed and much more often in black (seven out of eight times) than in white. Thus, while the appearance of a fixation cross helps the reader to perceive the subliminal words during that level, the reader is more likely *not* to register the black subliminal words. This perceptual sleight of hand echoes the aesthetic of the piece itself, as when Poundstone announces the use of subliminal content in the paratextual entryscreens, while the work, of course, still hides that content.

Project plays with perception, leading it and misleading it, calling attention to our attention and how impressionable it is. The work purposefully and programmatically commingles distraction and attention as part of its literary poetic. In so doing, *Project* demonstrates how both registers are necessary to perception and to the act of reading.

BREAKING THE TACHISTOSCOPE (JEREMY)

Project presents us with a remediated tachistoscope, a timed visual apparatus, but unlike mechanical tachistoscopes, its effects are produced by a very different set of mechanisms and processes. Although Flash is meant to deliver a consistent experience across different platforms, *Project*'s behavior is not always predictable. Key differences between the way a mechanical tachistoscope might function and the way the actual code performs become apparent when *Project* malfunctions, particularly when the regulated timing of the Flash file loses control and speeds up to a blistering pace. By reading this breakdown we can better understand the roles of intentionality and accident in the work. We also come to a surprising realization about how speed operates in *Project*—and perhaps in digital media more generally.

When *Project* runs as expected, the remediated tachistoscope operates with clocklike regularity. New words and images tick by at regular intervals. Sometimes, however, all does not go as expected. Often, as *Project* runs, part of the already-fast work suddenly accelerates. While the music and background graphics continue to play at their usual rate, the sequence of icons and words speeds up. Images blur together, and words flicker at such speed that the story text becomes illegible before vanishing altogether. When this happens, all that can be seen, surprisingly, is the periodic flashing of subliminal words. It is not apparent to the reader why this acceleration has occurred, whether or not it is intentional, or if it will stop.

We initially dismissed this occasional acceleration when we encountered it in the course of researching *Project*. It appeared to be a mere unintended bug in the software.[25] Yet frequent reencounters led us to consider this acceleration to be a part of the work, whether intentional or not. What was the significance of the fact that, when *Project* breaks down, it does so not by grinding to a halt, but instead by speeding up? Upon closer inspection, we discovered that the acceleration effect is not a bug in the sense of a miskeyed line of code, nor is it caused by an incompatibility between the reader's current computer and the one on which *Project* was developed. Rather, it is caused by an odd interaction between how *Project* keeps time and a design flaw in the Flash platform. The problem emerges only if the computer on which *Project* is running temporarily slows down—whether due to browsing the Internet in multiple tabs, playing videos, or almost any significant demand on a computer's processor. When such a slowdown occurs, Flash attempts to keep things running on time by skipping a few steps in its instructions. It jumps ahead in the programmed timeline, and this action can cause a skip in the code. Like a clock whose gear slips so that the hands spin freely, a single skip in the code loop can cause the Flash animation to stop regulating time. This results in the loop playing as fast as the computer is able. A moment of slowed processing results in unchecked speed of display. The result is a very different *Project* indeed.

When Flash's temporal tactics cause *Project* to slip, they reveal the ways in which *Project* is a work of web-based art. Flash's catch-up strategy was developed to stream animation over slow and unreliable network connections. Consequently, while *Project* need not be viewed over the Internet,[26] it was created using software that always functions—and malfunctions—like a technology that was developed for the Internet. *Project* runs optimally only in one particular technological setting and context, and any changes to that context can have unintended consequences. In particular, its aesthetic may be altered by changes to hardware, software, or even other uses of a given computer at a given moment. In chapter 1, Jessica described *Project* and similar Flash-based works as primarily noninteractive. We can further complicate this; sudden acceleration is one example of the ways in which *Project* offers forms of unexpected interactivity that appear unintended in its design.

In digital media and digital arts there are several related critical traditions of exploring unanticipated outcomes as part of the aesthetics of a work. These outcomes may be celebrated either as happy accidents or as intentional creations. Two concepts in particular are helpful for understanding *Project*'s breakdowns: "glitch" in digital arts and "counterplay" in games studies. The word "glitch" originated as technical jargon; it signifies a slippage, bug, or error. When discussed in digital media criticism, a glitch has been described as an opportunity to understand mediation. In their entry on "glitch" in *Software Studies: A Lexicon*, Olga Goriunova and Alexia Shulgin describe a glitch as "a singular dysfunctional event that allows insight . . . a mess that is a moment, a possibility to glance at software's inner structure."[27] In the digital arts, "glitch" is an aesthetic of intentional error that finds beauty in the breakdown.[28] Contemporary glitch art is part of a long history of arts practice concerned with investigating the specific materiality of media—seen, for example, in Nam June Paik's use of magnets to distort the television, an artistic practice which calls attention to the nature of the cathode ray tube (Magnet TV, 1965).[29] Likewise, glitching performances of *Project* call attention to its nature as software art.

If the art concept of "glitch" is a celebration of digital accidents, then the game studies concept of "counterplay" is about causing such accidents on purpose—staging disruptive readings that go against the grain of a digital work's design. Nick Dyer-Witheford and Greig de Peuter describe counterplay as "acts of contestation within and against the ideologies of individual games."[30] While glitching usually emphasizes a surprising behavior that arises out of the materiality of the work, counterplaying additionally grants one license to modify that materiality—hacking, modding, remixing, or reshaping the work to other purposes and other aesthetic agendas.

Considered through the lenses of glitching or counterplaying, we might understand a disruptive reading of *Project* as anything that breaks free of the prescribed forms of reading which are imposed by the work, whether through material accident or intervention. Each potential glitch becomes a different opportunity for counterplaying *Project*, if we choose. By seizing control of the conditions of speed that govern the work's reception and intentionally speeding up the work, we can change the text into a series of sporadic subliminal words. Alternately, we might prevent the work from displaying any visual elements other than the "distractions."[31] Or we might overlay the entryscreen paragraphs atop the still-running work.[32] The possibility of such transformations is a part of the work, and, indeed, a reader may happen upon any one of them by accident. With more effort, more dramatic alterations are possible—such as intervening in the source code to entirely remove or replace some element of the text or images that play through *Project*'s scope. Breakdowns, glitching, and even counterplay are already part of the real (rather than the ideal) ways that *Project* is read and may be read. Each transformation has its own implications for the significance of the work. As an example, let us return to our initial acceleration "bug" and consider it more carefully.

When *Project* accelerates, it also reveals something that was hidden from us by the work's normal functioning: a way in which our historical relationship to speed has continued to change. As discussed earlier in this chapter, the purpose of tachistoscopic mechanisms was (as its name suggests) swift-viewing. This swiftness was achieved through acceleration, with devices such as high-speed shutters operating ever-faster in order to observe ever-diminishing fractions of a second. However, contemporary computing already performs operations at sub-millisecond speeds, durations too short for human perception. When functioning normally, *Project* uses code not to *accelerate*, but to *decelerate*. The code is a regulating mechanism that restrains the imperceptibly fast cycles of the computer, limiting them to the sub-liminal and liminal time scales that are appropriate for human readers. When a physical tachistoscope malfunctions, its shutter slows or stops. Its technique of acceleration yields to a stillness. By contrast, when *Project* malfunctions, its technique of deceleration may yield to unchecked speed. When both operate normally, we might say that the mechanical reading machine strives for speed, while the digital one works to impose slowness. While it is perhaps counterintuitive, the work is not speeding up poetry to computer speed, but is instead altering the rate at which the machine reads the text, slowing it down toward a human time scale. In fact, staged slowness may be a fundamental property of many electronic literary works, and of digital textuality more generally. If the way we normally read *Project* is actually a form of slowness, this suggests an even more radical approach to interpreting the work: in complete stillness.

　■

How might we read *Project* in a state of stillness? And, if we were able to do so, what might we find? *Project* pours across the screen in an irreversible flow, whether as a steady stream or a rushing torrent. Yet, the experience of reading *Project* tends to arrest us in this shifting present, impairing our ability to reflect upon its past or anticipate its future. The work thus produces a paradox of stasis and mobility. In the beginning of this chapter, Jessica discussed the paradox Jonathan Crary identifies as central to the emergence of the modern, viewing subject and the tachistoscope's role in that development. In addition to occupying this general subject position, the viewer of *Project* is arrested in the moment of reading in a way that is specific to the work's digital nature.

Due to the lack of user control, each moment of *Project* is irretrievable. Due to computationally randomized elements, each moment is also unique. While the story word sequence is always the same, rerunning the piece will always create a different conjunction of colors, icons, words, and pictures that frame, obscure, emphasize, or interrupt in different ways. Many moments in *Project* are both unique within a given playthrough *and* unlikely to be exactly repeated even if we replay the work thousands of times. Heraclitus held that we cannot step twice into the same river. Because of its combinatoric variability, the experience of reading *Project* encourages both disorientation and acute awareness of the ephemerality of each moment.

In our previous chapter, Jessica suggested that *Project* draws a parallel between the world of the Pit and that of the reader. Just as the characters fail to understand the Pit because they cannot access it in its entirety, so too do we readers also suffer from a similar inability to map out and orient ourselves within the work as it flashes by. But we *can* navigate this river in ways other than stepping into it and diving deep; there are also boats, levees, and dams—other ways and techniques for taming these rushing data streams. Earlier, Mark used decompiling software to enable close reading of *Project*'s source code. Here, we extend that approach from an archaeology of the mechanism to an archaeology of the visible images presented by *Project*. Specifically, we will excavate the contents of many moments on-screen that have been compiled within a video recording. By transforming *Project* from a moving animation into a still image—by arresting it, as it arrests us—we can learn a good deal about the work. In particular, and perhaps paradoxically, we learn about how time works in *Project*. The effort to dam the flowing river allows us to focus on its duration: the duration of its story cycle, the duration of its "distractions" (which Mark described earlier), and the way that those distractions act like stanzas to structure a temporal reading pace and poetic prosody for the text.

This is not the first time that we have considered stillness and the screen. In our previous chapter, we interpreted the visual layers of a single still screenshot—a "biohazard poppy"—in order to explicate the various elements engaged in producing the palimpsestic effect. In this section, we move from examining a single, frozen screenshot to examining the entire frozen work. To read *Project* in a state of stillness, we create a single large image of one entire playthrough of *Project*.

The visualization in Image 1.1 presents a "montage" view. This montage illustrates one full cycle of one unique playthrough of the *Project* story text (including the subliminal text flashing between screens). Each small square is a new image of the screen (a screenshot) taken from that recording; they proceed temporally in reading order, left-to-right, top-to-bottom, like the words in this paragraph. For this reason we can think of the montage view as presenting a page-like view of a *Project* playthrough, as it combines the contents of the digital medium by using an arrangement that recalls familiar print formats.[33] The visual material was initially captured in a video recording of the playthrough. While initially totaling over thirty-five thousand frames, the recording was later reduced in two ways. First, we noted the point at which the story words begin to repeat, and stopped there: at nine minutes and forty-two seconds.[34] The stopping point is indicated by the solid black bar at the bottom of the image. Second, we reduced the speed of the recording to twelve frames per second, or 6,983 frames total. In this montage, those frames were then arranged in 120 columns and 59 rows. Each horizontal row represents a ten-second duration in the recording; six rows summarize one minute of *Project* playing. Tracing a finger halfway across the montage marks off five seconds, while tracing halfway down the image skips forward almost five minutes. When used in this way, the montage serves as a map of time, a geography of animation events as if seen from great heights.

Our technique of connecting many small screenshots of different moments together into a single montage view is drawn from the fields of data and information visualization.[35] In particular, it is one example of an uncommon approach that Lev Manovich defines as "media visualization":[36]

> Media visualization: creating new visual representations from the actual visual media objects, or their parts. Rather than representing text, images, video or other media though new visual signs such as points or rectangles, media visualizations build new representations out of the original media. Images remain images; text remains text.

Manovich also describes this as "direct visualization" or "visualization without quantification." For Manovich, the significance of this approach is that it dispenses with the principle of reduction—of representing each image as a point, for example—that has characterized information visualization techniques for over two centuries.[37] By refusing to reduce, a media visualization allows media to be differently represented while still preserving many media-specific aspects of the original.

When reading *Project*, the immediate consequence of a montage approach is not a specific interpretive discovery, but rather a *breakthrough in legibility*. The montage changes not our specific understanding of what we read, but the very forms of reading that are possible. In order to understand these new possibilities, consider what the page-like aspect of the montage reveals in comparison to what was revealed by our earlier discovery of BP.txt. Like the montage, this source code file affords us a way of viewing the one-at-a-time words of *Project* together, as if on a page. However, as Mark's source explorations showed, BP.txt contains two separate sets of words, and these sets appear *prior* to being interleaved into a single stream by the running *Project*. Both the montage and the source code make it possible to browse the complete text of *Project*, but this complete text is read and written in radically different ways. Just as a screenshot enables us to contemplate patterns on a single screen, and just as the source text enables us to reflect on patterns throughout the narrative, so too does our montage assist us in considering patterns in *Project*. The montage shows the work spread out over minutes rather than instants. It thus allows us to consider how *Project* behaves as a process over time.

What is the temporal structure of *Project*? Just as a poem might be measured out in syllables, feet, words, lines, couplets, or stanzas, time in *Project* is structured by different durations—that is, things change at different speeds. We can engage these speeds by reading the montage at different distances. Up close, our eyes wander across the spaces of each small square screenshot, noting its contents. Leaning back a bit, we read (left-to-right) the row of imagetexts in a colored band. From a distance, our view of words and icons fades away and is replaced by bands of color—indicating the larger-scale temporal phenomenon that structures the work. Leaning in to examine individual frames, we can make out the small text of subliminal words in some frames. Because the montage shows that subliminal words are never repeated in two consecutive frames, we know that they flicker on screen for less than one-twelfth of a second. We may also recognize the longer flash of a single word, generally seen here in groups of three consecutive frames, or one-fourth of a second per word—a beat of about four words per second.

How long does *Project* last? Or rather, given its endless looping, how long before the story repeats? Searching the source files gives us various *lengths* of the work (2,483 words, 144 lines, etc.), but it cannot easily provide a *duration*. That duration is specified nowhere in the code, but instead is an emergent behavior of *Project* as a process. This montage, by contrast, makes determining the number of words quite difficult. Yet, it does enable us to discover the play length almost immediately; we can quickly browse our montage image to locate where the unusual first word, "Sinkholes," is repeated. (This happens after about nine and a half minutes.) Cropping the content here, after the last word, offers its own moment of insight. In attempting to mark where *Project* "ends" in the montage, we must engage with its never-ending nature and impose our own end point. Indeed, before being cropped, the enjambment "deeper Sinkholes" indicates how the final line extends in a jarringly ungrammatical turn, which is revealed to be a return of the first sentence.[38]

As we browse the lines of our montage, we may imagine time ticking in analog circles—like a "second hand" marking off each word, while an "hour hand" traces each full story cycle. Is there a "minute hand" missing from our temporal model? Is *Project* organized by some conceptual unit larger than the individual word, yet smaller than the entire work? Just as lines, stanzas, or cantos might structure a long print poem, what structures the textual rhythms of *Project*? Our montage suggests several answers.

When viewed from the distance enabled by the montage view, one of the most striking aspects of *Project*'s structure is its rhythmic changes in color. Instead of words, we see color bands of blue, brown, and black with occasional stripes of yellow, purple, and white. Mark's previous investigation of the source code has already prepared us to recognize these dramatic changes in background created by the "distractions"—although the pattern of their durations was not immediately apparent from viewing the code. In the montage we can see that the distractions vary in length, but in a particular way. Creating new visualizations of subsequent playthroughs will always reveal differences in particulars, yet similarities in this pattern. Each playthrough is unique in the exact number, sequence, and durations of its distractions but fairly consistent in frequency and distribution. Over many playthroughs we came to notice that these small color bands are always of the same exact duration. At their smallest they mark off lengths of approximately eight-tenths of a line, or durations of about eight seconds. Once noticed, it becomes apparent that the longer color bands are all multiples of this basic unit—sixteen seconds long, twenty-four, etc. Laid out before us in color, this visible regularity may seem so obvious that it is as if we have always seen it—that is, we may immediately forget the ways in which the temporal pacing of *Project* remained a great mystery, even after multiple viewings. And yet, these eight-second beats were not obvious. While immersed in the experience of *Project*, eight seconds is an almost unimaginable length of time, and this long duration is a surprise—the distractions, both as they are described in code and as they are heralded on screen, at first appeared to be mere transient events. Instead, the regularity of the distractions reveals underlying order to the chaos of *Project*: a metronome, slowly ticking.

What causes this eight-second beat? Examining the text of the source code reveals no place where such a duration is specified. Had we *only* examined the source code, we would never have found the pattern we see in the montage. However, once noticed, we can return to the source code for an answer. As it transpires, a new distraction is chosen each time the main audio loop file finishes playing, and this audio clip is exactly eight seconds long. Background music thus serves as both the audible and the visible heartbeat of the work. This insight arises out of a silent and still visualization, but it suggests a complementary way of returning to Project and experiencing it differently: close your eyes and listen.

We turned to this investigation of color in search of "stanzas" in the work, but we have not yet established how the audio-color rhythms of the distractions can be tied back to the words appearing on-screen. Leaning in closer, we can see where the durations of the distractions fall. When a sudden change sweeps across the screen, the color contrast acts like a line break, separating phrases such as "Workers pulled up / core samples" or "behind them / a great chasm opened." However, due to the nature of this montage as one specific recording, we cannot know at first whether these word boundaries will change arbitrarily with each playthrough or if they persist across every viewing of the work. Should we understand the visual breaks that the distractions create between word groups to be a form of chaos or a form of order? One solution is to create and compare many montages. This process reveals that, in fact, distractions *do* structure *Project* in much the way that stanzas act to structure traditional poetry, marking off groups of words at regular intervals.

We have already discussed the story words in terms of three temporal scales: the word-instant (a subliminal flash), the word-moment (a sub-second duration of a single story word), and the story-playthrough (an approximately nine-minute runtime before the story text loops and begins again). To these we can now add a fourth temporal scale: the stanza-distraction (an eight second period that marks discrete phases of color, animation, sound, and text). Beginning in a search for stillness, our visualization laid *Project* out as if on a page, then led us deep into an investigation of its temporality, and now, in the idea of distractions as stanzas, brings us back to the idea of a page once again. Reading our visualization of *Project* has brought the poetic logic of the screen into productive tensions with the poetic logic of the page. As this exploration of the work's temporality has shown, new insights may arise out of such comparative approaches to different media-specific forms.

PERSPECTIVE AS INTERPRETATION (JESSICA)

Changing the way we see changes what we see. Jeremy's visualizations illuminate the benefits of approaching *Project* from different perspectives so as to see the work in new ways. Specifically, his images illuminate parts of *Project* we cannot see up close and thus serve to support a form of distant reading. "Distant reading" is a buzzword in the era of big data, and it often describes critical strategies far different from (or even oppositional to) that central tool from the toolbox of literary criticism: close reading. Rather than depict a binary between close and distant reading, Jeremy's visualizations support critical movement between close reading and distant reading, and, moreover, promote reflection upon their symbiotic relationship.

Franco Moretti presents distant reading as an alternative to close reading. Distant reading, he argues, understands distance not as an impediment to analysis but as "a specific form of knowledge," a perspective that presents "a new object of study: instead of concrete, individual works, a trio of artificial constructs—graphs, maps, trees."[39] Moving "from texts to models,"[40] distant reading analyzes a large corpus of data (e.g., the history of detective fiction, the epistolary correspondence of an entire era, or every play or poem by a single author) rather than a single text. The goal is to understand literature as "a collective system, that should be grasped as such, as a whole" rather than a field represented by exemplary cases.[41] But, as our engagement with *Project* shows, distant reading need not force a choice between text *or* data. Jeremy's visualizations turn the literary work into a data set and produce maps of this data that promote new ways of seeing the work. "A good map is worth a thousand words," Moretti writes, because a map "produces a thousand words: it raises doubts, ideas. It poses new questions, and forces you to look for new answers."[42] Jeremy's visualizations translate *Project*'s Flash-based temporal animation into spatial parameters and visual documentations. They create maps of the work that expose programmatic patterns in its coded performance and thus raise new questions about it. These visualizations are not ends in themselves but are interventions into the process of interpretation. Consequently, these images suggest that distant reading can entail a conscious effort to stand back from an object of study (including a single literary work) and use that distance to pursue a fresh critical perspective. Distant reading can, in other words, lead us back to close reading.

When we return to *Project* via Jeremy's visualizations, we notice how the narrative itself performs shifting between close and distant. It zooms in to describe the specifics of the Pit and life around it; then it zooms out to show the Pit's wide-reaching impact. This shifting in narrative perspective is, to be sure, not what Moretti means by "distant reading," but it does perform perspectival shifts in ways that invite the reader to consider how movement alone might payoff in reading *Project*. For example, consider how the narrative zooms in to focus on a particular textual genre: brochures. The text states, "Mentions of the Pit are conspicuously absent from area real estate brochures and Chamber of Commerce publications." Yet this absence is complicated when the narrative takes a distant reading approach to examine this genre as a data set. The text identifies patterns of rhetorical practices in the real estate brochures for property around the Pit; they use certain "circumlocutions" to "describ[e] the general region as a geological wonderland." These circumlocutions not only invoke the image of the Pit but also suggest that a certain lacuna results from reading too closely, either the brochures or the Pit they reference.

However, even when obscured, the Pit is a constant presence in the narrative. It is both a real place and a poignant symbol, and in both cases it influences the consciousness and cultural practices of those living in the area. But it takes close and distant reading practices to register this to be the case. We are told, "The Pit has become an integral part of life in the region." This succinct statement is then elaborated upon by numerous examples of how the Pit extends beyond an actual sinkhole. It is not just a singular location that invites close reading but is also part of a vast network of visible and imperceptible cracks—in the ground and in the psyches of those living in the area—which require distant reading in order to trace their connections and implications, to read and interpret. The narrative tells us, "Children and to some extent the adults of the area are subject to recurring dreams and nightmares about the Pit." Even when it is not visible, when people are asleep, the Pit is present and potent. The Pit is everywhere and nowhere, but its patterns, boundaries, and impacts are often best seen at a distance.

Consider, as a kind of analogy, a different kind of distant reading via a technologically enabled visualization machine: images produced from a satellite. In particular, consider the famous photograph of the Earth known as "The Blue Marble," taken by the crew of the Apollo 17 spacecraft in 1972 at a 3,000 miles distance from the Earth.[43] The photograph, produced from space by a technological eye, dramatically reframed the way people perceived the world on which they lived by displaying the "blue" aspect of our (primarily water-covered) world, which visually contradicted the daily, lived experience of most land-dwelling humans. The satellite image taken from outer space inversely produced new ways of understanding, not distance, but life close-up on Earth. Media studies pioneer Marshall McLuhan, reflecting on the momentous effect of Earth's first man-made satellite, provocatively claimed, "Once *Sputnik* went around the planet, Nature disappeared;

it was enclosed in a man-made environment, and Art took the place of Nature."[44] McLuhan's enigmatic pronouncement suggests that *Sputnik* provided a new way of viewing Earth, not only from a distance but also from the purview of a man-made device that presented the Earth back to us as something shaped by man—in other words, not as Nature but as Art. Jeremy's spatial montage of *Project* operates differently, to be sure, than a satellite, but it does similar work for our understanding of *Project*: it maps the digital work in ways that support new ways of perceiving it by presenting a vision of the work as a whole.

Yet, this vision of the total work is a fantasy, a fiction—more Art (to employ McLuhan) than Truth. Neither distant nor close reading offer a complete or totalizing view but, instead, serve to remind us how perspective is always performed through constraints and customs, some of which are produced by our scopes and reading machines. In "Walking in the City," Michel de Certeau explores the desire of achieving a godlike, omnipresent perspective, and, to do so, he imagines a distant perspective for reading. He wonders, "what is the source of this pleasure of 'seeing the whole,' of looking down on, totalizing the most immoderate of human texts," in this case, the city of Manhattan.[45] De Certeau notes that the desire to see the entirety of the visual plane has inspired experiments in viewing technologies and artistic techniques, from the invention of perspective in Renaissance painting to the panoramic views made possible from the tops of skyscrapers. "The totalizing eye imagined by the painters of earlier times," he writes, "lives on in our achievements."[46] Jeremy's visualizations might be considered the latest such effort or "achievement." These achievements, however, have their ideological flaws and faults.

De Certeau's essay opens at the top of the World Trade Center (a view no longer accessible) where "elevation transfigures him [the viewer] into a voyeur. It puts him at a distance."[47] This perspective grants one the ability to see the city-as-text in its entirety: "It allows one to read it, to be a solar Eye, looking down like a god." While this spatial distance is not the same as Moretti's data-based distant reading or the far-distant photograph of Earth taken by a satellite, it does share with them (and also Jeremy's visualizations) the effort to use technologies to impart spatial distance in ways that transform the viewer's relationship to what is seen. But, there is a limit to such "spatial practice," as de Certeau calls it. "There is a rhetoric of walking"[48] at street-level in the city—the equivalent to close reading de Certeau's essay—that cannot be appreciated from a distance. "The ordinary practitioners of the city live 'down below,' below the thresholds at which visibility begins,"[49] de Certeau writes, and these pedestrians see the world around them from another partial perspective—a close one. This view remains inaccessible to those who do not walk the city streets but instead stare down from great heights. We might consider de Certeau's description of "ordinary practitioners of the city" as representing traditional modes of reading a literary work by walking, wandering, and experiencing it closely. This ordinary practice is not replaced by the ever-taller, Babel-like distant views enabled by various technological advancements. Indeed, de Certeau's essay and our experience interpreting *Project* show the opposite. We need both.

In *Reading* Project, we pursue two main technological interventions, reading the code and producing visualizations, which are both attempts to access new vistas from which to observe *Project* so as to produce interpretations of it. But, we do not abandon the mode of "walking" around *Project*, of interpreting its on-screen poetics and its resulting effects. Were we to focus solely on Jeremy's spatial montage maps or Mark's code renderings, we would lose the ability to examine the poetic experience of the piece. Digital methods of distant reading might produce a viewing experience akin to the godlike view de Certeau likens to "Icarus flying above these waters,"[50] but we know what happens to Icarus. There is danger in abandoning the ground altogether or in rejecting the trusted reading practices that help us navigate texts. Instead of choosing one practice over another, we need to develop hybrid reading methods that combine distant and close reading, methods that employ big data visualizations and pedestrian practices, all in the service of supporting our age-old endeavor to see and understand our world.

Examining *Project*'s remediation of the tachistoscope required us to step back from the work in order to read the reading machine. In the next chapter, we look through the tachistoscope and various other reading machines in order to zoom in and analyze the subject of *Project*'s tale—the Bottomless Pit.

CHAPTER THREE **BOTTOMLESS PIT**

▪ ▪ ▪ We Are Drawn into the Pit

From an online chat:

12:07 P.M. **JESSICA**: Ok, I figured out what I need to do . . . thanks, in part, to Mark's helpful marginal comments and Jeremy's helpful outline in the Table of Contents. So thanks, guys!

12:09 P.M. **JEREMY**: Great! Glad it was helpful—I'm orienting myself as well. I'm really getting excited about feeling this sequence into an argument.

12:10 P.M. **MARK**: Okay, I think I need to jump down to the bottom of this document for a while, who's got the winch?

12:11 P.M. **JEREMY**: As long as you use a novel mechanism for lowering yourself, what could possibly go wrong?

12:11 P.M. **MARK**: :D

12:11 P.M. **JESSICA**: watch out for the birds' nests . . . and their nidificatory limits!

At some point in the process, we realized that a bottomless pit had sucked us in. This dazzling, hypnotic work had triggered our desire to measure and mark it, to explore and explain its poetic expanse. Our efforts took the form of different types of map-making, from mapping the geographic nodes of the story onto an actual map of America to Jeremy drawing an illustration of the Pit's depth. This latter effort proved to be a signal interpretative breakthrough. Jeremy described this visual representation of the Pit as "a kind of proto-graphic that shows at what depth various events and descriptions are identified; and, for my own amusement, I added the world's tallest building, deepest mine, and largest canyon to the chart for context." (See figure 3.1). This method of indexing the work turned the Pit into something visual and concrete; it altered the way we understood the Pit and, even, the work as a whole. After placing the fictional Pit in relation to actual tall buildings and deep canyons, the illustration promoted comparison and provided a new perspective for approaching the work through a particular focus on the Bottomless Pit. For, if the blind midge that is discovered in the Pit lives at a depth just below the world's deepest canyon, what other connections and contexts to real-world depths might we make?

And, moreover, what kinds of interpretative footholds might these narrative details support?

We began to measure and mark up concrete facts and elements in the work: Where exactly is Beale Pike? When did Hoar House fall apart? How far down exactly until optical mirages appear? At the same time, the margins of our manuscript grew crowded with dialogic comments—ideas for new research trajectories, supporting citations, disagreements. As time passed, we started to see a parallel between Poundstone's tale of a bottomless pit and our own writing. The Pit became emblematic of interpretive process—whether charting the depths of a deep abyss or exploring the layers of a complex text.

THE NIDIFICATORY LIMIT: LOCATING AND MAPPING THE PIT (JEREMY)

The Bottomless Pit is the central preoccupation of *Project*. The Pit is constantly described yet remains unknowable in many ways, some overt, some subtle. Its depths are measureless; the senses fail when under its influence, as do natural instincts. Even the Pit's location is unclear. It can be found only in relation to other places, and these relations are uncertain, shifting, and subjective rather than cartographic, cardinal, and absolute. We begin our critical excursions in the spirit of mountaineering or caving by attempting to map the location of the Pit geographically (by tracing place names and directions), then charting it geologically (by compiling details gleaned from *Project*'s text). What do we know about the Pit, and in what specific ways is it unknowable?

Geographically, the Pit has no explicit location. Instead, *Project* situates it in relation to a network of roads, towns, buildings, and regions. We learn in the first sentence that the Pit is in the area "around Bluefields" where construction of a toll road, "the Beale Pike," was initially planned and then rerouted to avoid it. This toll road further offers a connection between "Breezewood and Roanoke Park," but each of these places (and indeed every place in the text) describes where the Pit is not. The named locations are themselves ambiguous and unlocatable. Beale Pike may be an existing road that is being expanded or an intended road that remained unopened after construction failed. Miltown and New Lebanon may be the names of local towns, churches, or historical societies. Turning to a map, can we locate these ambiguous names in a likely region? Communities named New Lebanon can be found in Ohio, Pennsylvania, New York, Indiana, and more, while roads and boroughs named Miltown appear throughout the United States. These names evoke a sense of place that could be east of the Mississippi River, or almost anywhere, allowing *Project* to convey its story in regional terms while simultaneously telling an American tale.

Just as the story cannot be located on a U.S. map, it is not possible to draw a local map of the Pit and its environs. This is because no place is described in spatial relation to any other. We cannot know whether Carbondale is north or south of Bluefields, near or far from it, or perhaps within it. Instead, each place relates only to the Pit, and that all-important and defining relationship is never expressed in compass directions or in miles. The Beale Pike route was selected for "its distance" from the Pit, while Carbondale "was considered to be a vast distance from the Pit." This abstract "distance" seems particularly odd in contrast with the detail, precision, and nuance found elsewhere in the narrative. The text is replete with times ("12:57"), dates ("1962"), measurements ("200 feet"), and close observations. For example, the destruction of Hoar House is described in detail that evokes a scientific record of the event: "Hoar House was pulled apart in the ground stress accompanying the 1993 subsidence its timbers and foundation stones being scattered in the characteristic rhomboid pattern. The debris was pulled into the Pit." In this, one of many "subsidence events" throughout the story, the unstable soil of this karstland region is both scientifically characterized and at the same time personified in a way that comes to signify the agency of the Pit itself, a distant actor which actively "pulled" Hoar House and its debris. In fact, housing damage signifying the Pit's influence appears in a "marginal zone" which extends "far beyond that where measurable subsidence has occurred." When we attribute this damage to a personified Pit, that Pit is both elsewhere and also everywhere that its effects may be seen. It cannot be located or contained, and its omnipresent influence transforms our experience of space. Location becomes abstract; geography loses both direction and proximity. If the Pit can act at great distances, how could one meaningfully measure a distance from it?

Distance becomes affective in the presence of the Pit. When the Beale Pike route is "selected for its distance from the Bottomless Pit and the perceived need to allow a generous margin of safety mandated not by necessity but by the psychology of the people in this region," this "distance" is meant to establish emotional safety rather than physical security. What engineers are mapping is not geographical or geological but the psychological "conceptions" of locals. If "areas once viewed as remote from the Pit are in fact slowly sliding inward," then what appears far from the Pit may be drawn near, and anything outside may fall in. Distinctions collapse; differences prove illusory. The region around the Pit is already within its sphere of influence, and thus in a sense already inside it.

It is perhaps fitting that a pit of immeasurable depth exists at the center of an undefined region. Indeed, part of the Pit's fascination is that it is unmappable: "Compasses and dip needles act erratically near the Pit." Just as the unfathomable depth of the Pit attracts visitors to its edge, so too does its lack of geographic certainty create poetic tension for the reader. In both cases, what is immeasurable and thus enigmatic becomes meaningful. Yet this uncertainty and unknowability is only true to a certain degree. While the text describes horizontal distances that are relative and implicit, it describes vertical depths that are absolute and explicit, measured and quantified in exacting detail, and striated into zones that are defined numerically, in thousands of feet. These zones are then further defined by regions, events, and species of animals that the narrative locates at precise depths (see figure 3.1). In a reversal, while the surrounding region dissolves into scattered impressions, it is the inside of the mysterious Pit that the story maps out and orders. Of course, the Pit's bottom cannot be measured due to a variety of phenomena, including shadows, hazes, dense fogs, and air pressure mirages. Yet what the story locates within the Pit is not its bottom, but the limits of knowledge, the depths at which vision, logic, and natural order fail and fade away by degrees.

The narrative provides a particular point at which visibility breaks down. We are told that at a depth of about four miles, "Kellogg was unable to see anything below 22000 feet, even his own lamp." Five miles of depth seems to be a limit below which nothing has been witnessed.[1] On reflection, five vertical miles is a surprisingly appropriate distance at which to find a boundary marker for the limits of human understanding, given that five miles is also the approximate height of the world's tallest mountains (Mount Everest, K2) whose ascents have been held forth as a dramatic measure of mankind's achievement. Kellogg himself eventually descends to the fantastical depth of 54,000 feet— which we can understand in context as being over twice the height of

Depths of the Bottomless Pit

0 ft	Passion play pavilion (S rim), casino construction site (S rim), railings	
2,000	Detritus (SE rim) [2,717 ft tallest skyscraper in the world, Burj Khalifa]	
4,000	3,340 ft: lowest bird nests found, "nidificatory limit"	~1 mi
6,000	[~6,000 ft depth of Grand Canyon]	
8,000		
10,000 ft		
12,000	[world's deepest mine, TauTona Mine, ~13k ft]	
14,000	Kellog initial exploration to view extra-galactic nebulae at midday	
16,000	[world's deepest canyon, Yarlung Zangbo Grand Canyon ~15k ft]	
18,000	Fleas discovered, e.g. a blind midge (cinea horribilis)	
20,000 ft	"Haze and shadow permit little visibility below the 4 mile depth."	
22,000	"Kellogg was unable to see anything below 22000 feet, even his own lamp"	
24,000	~ Magnesium flare max. visibility, est. 4 min. free fall (240s * ~100ft/s term.vel)	
26,000		~5 mi
28,000	[world's tallest mountain peaks, Mount Everest and K2, ~28-29k ft]	
30,000 ft		
32,000	~ "Dense fogs have been reported at lower levels"	
34,000		
36,000	[world's deepest seafloor, in the Mariana Trench, ~36k ft]	
38,000		
40,000 ft		
42,000	~ "At still lower depths air pressure creates mirages"	
44,000		
46,000		
48,000		
50,000 ft		
52,000		~10 mi
54,000	"In 1962 Kellogg perished when an ambitious two-man winch broke"	
58,000		
60,000 ft ...?		

"quotation"	direct excerpts from the text
~ approximate	estimated depth, when no measure is given in the text
[compare]	famous tall/deep structures, not mentioned in the text

FIGURE 3.1: Depths of the Bottomless Pit. (Table by Jeremy Douglass.)

Mount Everest, further than the world's tallest skyscraper (about 3,000 feet), its deepest mine (about 13,000 feet), or even the deepest known point on the crust of the Earth, below the ocean at the bottom of the Mariana Trench (about 36,000 feet).[2] However, Kellogg never returns from the depths to tell his tale. Like the flare, he passes out of sight. The Pit appears to contain some kind of boundary, like the event horizon of a black hole, near which nothing can be seen, and from beyond which nothing can return. As the text succinctly states, "Visibility in the Pit is a complex matter," and this could serve as the thesis or slogan of *Project*. The work explores the complexity of vision by telling the tale of a Pit that cannot be mapped or even completely seen.

Despite the fact that vision is disabled in the Pit, *Project* provides detailed clues for mapping the Pit's depths and for determining the exact point where sense (not just vision) is lost. The narrative describes the location where birds lose their sense of direction. "Flocks of birds are sometimes observed flying down into the Pit," and, "The flocking behavior may be an instinct triggered by the absence of a ground sense." But there is more. The narrative uses the behavior of these birds to chart sense and depth via "the so-called 'nidificatory limit,'" a scientific phrase which Poundstone coins to indicate a level below which birds can no longer engage in nest-building (nidification).[3] "Nests have been found down to 3,340 feet," but "Near the so-called nidificatory limit nests become disorganized irregular composed of bizarre elements." The nidificatory limit is one demarcation of where natural order breaks down. Birds forget how to build nests, and their loss of instinct serves as a canary in a coal mine, signifying the breakdown of all meaning-making in the presence of the Pit.

As they approach the limit, increasingly disordered nests are made of detritus, "composed of bizarre elements (wire debris pebbles hard candy chewing gum religious tracts)." Nest disarray reveals how the Pit threatens the concept of nest-building and social order. Human homes built in proximity to the Pit also suffer and become increasingly incoherent assemblages. The text makes the comparison between the birds and a local Carbondale resident named Little, who reaches his own nidificatory limit. He is found nesting outside a home in absolute disorder: "(a satellite dish a construction crew's portable toilet and a microwave oven and cooler plugged into a portable generator)." What is lost is not only a sense of how to make and keep a house but also the sense of what a home is and why it matters. Through the example of Little's strange and defamiliarized abode, *Project* exposes an extreme disruption of meaning-making. Words and objects appear in unexpected juxtapositions—a satellite dish does not accompany a television, but instead a portable toilet. As relationships between objects and how they work together shift, so too shifts the meaning of the "home" assemblage they comprise. The communities outside the Pit (and yet within its influence) may have their own nidificatory limit, a zone where our struggle to make meaning slowly fails, and the construction of our quotidian, everyday world breaks down.

AN ALLEGORY OF MEDIA SHIFT (JESSICA)

Jeremy's writing about the nidificatory limit prompted me to think differently about *Project,* to see connections between this recent work of digital literature and the deep time of media history.[4] In particular, I started thinking about very old ways of storing memory, mnemonic devices that Mary Carruthers describes in her seminal book on medieval memory, *The Book of Memory.* Carruthers examines the role of memory in medieval scholarly life and the specific mnemonic techniques employed by scholarly readers in the centuries preceding print. What seems like a strange connection—digital literature and medieval memory—became a central point of intersection through the intervention of Jeremy's illustration. Carruthers describes a genre of mnemonic devices that employ visual locations as storage places for specific memories. This "long-standing chain or—a better word—a texture of metaphors," she writes, "likens the placement of memory-images in a trained memory to the keeping of birds (especially pigeons)."[5] Medieval memory thus depended upon the imagery of birds' nests. By way of example, Carruthers explains that the first-century Roman writer Martial (Marcus Valerius Martialis) "uses the related word *nidus,* 'nest' or 'pigeon-hole,' for the place where his book-seller kept copies of his work."[6] Carruthers suggests that the etymological history of "pigeon-holes" to denote physical compartments for storing documents has a parallel to more intangible storage places in cognition and memory. "Birds are a common image for souls, memories, and thoughts throughout the ancient world," she writes, and this "metaphoric relationship of birds, especially pigeons, to thoughts and memories persisted in the Middle Ages."[7] This history leaves its trace in the multitude of remediations that reconfigure pigeonholes and nidificatory limits as metaphors for memory storage. And, as Jeremy showed, this history reaches us in Poundstone's digital narrative.

Pursuing this connection, we can extend our understanding of the allegory *Project* presents. If the nidificatory limit serves to mark the depths at which birds can make stable nests—and, by way of Carruthers, the ways in which we archive and remember—then we have reached a nidificatory limit of sorts with regards to our ability to comfortably inhabit the usual "nests" of literary criticism. To read *Project* is to encounter a nidificatory limit: traditional interpretive practices and readerly expectations falter when facing this fast-flashing work. *Project* is very much about exploring the limits of our abilities to measure and map. But, using the concept of the nidificatory limit, we might also understand *Project* as describing, invoking, and aestheticizing the ways in which we read by measuring. We count the remaining pages in a book or the percentage remaining on a Kindle in order to determine our progress with a narrative; we draw diagrams and marginal notes to track characters and plot twists in complex narratives. While reading, we allot our attention, we focus and retract it, and we use mental and material strategies to do so. Such quantitative actions often happen unconsciously, but they always happen with and through specific reading technologies and techniques adapted to them. Whether these devices are conceptual pigeonholes in medieval mnemonics, dog-eared pages, or digital "memory sticks," they are all constructed for specific reading contexts, technologies, and purposes. New reading situations challenge these practices and illuminate their pitfalls. Certainly, this is part of *Project*'s poetic purpose, with its presentation of the Pit and description of readers' attempts to measure it.

Project presents an allegorical tale about adapting reading practices to a changing media environment. The narrative about a Bottomless Pit portrays a parallel between its diegetic world and the reader's own by focusing on the trials and tribulations of specific readers, people who journey to the Pit with the intention of explaining it using traditional methods and who, inevitably, fail. One such reader is Nelson Playfair, a geologist "who had experience with deep wells," and he brings to the Pit his expertise in devices for assessing them. But media-specificity matters, and "Playfair's attempts to measure the depth of the Pit by triangulation failed." The stated reason for the failure: "poor visibility at the lower levels." His techniques for lighting up his reading space did not transfer from deep well to bottomless pit. He could not see, so he could not read. The next line of the narrative implies that failure to read the Pit is not simply a failure of Playfair's inappropriate reading technologies (i.e., illuminating machines). There is a larger, more systemic problem: "The Pit is not an isolated phenomenon. It is only an extreme case of what has been happening all along in this region where integration of geologic layers has become compromised." As Playfair warns, "You're really not on solid ground anywhere in this region." The Pit, like the work containing it, is not a one-off situation but is symptomatic of larger, systemic change. In the face of this larger crisis, readers in *Project* are inspired, rather than deterred, by Playfair's statement to approach the Pit. Readers of all sorts—from geologists to neighbors and tourists alike—journey to the Pit to explore and explain the situation.

Similarly, *Project* invites its reader to pour attention into the vortex at the center of the computer screen; and, like those who stand at the rim of the Pit, we too approach *Project* ready to throw at it every last tool from the literary criticism toolkit. We can look for poetic elements in the text, seek out connections between images and text, and consider the moments of tension and paradox (to use those New Critical terms) as places to begin excavation. Yet, there is so much to read, see, and hear in this work and also so much that we are not supposed to see: subliminal words, computer code, bugs from versioning, etc. As readers, "It is possible to lose all sense of direction in the vicinity of the Pit." It is easy to become disoriented, which is why collaboration is vital to reading this work (and other digital, multimodal works like it). The narrative shows, and we can substantiate, that we need more and, indeed, different kinds of readers and perspectives to examine this Pit. One tool, one perspective, does not serve all.

In addition to Playfair, *Project* provides another exemplary reader, Chandler Moody. The nineteenth century "sign painter inventor libertine and atheist" approached the Pit differently than Playfair, for, rather than bringing his own knowledge to bear on the Pit, Moody "collected all that had been written about the Pit." (This collection becomes the New Lebanon Historical Society, which then falls into the Pit.) "Moody complained that maps of the Pit are of limited and at best temporary value," and his assessment imparts an important point. Maps—and, indeed all tools and techniques used to define emergent knowledge forms, whether expanding sinkholes or digital poetics—should be considered of "limited and at best temporary value." This limitation does not require readers to dispense with map-making, cartography, and close reading altogether. On the contrary, instead of throwing away (or throwing into the Pit) the older techniques, we need to continually reassess and renovate our reading practices to adapt to the changing ecology.

Project makes this point many times and in many ways. Along with warnings articulated by Playfair and Moody, the narrative ends with the following sentence, "In recent years the Pit has both widened and gotten alarmingly deeper." This final statement implies that both the Pit and readings of it will continue to expand. This suggestion is re-inforced formally, for the work does not stop, pause, or loop back to the "Start" screen; it just plays continuously, repeating its text without a discernible break. The story about a Bottomless Pit thus becomes a bottomless pit for reading and for reconsidering our reading practices.

THE DEEP, LAYERED PIT THAT IS FLASH (MARK)

Following the explorers and interpreters within *Project*'s narrative who descend into the Pit's layers to the nidificatory limit and beyond, we can descend into the layers of Flash to see the pit in which Pound-stone labored. The vertical field of the Flash authoring environment offers a kind of depth-viewing that has its parallel in the narrative. The parallel between a deep (bottomless) pit and the media-specific tech-nologies enabling it invites critical analysis of this relationship. I take up this invitation and pursue the Flash files as a way of reading the Pit by exploring the depths of this authoring interface.

On its face—or interface—the Flash authoring environment ap-pears to offer a simple software analogy for the Pit. Since the layers on the screen, for the most part, indicate the depth of the images on the z-axis, the design interface gives the programmer the sense of build-ing up from or descending into the pit that is Flash. To be clear, if an image is placed on a layer beneath another on the timeline, that image will be obscured by the image on the higher layer. Because of this cor-relation between layer and z-axis, when we made our archaeological discovery of the .fla source file—by decompiling the online version of *Project*—we found what looked like a map or depth chart of vertical slices of the finished piece. However, like the Pit itself, which resists

FIGURE 3.2: Flash authoring environment view of *Project* source code with image assets placed on a stage. (Screenshot by Mark Marino; with the permission of William Poundstone.)

any straightforward measurement or containment, this representation of Flash is also misleading. The layers present a visual interface for positioning images in the movie, but they represent only one of several methods for doing so. This view of the pit of *Project* through the source files is yet another slippery and shifting surface on which we struggle to construct an interpretation of the piece.

In order to understand the distinction between the images that are displayed when the .swf file is executed and the images that are positioned in the authoring environment, it is important to know how Flash's .swf and the .fla files differ. The .fla is the authoring file that contains all of the assets (images, sound files, animation sequences), levels, and ActionScript. On the other hand, the .swf is a display file that is placed on web pages for readers to encounter and experience as an audience. In the .fla file, assets can be placed on the stage visibly or placed there invisibly so that they can be moved or made to appear in the .swf. In other words, placing an asset on the authoring stage (in the .fla) does not translate into the immediate display of that asset in the animation on the browser (in the .swf) but rather indicates that the image or sound will be loaded at the time noted in the keyframe, so it can be displayed or played at some point in the animation. Consider the images in figure 3.2. They have been arranged together, on a layer the author labeled "Invisible Assets," beneath a blue square of background and the pulsating blue target (both of which I have dragged aside for clearer viewing). However, during the course of the playthrough, the images are not displayed beneath the square or the target. When the movie reaches this point, the images are loaded but hidden behind the background until they are summoned forth one at a time to be combined with text and icons. Once these assets have been loaded, they can be positioned by the code at a later time. This distinction reveals Flash to be not merely an environment for laying out images but one for visually interfacing with programming constructs. As a result, unlike what she sees in the authoring environment, the viewer of an exported Flash .swf sees not a series of frames in a filmstrip or a stage but, rather, a flow of manipulated information loaded over time.

It was tempting, when I first saw the decompiled code and then Jeremy and Jessica's work on the nidificatory limit, to think of myself as a Kellogg exploring the Flash file as the material manifestation of Poundstone's Pit. However, the bottom falls out of this depth metaphor. Aside from background color, which can also be changed by the code on higher levels, nothing in the Flash authoring environment can be placed on a level so low that it cannot be immediately called back into the foreground by the code. The Flash interface, like the Pit, cannot be reliably or consistently mapped. These contradictions mark the nidificatory limit of Flash's visual metaphors, as these comforting and familiar metaphors have now proven uninhabitable. Meanwhile, the code that the GUI manipulates continues to be effaced by these authoring metaphors.

Returning to the narrative, we see that the tale of the Bottomless Pit ends by describing an effort to capitalize on the Pit by building a casino near and, in part, over it. Plans for the "3,000-room Indian casino" are abandoned, however, for "the Pit has swallowed part of the safety rail system encircling the Pit's perimeter." Unlike the ill-fated casino, which is "cantilevered over the Pit," the GUI of Flash presents metaphors that appear *in place of* (rather than above) the levels of code. The effects of this code can be seen, yet the code itself cannot be fully accessed. Press upon those metaphors just a little, and they tumble into the pit of information representation. The GUI proves to be an unstable surface that attempts to make programming more concrete.

BRINGING DEPTH TO SURFACE: A VOLUMETRIC VIEW (JEREMY)

Mark showed how *Project's* programming interface evokes and then calls into question depth-based metaphors, and with this perspective we can now zoom out to see the ways in which the reader's screen can be understood as possessing depth, albeit of a different kind. In this section we investigate *Project's* screen anew by constructing new ways of seeing its aesthetic—in particular, by using metaphors of depth to create new views of the work and perspectives for understanding how *Project's* interface changes over time.

First, we will continue our reading of the casino tale, considering how this narrative thread frames one way of reading the Pit's depths. Our visual excursion into the depths of *Project's* screen space will use the visualization technique called "volumetric views." Such visualizations are usually employed for examining patterns in image series. Applying this visualization method to *Project*, we see that the volume view highlights the surprising stillness at the edges of the screen throughout the animation. Identifying this pattern leads us to investigate the tensions between stillness and action in the work, both visually and figurally. Next, we will make our visualization partially transparent and see something different. We will recognize a figure for the Pit itself, explore the ways in which this figure is visually inverted, and then consider the implications resulting from this image.

We begin with the casino tale, which marks the end of each story cycle in *Project*, and which Mark described as offering us an entry point for deconstructing depth metaphors. This part of the narrative offers a striking fantasy of the unseen, and it introduces a new perspective on depth. The construction site of the never-completed casino "was to have featured a spectacular glass ballroom cantilevered over the Pit," the text states, and "Guests would have viewed the glorious abyss opening beneath their feet according to promotional literature." The casino ballroom is both a spectacle and is specular. It is designed as a viewing apparatus, with a floor like a giant glass lens, aimed down. Yet this lens is unlike the many scopes we have previously discussed. Playfair uses viewing instruments for measurement, and his purposes are defeated by "poor visibility." By contrast, guests of the ballroom use its glass floor to celebrate the imperceptible. They do not see the bottom of the Pit, but the Bottomless itself; they experience (and presumably take pleasure in) their own inability to see. Or more accurately, they *would have* witnessed this bottomlessness and inability to see had the ballroom been constructed. But it was never built, so the unseen went unseen. Only pamphlets publicizing the construction project remain present and visible; this paper detritus anticipates and represents the un-seeing that never came to pass. The casino is merely a set of unworkable construction plans. Its lack of substance serves the narrative by illustrating the fact that any project to understand the depths of the Pit remains hypothetical.

The Pit is referred to as an "abyss" just once, in this final scene. The word is both evocative and precise, coming as it does from the Greek *abyssos*, literally "without" + "bottom." While geologists, explorers, dreamers, and worshipers all sought or imagined various bottoms to the Bottomless Pit, it is the land speculators and gamblers who embrace the idea and aesthetic of the bottomless. They celebrate the abyss by introducing a provisional bottom-which-is-not-one in the form of the glass floor. It is perhaps no surprise that the plan for gazing into the abyss goes poorly for the casino and its financial backers. Indeed, any endeavor that contemplates the Pit seems to take on something of the Pit's nature, eventually becoming as ungrounded as that which it contemplates. As the saying goes, "when you gaze long into an abyss, the abyss also gazes into you."[8] Since the tale of the casino construction project comes at the end of *Project*'s narrative, readers already anticipate its inevitable failure. The proposal to install floor-stress evacuation alarms in the glass floor of the casino only underscores the expectation that walking on it is a very risky gamble. The question is never *if* a glass-bottomed ballroom will become as bottomless as its spectacle, but *when*. When will the mediation of absence become absence itself? How suddenly will the image of the Pit on the glass floor become a pit of empty space?

The answer is a paradox. Casino construction halts because its structural failure is inevitable, and yet, precisely because the ballroom floor will inevitably fail, no floor is ever built; thus, it will never fail. For this reason, it has, in some sense, already failed. Metaphorically, investigations of the Pit that attempt to capture it, map it, or rationalize it are "pre-failed" endeavors. Any simplified 2-D view of the Pit may give way without warning, and when such flattening attempts shatter, they fall back into complexity and depth. In this sense, the ballroom floor sequence cautions us that deep understandings (with all their dangers) are actually the only options available to us.

The casino tale in *Project*'s narrative serves to strengthen the parallelism between readers of *Project* and viewers of the Pit. We have been exploring this parallel in other ways and places, but here, the casino tale highlights how readers of and within the diegetic narrative encounter analogous challenges based in dimensions of space and time. For characters in the narrative, the challenging dimension is spatial: the measureless depth of the Pit. For readers of the work, the challenging dimension is temporal: the uncontrollable speed of *Project*'s screen.

Both in the narrative and on the screen, space and time are deeply connected: space consumes time. In the narrative, the Pit is an object defined by its own absence (a missing volume) as well as by various historic artifacts that are ephemeral due to being constantly consumed by the Pit. Through ground-shifting "subsidence events," objects and locations fall into the earth, and in doing so disappear into the past: problems of unstable geography become problems of unreliable memory and absent history. At the level of the screen's interface, viewers of *Project* also find themselves reading without access to records of their reading experience. Just as the Pit consumes Hoar House and thereby denies local people the ability to read and reflect on their ephemeral cultural history, so too does *Project* consume itself before the readers eyes, denying the ability turn back a few pages, browse, or even linger on the disappearing text.

We have already created records of *Project*, as in the case of the visualization of a montage view (in the previous chapter). As we saw there, the montage drew our attention to the durations of the story cycle and the distractions, highlighting how phases of visual distractions structure the words of *Project* in stanza-like and page-like ways. This time, we return to methods of visualization but with a difference. Instead of multiplying the presence of the screen through tiling, we will move from flatness to depth by stacking many screenshots together into the form of a 3-D object, here called a "volume view."

Before reading volumes, however, we must first understand their purpose. Volume views are used for examining patterns in image series. In diverse disciplines from the sciences to the digital arts, a volume view (sometimes called a volumetric view) may reconstruct a 3-D model of a brain out of many images of "slices" taken at different depths, or instead assemble a deep image of the night sky, or perhaps present a large sculpture out of time-based processes such as stock market behaviors or internet traffic. Applications can range from concrete models of the physical world to abstract representations of processes and concepts. Our approach to visualizing *Project* as a volume lies somewhere between the concrete and the metaphoric. We will combine the two given dimensions of the screen with the third dimension of time. A video recording of one playthrough of *Project* is transformed from a series of 2-D images over time (x, y, t) into a 3-D object in space (x, y, z). Continuity of every moment in time becomes continuity of the images in depth, and the object becomes a "solid" as each pixel is packed tightly next to its neighbors in both time and space.

To understand the process, picture a recording of a single playthrough of *Project*, with each frame of the animation arranged in linear sequence, as on a celluloid film strip for a movie projector. Previously, we created a montage by rearranging these frames alongside one another in rows and columns. Now, however, to create a volume, we instead arrange the images in a stack, in the manner that slide images for a slide projector may be stacked in long boxes when not loaded in a carousel. Time exists in the movie reel as a column, or a vertical procession from image to image along the strip. Time in the spatial montage is laid out in a series of rows, arranged left-to-right and top-to-bottom much like printed prose. In the box of slides, however, time has *depth*, and time moves from the first slide at the front of the stack to the last slide at the back. Fusing these slide-images together into a solid block of glass produces our imagined volume view: a single object that we can now remove from the box and hold up to the light. We can now inspect the object in both time and space from any angle.

FIGURE 3.3: A volume view of *Project*, presenting a left-to-right time series of screenshots in 3-D form. (Visualization by Jeremy Douglass.)

Our visualization is produced according to a software version of this method,[9] first by taking a video recording of one playthrough of *Project*, then loading images from it at a rate of one frame per second of video, then arranging the pixels of each frame along a z-axis to form a visual volume. The result is a virtual 3-D object that can be rotated in our software and viewed from any direction. As shown in figure 3.3, the first frame appears on the left, while our playthrough proceeds in time toward the right. From this vantage point, the edges of each video frame are stacked together to create the sides of a box, much as the edges of book pages sit together to form the fore edge of a closed book. Indeed, the text and images of the work are similarly closed to us in this view. We are departing from the print metaphors that we used extensively in the last chapter while reading the montage. If the montage presented the conceit of open pages and multiplied our view of one screen into many, here we witness the fusing of those many screens into a continuous whole.

By comparison to the frenetic montage, this volume view of *Project* looks calm, almost placid, in its presentation of the now-familiar bands of blue, black, white, orange, and pink. Just as the rings of a tree may record a history of rainy seasons and of fires, these bands record the distractions of one specific playthrough. This material sampling of *Project* also suggests an even more appropriate analogy—the geological "core samples" from the failed Beale Pike construction site at the opening of the story. Core samples are taken to reveal the structure of the underlying ground, and these cross sections of the Earth may also be images of its history, for they go back in time as they go deeper. Or, we might say, core samples might afford such understanding *in theory*. In practice, seventy-three workers perished at the Beale Pike site after they "pulled up core samples" yet judged that the "soil problems . . . were not considered serious." As we create something in order to help us better understand *Project*, we should take caution from the failed construction projects that delimit its story cycle. In interpreting our volume visualization, we must ask not only what we are seeing, but also what we are not seeing.

What we first register while examining our volume is its surprising simplicity. Flat bands of color indicate that edges of the screen are surprisingly stable. This stability is something that is not readily apparent either when viewing the work or examining the montage view. Yet, the volumetric view makes clear that there are no slow gradient shifts and no speckles of large shapes entering or exiting the screen. Instead, the image shows a stable frame around the edges of the screen. A space of inactivity appears which stands in a stark counterpoint to the visual hyperactivity at the center of *Project*'s screen. The simplicity of the edges in turn focuses our attention on the unseen complexity that we know is missing from the visualization—the flashing and pulsing of words and images that we know exist but are hidden in this view. There are tensions here between exterior simplicity and interior complexity, between outer areas on the screen associated with slow changes and inner areas associated with fast changes. If *Project* is, as we have repeatedly observed, characterized by constant changes and rapid speed, then our volume view emphasizes that changing is not *all* that the work is and does. In some ways the work is remarkably stable over time. Changes are not random, but instead follow consistent patterns.

Because we want to know what shape or pattern the hidden complexity takes, we peer into the depths of our volume. To do so, we now move to further transform our volume view by using a "volume threshold" visualization technique. This technique makes our volumetric object appear partially transparent.

What this transparency reveals is a pulsing core that runs lengthwise through the center of the volume. This core or tunnel is formed from many images of circular rims arranged in a series over time, and it might present a visual analog to the figure of the Pit itself, albeit glimpsed from a slightly different angle.

FIGURE 3.4: A volume threshold of *Project*, using transparency to show screen activity inside the 3-D volume of screenshots. (Visualization by Jeremy Douglass.)

Textually, visually, and conceptually, there are many ways in which *Project* suggests that its readers are metaphorically gazing into a pit. Earlier, Jessica suggested that the Pit at the center of *Project*'s narrative has its formal parallel in the circular design on the screen, and she drew an analogy between readers focusing on the pulsing vortex and diegetic readers gazing into the Pit. The narrative provides many examples of characters who contemplate the Pit: geologists like Playfair, historians like Moody, artists like Church, as well as many unnamed construction workers, engineers, tourists, and even hypothetical casino guests. Like these characters, we as readers gaze into the screen of *Project*, and the tunnel form that appears in our volume threshold appears to confirm our concept of the screen as Pit-like. And yet, our expectations are also contradicted by the brightness of this image. What we *do not* see in our visualization is a Pit-like absence or darkness at the center of *Project*'s screen. Indeed, our visualizations and code explorations reveal that we never confront absence, not even for one moment. *Project* never presents the opportunity for its reader to stare into the Pit, for, unlike the casino guests, we as readers do not gaze into the emptiness of a "glorious abyss." Instead, we gaze into a glowing presence full of vibrant activity.

While the visual composition of *Project*'s screen imitates the form of the Pit, it also presents the antithesis of that form by inverting dark emptiness into bright fullness. This visual inversion has interpretive implications for where we locate the reader's perspective. If, rather than the dark earth, we see the bright sky, this suggests that we readers are not looking into the Pit, but are instead looking *out* of it. When words and icons appear and disappear in the center of a Pit-like circle, they may be raining down from above rather than falling out of view. This change in our understanding of the spatial relationship of the readerly subject to what they are reading has implications for how we interpret one particular reader figure who is situated within the Pit and who gazes up toward the sky: the astronomer and explorer Kellogg.

Project's narrative tells us that Kellogg mistakenly believes that descending deep enough into the Pit will eliminate the obscuring blue of daytime, such that he then "would be able to view extra-galactic nebulae at midday." Unlike Playfair, who uses instruments to view the Pit, Kellogg plans to use the Pit itself as his viewing instrument. For him, the Pit's purpose is not to see into the earth, but to see out of the earth and into the sky. Indeed, if the uncharted depths of the Pit and the outer reaches of the deep sky both represent limits of human knowledge and understanding, then Kellogg's gambit is that these two limits are connected.

Kellogg fails in his initial aspiration to view the deep sky, and his failure is instructive. Kellogg descends to a depth where he is unable to see "even his own lamp held inches from his eyes." Yet, the failure to see either far beyond the Pit or deep within it does not stop him, it merely refocuses his attention on the Pit itself. Whether investigating the Pit's rim or its depths, we learn that "Kellogg was the first to describe many famed optical phenomena of the Pit," including inexplicable darkness, mysterious silhouettes, and odd lights. He attempts to scientifically "describe" visions that are also interpreted by local myths and legends, as when "Kellogg described the odd lights seen on moonless nights, locally supposed to be the spirits of brigands or lost men." In fact, he actively participates in creative interpretation and myth-making about the Pit. "A theme of Kellogg's writing," the text continues, "was that the Pit was related to the Pit of Conklin or more often the Well of Conklin, a subject of local legend held to contain malign influences lethal to travelers." Such themes become his poetic preoccupations, and as a creative writer for popular publications such as "Libido," Kellogg's descriptions of the Pit "varied with his reading popular tastes and motion pictures and television programs he had seen." When considered alongside Kellogg's self-reported inability to see anything in the deep Pit, these varied descriptions and their sources suggest a kind of creative solipsism. Instead of providing Kellogg with a telescope for gazing up at the sky, the Pit acts on him as a sensory deprivation chamber and thus refocuses all his attention on the contents of his own mind. For Kellogg, this "lair of vortices and fantastic beings" becomes a liminal zone of imagination and a source of inspiration, the narrative suggests, for literature.

Project's narrative suggests one other answer to who gazes up out of the Pit, and that answer is troubling. In a section on suicides, we read that "at least 23 people have attempted suicide by jumping into the Pit," but the motives of the survivors and the dead alike are left unclear. We only learn that there is "a reported tendency to jump involuntarily." This odd compulsion to involuntary suicide occurs when victims "lose all sense of direction in the vicinity of the Pit," and this disorientation may be due to an unexplained optical illusion that inverts space. Returning to the text with the perspective gained from our volume view attunes our attention to such lines as the following, "One individual questioned by police reported the illusion of transposing the sky and the Pit." While Kellogg strove to intentionally connect Pit and sky, others suffer from any accidental conjunction of these two spaces. For the involuntary suicides, connecting Pit and sky is an illusion. Mistaking location and inverting perspective can be a dangerous thing.

When considered together, Kellogg's explorations and the fates of the involuntary suicides both present allegories for interpretation that depend on a surprising inversion. Descending deeply into something for the purpose of seeing clearly from its depths is a suggestive (if sly) metaphor for close reading, for close reading presents a text as a space that must be entered and understood from the inside out. In a broader sense, if we readers already occupy the Pit, then perhaps the Pit symbolizes not only the unknown but also the familiar world we live in. Its enigma is not only supernatural but also natural; mystery is a normal part of life in all its inherent unknowability. Just as Kellogg vacillates between gazing into the Pit and gazing through it, we readers switch back and forth between interpreting the Pit as an alien other space and using the Pit to illuminate the quotidian. By contrast, the fate of the suicides suggests that the danger of confusing the map for the territory or the viewfinder for what is viewed. In this light, choosing to read the Pit as an allegory of our shifting media landscape signals not only a crisis but also a kind of trap, and one that is most dangerous at the moment we leap to embrace that which it does not contain.

We live in an age of anxieties, many of them associated with the digital zeitgeist: crises of poetic creation, production, distribution, and reception; crises of the book, print media, publishing, literature, the humanities, the academy, and scholarship, to name but a few. However, crises, enigmas, and pits do not always need solutions, *Project* tells us. Rather than offer a path toward change, our efforts to respond may be more important in how they register the risk and promise of our desire to rethink what we know. Even our own collaborative effort in this book exemplifies this point, for as we try to rethink literary criticism for digital poetics, we are actually responding to a shifting media landscape with an expedition that is simultaneously a leap into the unknown.

THE OPTICAL UNCONSCIOUS (JESSICA)

Jeremy's visualizations capture the animation and present it back to the reader in ways that enable us to see it differently by allowing us to see *more* of it. The screenshots capture every screen of *Project*, and the montage view allows us to see, all at once, the work's visual elements that escape perception or do not register consciously during its temporal performance. Jeremy's efforts to read the images he makes, to make meaning from them, is both distinctly new but also part of a longer lineage of thinking about how we think *through* reading machines and how media machines impact what we can know. To explain and to put his work in context, I pursue an analogy between Jeremy's digital data visualizations and Walter Benjamin's concept of the mechanical optical unconscious.

In "The Work of Art in the Age of Mechanical Reproduction" (1936), Benjamin describes the "unconscious optics" of the cinematic camera, which make visible that which we see but do not consciously register.[10] We may use photographic and cinematic cameras with the intention of recording our individual vision of the world, but these machines actually capture more than we are capable of seeing and knowing. In so doing, such technology transforms what and how we can know in the modern world. Benjamin writes, "The enlargement of a snapshot does not simply render more precise what in any case was visible, though unclear: it reveals entirely new structural formations of the subject."[11] Consider the scientist who uses a microscope to view the world at the subatomic level or the volumetric view that stacks all screenshots of *Project* to reveal spaces of stasis in the flashing animation; these acts of technologically enhanced vision provide new ways of seeing and new things to see. For Benjamin, this technologically enhanced vision is not just about seeing new things in the external world but also about recognizing what and why we don't see. Benjamin suggests as much when he claims, "The camera introduces us to unconscious optics as does psychoanalysis to unconscious impulses."[12] The camera (particularly the "filmed behavior" of cinema) functions, for Benjamin, as both the unconscious and the psychoanalyst; the technology captures and "introduces us to" what we have seen but not perceived—or what has passed before our eyes without being perceived.[13] We might take this a step further, as *Project* will invite us to do, and suggest that such technologies introduce us to our own unconscious.

Project is very much about how technology affects human consciousness and, in particular, our reading practices. Indeed, we could say that *Project* performs an aesthetic version of Benjamin's optical unconscious: the work presents technologized speed in such a way that it exposes and makes us conscious of (even as it obscures and distracts us from) the computer's role in the otherwise seemingly private and unmediated practice of reading. Understood this way, *Project* invites the kind of technologized readings that Mark and Jeremy pursue, which are each efforts to expose the functioning of the optical unconscious. Consider how Mark's exploration of code showed how *Project* employs its animation software to present "distractions" and "fixation crosses" that intentionally distract and refocus the reader's attention at certain moments. In the case of Jeremy's visualizations, these technologized images offer, à la Benjamin's concept of the optical unconscious, an opportunity to reflect upon ("introduces us to") the operations of our own unconscious. Or, perhaps it is more accurate to say that Mark and Jeremy's computational interventions support reflection upon how machines mediate our reading practice and shape our conscious perception. For Jeremy's visualizations freeze the animation and make the fleeting content visible and static so that it can be examined, but his images also expose the workings of the Flash software and its processing. The visualizations create, in effect, a kind of timeline like the one Mark encountered in the decompiled files. The computational images support an interpretive reading of the work that a human reader alone could not perform, one attentive to that which Flash's tween algorithms blur and *Project*'s speed purposefully obscures.

Through its use of speed, animation, and random events, *Project* focuses its reader's attention on the role of the computer—the reading machine—in determining what will be read, perceived, and known. In so doing, *Project* illuminates the fact that reading involves conscious and subconscious cognition, both of which happen through reading technologies. *Project* aesthetically exploits the role of the unconscious in the activity known as "reading," and it does so in ways that prompt questions about what constitutes that central cognitive and critical act.

TWEEN (MARK)

The optical unconscious is not only relevant to considering the role of the human reader interacting with *Project* as digital literature; it can also describe the experience of the programmer-artist who interacts with the Flash authoring software, encountering visuals that are only produced when the .swf is executed. This is particularly true when we return to our consideration of Flash with the insights provided by Jeremy's work with visualizations. Jeremy uses highly specialized technological scopes to photograph a conceptual middle, an in-between that does not actually exist in the Flash files but is made present in their performance capture. From the vantage point offered by the Flash files, only the beginning and end points of many of these animations have been determined. There is no middle, only an algorithm that enacts the connection between point A and point B. Flash sutures these connections, to adapt a metaphor from film theory. That is why Flash can be described as offering, in Julian Sefton-Green's words, a "liminal experience" between the layers of visual manipulation and the code that enables it.[14] The liminal, or even the subliminal, in Flash is epitomized by its signature animation visualization: the tween.

The tween is the animation element that creates action between point A (at one keyframe, or moment in time) and point B (at another keyframe). It fills in the scenes between keyframes and thus creates action where none existed before. The tween names the in-between (hence "tween") motion that functions to move and morph graphics. Flash calculates the transitions between the keyframes and moves the lines along their predetermined trajectories. The movements of the tween are produced not by the programmer/designer but by the program. The author designates where the tween will appear, and the program generates the animation. As a programming tool, the tween saves countless hours of human labor (which in contemporary mainstream animation production is often outsourced to animators in lower-wage labor markets) because one does not have to fill in each frame of a movie or to rely merely on the persistence of vision to create the illusion of motion. In the graphical display of the Flash interface, a tween is represented by blue highlighted frames between two keyframes. Black circles indicate the keyframes, while an arrow stretched between the frames identifies where the tweening will occur. For example, to produce *Project*'s pulsating blue targets in the background, Poundstone created a MovieClip[15] in which the first keyframe shows the concentric rings in a small state and the second keyframe shows an expanded version. The arrow in between these two keyframes and the purple frames it covers mark the frames where the expansion is calculated and drawn by the tween effect. This unique color designation on the timeline of the authoring interface gives evidence of the special status of the tween in Flash.

Tweens are an aspect of Flash animations that are designed to elude our attention, to appear seamless, but *Project* offers an opportunity to turn our attention to them, both as formal and poetic devices. Tween is a visual metaphor for a process whose effects can be seen but whose methods and code are unseen. The effects appear to be occurring on the surface of the interface at the command of the programmer, but they are actually dependent on the calculations of the software and the processing of the computer platform that remain hidden but for their on-screen, runtime effects. Tweening thus represents a realm of authoring that is on the border between purposefully arranged visuals and programmatically determined movement.

Unlike the optical unconscious of film and photography that Jessica discussed earlier, the tween does not capture reality for playback; it instead mathematically simulates the movements of a reality. It is a metaphorical name given to the process that represents in-betweenness, for the tween creates streaming movement from discrete states (the individual keyframes in the Flash interface). The tween therefore represents a liminal zone in between the fixity of the GUI and the unseen calculations of the code, between the effects that the programmer determines and the results of processes that can only be observed. With the tween, the .fla file shows but does not reveal the activity of the software. In this way, the tween is the inverse of the "optical unconscious" because it is that effect which is perceived but whose production processes remain hidden even when observed through the reading (and writing) machine of the authoring environment. The tween produces programmatic and visual in-betweenness, but it marks one way Flash operates at the liminal state of human intention and action. It is, therefore, the tween—the device that enables the in-betweenness of this digital poetry—that enables *Project* to produce a poetics of simultaneous flow and flicker, presence and absence. It is thus a perfect poetic device for a work, *Project*, that is very much about the liminal and subliminal and what lies between.

DETRITUS AND UNCONTAINABILITY (MARK)

Thus far, we have been exploring how *Project* invites us to seek and excavate its unseen elements and technological aspects. Combing through *Project*'s Flash source files is another way of exploring its obscured and unseen content, a way of working to understand the hidden logic and assets that make the piece function. The search uncovers elements of the production file (.fla) that do not appear in the playable file (.swf) and which offer great fodder for interpretation. Like the detritus that litters the Pit, these items persist in the Flash file as discarded drafts and undeleted notes. They bear their labels for use in a movie that does not play them; their contents do not appear on-screen. We might say that this coded detritus is latent content that, when made manifest to us excavators, can tell us much about *Project* as a whole.

Reading the code, we have access to the uncovered signs of artistic process. The .fla file contains animation sequences, empty layers, and sound files that were never used in the finished .swf. For example, the Flash file reveals ten layers marked "inaudible," containing empty keyframes, a ghostly trace of Poundstone's path, and a reminder that the Flash file is a snapshot of a creative process. As a further sign of the evolution of this work, the level 1 distraction uses an instantiation of a movie called "inwardgradient" that displays a pulsating target of shades of white and blue; however, that instance is called "level4Effect," suggesting that Poundstone had originally used a different ordering of the effects. The discrepancy in the numbering system suggests previous versions of the piece, experiments gone wrong or proven unsatisfactory, that can no longer be accessed but whose trace lives on in the code as part of the signification system. The assets also bear timestamps that mark their creation. Such findings reward the kind of approaches we pursue—creative hacking and decompiling, visualizations and code reading. Like the items that find their way into the Pit, this detritus collects in the code and, when excavated, attests to the fact that the Flash authorware is not just a writing program or platform that makes *Project* perform. It is also an archive for writerly processes and intentions, a collection of data that document the decisions about what stays and what gets discarded in the production of this work of digital literature. Although there are parallels to be made with the forensic study of other art forms, such as the use of X-rays to discover *pentimenti* or hidden versions beneath a finished painting, Flash-based digital art is different. Such work carries with it a formalized set of artifacts detailing its production, including digital timestamps and a library of assets, which can be accessed and read along with the final on-screen product.

Not only does the Flash source code file hold elements that have been discarded, but so too does the file which stores the text—BP.txt. This data file contains the entire text of the story, as well as the full list of subliminal words (which we will consider in greater depth in the next chapter). However, a few of the subliminal words in the BP.txt data file are never displayed while *Project* runs. This happens because the file lists 223 subliminal words, but the source code contains instructions to load only the first 200 of these words into memory. The final twenty-three words are never loaded and thus are never displayed as subliminal text, although they remain in the code:

> *nuclear earthshaking covariate wrongful dogfish physiochemical edict registrable soliloquy escape Evans Kowalski know distant amiss Adelia Conway mayor impute convolute Henrietta successful semantic*

This list of the unused words has much in common with the other 200, discussed at length in chapter 4, in that they initially do not appear to follow any pattern, whether word length, word type, or subject matter. The words "earthshaking" and "mayor" stand out, however, as having relevance to a story about geological sinkholes and civic communities around it as well as the literal and figural fault lines that connect them. They will never be shown as subliminal words; they are a remnant in the text file, a ready reserve that the software never taps. Having discovered these hidden subliminal words, readers can try to evaluate why these were not included in the final set, why Poundstone stopped at 200, and why he did not merely delete these extra words, as he might have with a mere keystroke.

Remnants of the production process are, no doubt, part of any work of art (just think of the unhappy fly who landed in Jackson Pollock's paint[16]). But, there is an aspect of this fact that is distinct in digital art. If the work functions as the creator desires, there is no technical reason to go through and discard or delete the detritus from the work's source files. While artists working in open source, freeware, and easily readable formats (like HTML and JavaScript) can expect readers to access their code, Poundstone used the closed, proprietary format of Flash; so he would expect most readers to only see the surface, on-screen content. On the other hand, not only were many of these assets easily accessed with a decompiler, but also Poundstone himself freely shared with us annotated versions of his source files. When the author is also the programmer, meaning is made at the level of the output and the level of the code. His choices at the level of code are part of his artistic act and, hence, they invite critical consideration.

Moreover, since the story itself reflects the various forms of trash—such as the "layer of coins smooth stones beverage containers fast food wrappers, and feral cats" that lines the bottom of the southeast rim of the Pit—the presence of these unseen but undeleted words takes on added significance. They are not only remainders, but also reminders that what we see on-screen is never the entire or whole work. Instead, we see the files frozen at the end of, or perhaps even in the middle of, a much longer process. This is particularly pertinent in *Project*, for this work is very much about hidden depths and subterranean processes. Indeed, our consideration of the subliminal words has led us to move from focusing on the presentation file to the production file. In so doing, we not only find additional detritus, remnants of the creative process, but also artifacts that demonstrate how digital literary objects can be archives of their own production.

THE PSYCHOANALYTIC PIT IN AVANT-GARDE POETICS (JESSICA)

The Bottomless Pit is the stimulus, subject, and symbol of dreams; it produces and represents trauma. For these reasons and more, the Pit—and the story about it—reflects the influence of Freudian psychoanalysis. Allusions to psychoanalysis appear before *Project*'s narrative even begins—in the work's prefatory entryscreens. On these introductory and informational screens, Poundstone explicitly situates *Project* within a tradition of artistic experiments informed by psychoanalysis, works that strive to access and represent the unconscious through conscious engagement with media. The idea that the unconscious is a bottomless pit has inspired avant-garde writing and art since Freud, but *Project*'s paratextual entryscreens identify the 1950s as a period of particular interest. In the entryscreen titled "Falling into The Void," Poundstone uses a synonym for "the pit"—"the void"—that expands and describes his literary project by connecting it to earlier poetic traditions. "The abandonment of conscious control, so much a part of 1950s avant-garde practice," Poundstone explains, "was likened to falling into the abyss."[17] Such "art bordering on the imperceptible" included concrete poetry, which "was described as a poetry of voids, i.e. blank spaces on the page."[18] It also includes, as Poundstone mentions, Yves Klein's "empty-gallery-as-art" and John Cage's silent musical composition *4'33"*, both of which foreground the invisible, silent, and illegible aspects of meaning-making by focusing on the contexts in which art is produced and accessed. In these cases, the gallery space and the theater, respectively, are illuminated by the artwork as well as by the mechanically enhanced arrangement of the viewer or audience in the space. Such art not only attempts to access the unconscious, it also exposes how technologies and techniques participate in this effort.[19] *Project* responds to and participates in this poetic tradition of accessing, representing, and even altering consciousness through media. Moreover, it operates at the avant-garde by moving this practice forward—addressing these conceptual concerns and poetic interests by employing digital technologies in strikingly new ways.

But, there is more at stake in *Project*'s reference to psychoanalysis than poetic engagement with the unconscious. There is a moment halfway through the story cycle when the narrative directly addresses and engages psychoanalysis; the story turns to analyze the dreams of residents living near the Pit, Freudian style. We learn, "Children and to some extent the adults of the area are subject to recurring dreams and nightmares about the Pit. Dreams of falling into the Pit are common." The fact that it is primarily children who dream about the Pit is notable because Freud understood dreamwork as offering access not only to the unconscious, but also to unfulfilled infantile fantasies: *"The dream is the (disguised) fulfillment of a (suppressed, repressed) wish."*[20] As *Project*'s dream section continues, the narrative begins to catalog the dreams of people living around the Pit, taking on a scientific tone as it classifies the dreams by way of their shared characteristics: "Often in the dream the Pit is ever widening and threatens the dreamer's home and familiar surroundings." The threat posed to dreamer's homes is actual; the Pit might actually swallow a home by destabilizing its foundation, but it is also symbolic. This is the nidificatory limit, the place where nests, homes, and laws of sociality fail. As *Project*'s dreamwork section presents the symbolic representation of fears, anxieties, and traumas associated with the Pit, the narrative adopts the tone of an analyst's report: "Feelings of anxiety despair fear abandonment and anomie are frequently reported." Psychoanalysis teaches that what is reported is not the whole story, and the other category of dreams described in *Project* prompts the reader to consider more traditional psychoanalytic interpretations of the Pit: sexual symbolism.

The text states, "In another locally common class of dream the dreamer finds him or herself already in the Pit and unable to scale its walls." The threat of falling into the Pit and being unable to escape echoes Freud's interpretation of the appearance of pits in dreams as a symbol for female genitalia. Freud's twelfth lecture in *A General Introduction to Psychoanalysis* twice references dreams in which a pit symbolizes a vagina. In the first instance, he shares a young woman's dream wherein she sees a deep hole in a vineyard, a hole that the woman (while dreaming) knows has been made by pulling out a tree. Freud remarks that the "dream deals with another bit of the infantile sex theory, namely, with the belief that girls originally had the same genitals as boys and that the later conformation results from castration (pulling out of a tree)."[21] Later in the same lecture, Freud recounts a man's story of a dream that includes a pit. The man dreamt of walking with his father: *"There are steps leading from this courtyard down into a pit, the walls of which are upholstered with some soft material rather like a leather arm chair."*[22] Freud explains that, after the man related his dream, "the dreamer himself translated all the symbols, even though he had had no preliminary knowledge of dream interpretation."[23] The dreamer describes his own dream in sexual symbolism, with "the pit as the vagina on account of the soft upholstering of its walls."[24] Freud suggests that the fact that this untaught man interpreted his own dream in accordance with Freud's theoretical equation of vagina = pit = castration or death[25] confirms the veracity of psychoanalytic dreamwork. (Leo Bersani famously repurposes this symbolic equation in his essay "Is the Rectum a Grave?" wherein he deconstructs the heteronormative sexuality of psychoanalysis for application in queer theory).[26] Although psychoanalysis and psychology moved away from dream analysis and phallocentric notions such as penis envy, Freud's lecture reminds us that pits in dreams—and thus artistic dreams of pits, including *Project*—invite interpretations based in sexual symbolism.

For our purposes reading this work about a bottomless pit that many men stare into, explore, and even die inside, the equation of vagina = pit propagated by Freudian psychoanalysis permeates the narrative and beckons interpretation. Recognizing that the Bottomless Pit in Poundstone's tale might symbolize sexuality and anxieties about it opens new ways of reading the work. In particular, this critical context situates the Pit as an object of fascination and intense attraction that draws readers (both within and of the narrative) into its depths. As with the sexual undercurrents in Freudian analysis, the fulfillment readers seek in knowing the depths of *Project*'s Pit is intertwined with a fundamental fear of losing ourselves inside it. Or, in line with the interpretative allegory we are pursuing in this book, wherein *Project* presents an allegory for the current context of media shift, critically examining this digital pit requires relinquishing parts of our interpretative past.

The interpretation of dreams section ends by suggesting, in a very Freudian manner, that the Pit is the subject of dreams and fixations even when it is not immediately and visibly present: "Even when dream content is not manifestly about the Pit residents dream of falling off cliffs or being stranded in crevices." The Pit's presence, we are told, pervades and remains readable even when it is absent. The logic parallels Freud's suggestion that stories about pits are always about female genitalia, castration, and sexual anxiety. Whether or not the Pit is a proxy for a sexual orifice, we will leave to Dr. Freud. Instead we note how the story endows the Pit with psychological force and symbolism so as to place it—both the Pit and *Project*—within a genealogy of textual interpretation and hermeneutics that reach back to Freudian psychoanalysis and, in so doing, challenge readers to wonder why.

GENRE (MARK)

Project strives to elude our ability to constrain and contain it. Like its central character, symbol, and formal trope—the Pit—the work revels in resisting interpretation. This is, we might say, its central ambition and poetic, yet this is also what connects *Project* to a specific narrative tradition. In the previous section, Jessica discussed *Project* in the context of avant-garde art focused on psychoanalytic poetics, and earlier we considered *Project* in the context of electronic literature. Here, however, I want to situate *Project* in relation to a different literary context: the prose tradition of fables, particularly tall tales. *Project*'s narrative about a large bottomless pit that inspires a crisis of meaning shares certain distinct conventions with tall tales. These stories inspire and disturb interpretation for their readers both inside and outside their diegetic text. Placing Poundstone's tale in this context shows how this digital text adapts and reimagines that particular genre and also how folk genres evolve in digital contexts.

The tall tale has a long and winding history that wends through print and oral traditions.[27] This type of story centers on a fabulous, inexplicable, enigmatic element—something taller, larger, and more fantastic than normal. In such tales, the "tall" element—the unusually large, mythical, or far-fetched—becomes the center and purpose of the tale. This element is often inscrutable, unknowable, or magical but it is always based on and in reality. This mysterious or otherworldly quality ties the genre to works of another tradition, from another part of the globe, magical realism, which also introduces the improbable or otherworldly into the natural order of things. Rawdon Wilson offers a lovely catalog of the characteristics of magical realism: "The copresence of oddities, the interaction of the bizarre with the entirely ordinary, the doubleness of conceptual codes, the irreducibly hybrid nature of experience strikes the mind's eye."[28] In this section, I will discuss these traditions together to note the confluence of their techniques that flow into Poundstone's tale.

The central figure in these tales is always larger than life, and the insertion of this mythic figure into the realistic landscape serves as a kind of touchstone or lightning rod—to illuminate the way the world works around it. This thing or person is typically both wonderful and threatening. Its presence disturbs the otherwise ordinary community it enters and inhabits. The tall element—the very large man, the very little girl, the man with enormous wings, or the inexplicable balloon hovering over a city—presents the community with an interpretative challenge: how to understand, explain, or name the unknown. These tales thus present a situation of uncertainty—the unresolvable nature of that troubling object of fascination.

As the pit becomes "The Pit" in *Project*, it grows to the mythological proportions of folk tales. *Project*'s flashing, digital interface—with its distracting visual and sonic effects—might obscure the more traditional and recognizable aspects of its narrative. But, it is worth considering how and why this work updates the tall tale genre. In particular, *Project*'s narrative bears a striking resemblance to two highly anthologized examples of the genre: Donald Barthelme's "The Balloon" (1981) and Gabriel García Márquez's "A Very Old Man with Enormous Wings" (1972). These two stories arise from different traditions. Barthelme is identified as exemplary of North American postmodern fiction while Márquez hails from "magic realism" from the so-called literary boom in Latin America.[29] Yet, their stories share a common thematic about the failure of hermeneutics to contain and explain the supernatural (the natural but extraordinary). Moreover, *Project* presents an opportunity to read these two print stories together and in new ways via a kind of literary triangulation.

Like the Bottomless Pit, the inscrutable objects in these two stories call forth unusual behaviors from the communities that try to understand them. William Scott could be describing Poundstone's piece when he calls "The Balloon" "a sort of allegorical poem in sociologist prose."[30] Barthelme's short story tells of a city-sized balloon that appears in midtown Manhattan and transforms the life of the city dwellers. The balloon becomes an enigmatic sign that the populous strives to interpret, but it also reconfigures the space it enters.[31] Its presence transforms perspectives of the space, turning the city into a new place—certainly a place to see and know anew—based on its presence, dwarfing the skyscrapers and displacing the sky itself. In Márquez's tale, the object of fascination is the man of the title. The man with enormous wings, who could almost be called an angel, challenges definitions and expectations of humanness. The story details how people respond to this strange man, how the community struggles to interpret the supernatural phenomena inserted into its midst.

Poundstone's Pit shares much with Barthelme's balloon and Márquez's man. None of these elements submits easily to being pinned down, yet the plots of these stories revolve around efforts to explain them. In Barthelme's tall tale, city-dwellers "engaged in remarkably detailed fantasies having to do with a wish either to lose themselves in the balloon, or to engorge it." As Maurice Couturier and Régis Durand write, "The New Yorkers begin by trying out their learned discourse (journalistic, sociological, psychological, economic) in their attempt to naturalize it."[32] In Márquez, "The curious came from far away. A traveling carnival arrived with a flying acrobat who buzzed over the crowd several times." Similarly, Poundstone's townsfolk are inspired to stage a Passion Play on the Pit's southern rim. This performance transforms the Pit into a backdrop, which is one way of reading it; in another, sermons interpret the Pit as an allegory.

Yet, like the old man with wings, the Pit cannot be coopted into a simple religious reading. Poundstone's initial description at first gives the Passion Play a kind of majesty: "The performance began with a costumed angel trumpeting followed by the meteoric appearance of a magnesium flare star that fell from the sky into the Pit remaining visible up to 4 minutes." Poundstone creates a sense of awe by drawing the reader's gaze into the pit after the flare star. After the Pit was "symbolically opened with a golden key, there issued great billows of smoke and a plague of locusts enacted by the release of 600 horned lizards caged in concealed locations on the perimeter of the Pit." The bizarre use of "horned lizards" to manufacture a plague subverts any attempt to tap into a more reverent reading of this Pit, and along with the addition of the key (how does one unlock a pit?), the embellishment seems an absurd imposition on what is otherwise described as a natural geological formation. This passage ends its religious vignette with an abrupt return to the human world when a "lawsuit brought by the family of a woman who fell into the Pit while trying to get a better view brought an end to the production." This tragedy abruptly ends the religious reading with a reminder that the Pit is a dangerous space around which readers must tread with care. It cares not how it is read, for every reading is a superimposition, an attempt to simplify the unknowable or name the unnamable.

Both Márquez and Barthleme's stories contain similar patterns of readings that alternatively elevate (in the case of the balloon) and ground (in the case of the winged man) their mysterious objects. Father Gonzaga, the parish priest of Márquez's tale, after failing to get a response from the winged man using Latin, decides on closer inspection that the man is "much too human: he had an unbearable smell of the outdoors, the back side of his wings was strewn with parasites and his main feathers had been mistreated by terrestrial winds." The balloon in Barthelme's story becomes a playground for "daring" children. While some citizens hang "green and blue paper lanterns from the warm gray underside," others "seized the occasion to write messages on the surface, announcing their availability for the performance of unnatural acts, or the availability of acquaintances." The mysterious objects reveal the nature of the community by compelling them to react and interact.

The struggle over what to do with these objects is a struggle over how to read them. Barthleme's text makes this explicit when the narrator says,

> There was a certain amount of initial argumentation about the 'meaning' of the balloon; this subsided, because we have learned not to insist on meanings, and they are rarely even looked for now, except in cases involving the simplest, safest phenomena. It was agreed that since the meaning of the balloon could never be known absolutely, extended discussion was pointless.

Meaning itself has been disrupted in these tales by these extraordinary and inscrutable objects. Poundstone takes up this genre with a tale he delivers via a browser-based platform, Flash, the dazzling advertising tool, to suggest the ways this crisis of meaning extends to contemporary, online commercial spaces.

ADVERTISING AND THE PIT IN THE MARKETPLACE (JESSICA)

Advertising is an aspect of contemporary culture that we encounter daily without fully and consciously comprehending it, and *Project* takes on this situation as a poetic challenge. The work turns attention to advertising by shining a spotlight on its operational aesthetics (subliminal messaging) and by employing its visual iconography (logos). In an interview with *The Iowa Review Web*, Poundstone states, "There is a museum of typography on American consumer product labels, and we never see it because we've learned to tune it out."[33] We do not look at the words to see what and how they say; rather, we look through them. Poundstone continues, "I say 'museum,' because it's not all contemporary. There are labels and logos that have been unchanged in decades, preserving echoes of fifties biomorphism, constructivism, and everything else."[34] The conceptual museum of advertising that Poundstone references is an archive of sorts, an archive of American capitalist consumer culture and the visual design associated with it. *Project* borrows from this archive for its visual poetics, employing icons from the realm of advertising for its flashing image-texts. The entire story text of *Project* appears atop images from advertising, icons from consumer culture depicting goods-turned-symbols: a martini glass, a camera, a film projector, a hair pick, etc. These icons are semiotic signs that exceed linguistic representation yet are instantly recognizable, comprehended without directed attention or consciousness.[35] Yet *Project* prompts us to pay attention to these icons and, also, to the formal poetics used in product labels from which they are drawn. The work performs media archaeology not only on the tachistoscope but also on advertising, for it explores how advertising affects consumers unconsciously through art (labels and logos) that deserves to be analyzed and archived.

As Poundstone suggested in his interview with *The Iowa Review Web*, there is much to read and examine in the mini-museums of American culture that we call product labels. He pursues this subject of investigation further in a recent book, *Priceless: The Myth of Fair Value (and How to Take Advantage of It)* (2010). In this nonfiction work, Poundstone explores how economic psychology impacts pricing and its presentation, from printed menus to Prada store exhibits to price tags displaying slashed-down numbers. In *Project*, Poundstone uses a condensed narrative to explore the psychology behind capitalism, advertising, and consumer culture. Indeed, one way of understanding this work—and of trying to get a handle on the Pit—is by focusing on its interest in advertising.

The narrative is packed with examples of people trying to bring the Pit to the marketplace, to profit off of it and control it through advertising. For example, "One commercial enterprise throws unwanted objects into the Pit for a fee." This effort is built upon exploiting the daily customs of locals. We are told, "It has become popular to throw small or valueless objects into the Pit." The Pit becomes a collection site for such detritus, and the act of throwing something away takes on meaning and becomes marketable. "People talk of casting something into the Pit when they mean to get rid of it with certainty" while they also "literally cast into the Pit last packs of cigarettes photographs of ex-husbands" and more. Rituals and common practices grow up around the Pit, and these customs become potential cash cows. Poundstone never misses an opportunity to suggest how popular traditions serve capitalistic enterprises. This is especially true of tourism, for "The Pit remains an attraction to travelers." The tourist site stimulates a local economy that depends upon the circulation of advertising narratives about the Pit as a religious or allegorical site, stories which then serve to promote the sale of "calcite spars sold at roadside stands as devil horns or Satan's jewel boxes." While circulating Pit narratives is good for one part of the local economy, it also has (pardon the pun) its pitfalls. Circulating stories about the Pit is particularly bad for the real estate sector of the economy. As a result, such businesses strive to censure proliferating narratives about the Pit: "Mentions of the Pit are conspicuously absent from area real estate brochures." The narrative spotlights one attempt, in particular, to recast real estate dangers as tourist attractions: the final construction project discussed in *Project*, the largest of all efforts to capitalize on the Pit, the three-thousand room Indian casino. But not even a top-notch advertisement with a seductive tagline can overcome the reality of cracking ground.

The Pit is a product and an advertisement, a material entity and a metaphor for it. Poetry and advertising converge in *Project*'s depiction of a pit that becomes the Bottomless Pit (a seemingly trademarkable name). So, when the narrative states, "Large cracks parallel to the Pit's rim have appeared in the ground where construction was to have begun," we know that these fissures not only suggest impending calamity for the casino but also signify that the Pit will continue to expand and, along with it, so too will imaginative and poetic efforts to capitalize on it and tell stories about it.

COLLAPSING THE PIT: A Z-PROJECTION VIEW (JEREMY)

Breaking down is a recurring theme of both *Project* and our readings of it. These breakdowns are always failures of separation or containment. Mark considered the failure of hermeneutics to contain the supernatural, while Jessica considered how advertising and poetry are united by artifice rather than separated by it. When the safety rail is partially swallowed by the Pit at the end of the *Project* story cycle, we are reminded that the world cannot be kept safely out of the Pit, and the Pit cannot be prevented from expanding into the world: exchange is inevitable. In our consideration of topics from detritus to dreams, we consistently return to these issues of inseparability. Indeed, the failure of the safety rail to mark the edge of the Pit also foreshadows the imminent failure of *Project* to mark its own end, as the first words of the story cycle appear on the heels of the last. The work runs on in a closed loop, endlessly inseparable from itself and as infinite as a circle.

It is perhaps characteristic of *Project* and its inversions that we set out in this chapter to grapple with the central mystery of the Bottomless Pit but return again and again to a different mystery of what we might term the "Edgeless Pit" and its undefined rim. In this section our return to the scene of the crumbling safety rail is the occasion for our return to visual approaches to *Project*'s screen, and in particular to interpretations of the visual element of the rim. We will explore how the rim does and does not circumscribe and delineate the experience of *Project*—both on the space of the screen and as it varies during a story cycle.

In order to investigate how the visual rim both changes and endures over one complete playthrough of *Project*, we will now transform our previous volume view. First, by visually "slicing" the volume in order to more clearly see its interior, we will focus on a third visual-temporal structure which complicates the binary oppositions of our previous readings by focusing our attention on the figure of the rim and its potential for reading *Project* in terms of liminal spaces. Next, we will use the method of "z-projection" to summarize the contents of our volume in several ways. While the montage view provided us with a kind of transcript of many screens and the volume view presented those screens as an object, each projection will work like a long-exposure photograph, summarizing many moments into an image. As we will see, a projection of all color over time confirms our intuition of how a *Project* screen typically appears, while a projection of change reveals how the rim both frames and is framed by text and icons—it expands and collapses, and does *not* consistently separate the hyperactive reading area from its placid surroundings. Yet, although the rim shifts, a projection of darkness confirms that the rim is *always* present. On the one hand, the visual rim fails to separate the inside and outside of the screen, undermining distinctions between what is and is not to be read and paid attention to. On the other, it is as stable over time as it is unstable in space. Indeed, its enduring and unbroken presence is the fundamental visual structure of the work.

Our previous method of visual interpretation proceeded by locating the visual figure of the Pit in the visual composition of *Project*, characterizing it, and then narratively locating characters and the reader in relationship to this figure. One basis for doing so in relation to the composition of the screen has been a distinction, highlighted by our volume views, between the static edges and the active center of the screen. In order to more carefully consider the question of activity on the screen and what readings it gives rise to, we will now transform

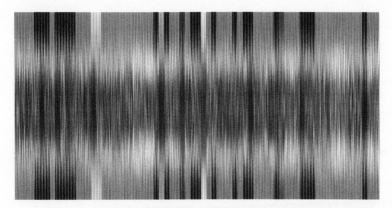

FIGURE 3.5: A volume slice of *Project*, sampling the screen's vertical center-line. Each line marks one moment. Horizontal patterns show activity at different screen heights. (Visualization by Jeremy Douglass.)

our visualization yet again, this time using a "slice" method to cut the previous 3-D volume visualization lengthways, opening it and revealing the center in detail. The cross-section approach of the slice offers an opportunity to closely read screen activity as it occurs horizontally or vertically throughout the work. Should our visual readings of the Pit arise out of binary oppositions between edge and center? Or is there a third way?

In our slice of the volume, time still proceeds from left to right, with each vertical line marking one moment in time. As in the original volume view, we can still see slow changes in simple color bands running along the top and bottom of the image, which correspond to the edges of the screen. As in the threshold volume, we can also see a highly active core, with the gray blur that runs left to right marking the constant shifting of text and icons at the center of the image. What we also see in our volume slice, however, is not two zones of activity but three: between the center and each edge is a pale band that marks the movements of the rim—always present, ever-shifting, faster than the background, yet slower than the center of the screen. Revisiting our earlier threshold volume, we can recognize that the Pit-like figure contains not only text and icons, but also the rim itself. Both visually and in the narrative, the silhouette of the rim is a liminal space that frames the Pit and is, at the same time, part of it—both without and within. In order to bring this silhouette into clearer focus, we will now switch to a different 2-D view of our volume: a z-projection.

What is a z-projection? This form of visualization combines all of the frames in *Project* into one frame, summarizing how the work varies over a full playthrough. Two simple analogies help explain this process. The term "z-projection" can be understood as the result of projecting light through our volume view along its z-axis (time, depth) and out onto a screen. The resulting z-projection combines many images into one, as if its light were filtered through a series of many transparent slides. A second analogy clarifies the results we may expect of z-projection. In long-exposure photography, light from many different instances accrues and forms an exposure over time on photographic film. The resulting exposure combines many different moments into one image, often with blurring that indicates the compression of time. You know these images: a streak of color that records a car in motion or a person with a multitude of blurred arms that actually indicate the movement of two limbs. The process of z-projection likewise superimposes motion as blur.

Yet z-projections are not created through filters or exposures. Instead of being determined by the properties of media such as photographic film or transparency foils, each z-projection is the result of a different algorithmic operation, and so each must be understood according to its own logic in order to support interpretive arguments. Here we consider three operations: a mean, standard deviation, and minimum z-projection.[36]

How should we read these three projects, and what do we observe? Let us consider each in turn. The first projection creates an image of *typical colors* and where they are found on the screen, by calculating the mean, median, or modal color values of each pixel. This image indeed looks something like a blurred photo of *Project* itself, and confirms our intuition of the work's typical or archetypal form: a blue background, a pale rim, an indistinct white image, and black text. Yet this is not a typical screen selected from our playthrough. This is instead an amalgamation of all screens into *the* typical screen, not as described by a person, but as described by our machine collaborator. While the program does not understand this screen in the way we do, it reads in ways we cannot. Its observations are a source of productive defamiliarization, for they make our subject strange to us so that we may encounter it with fresh eyes. In contrast to our own perceptions, our algorithm is exceedingly simple but exceeds both the scope of our memory (by capturing every moment completely and weighing each one equally) and

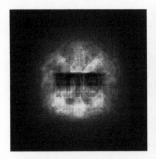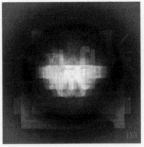

FIGURE 3.6: Three z-projections of the *Project* volume. Each pixel in a z-projection summarizes all values of that pixel on-screen over time. 1st: Color: mean value per pixel—center is black due to text, edges are light due to the predominantly blue background. 2nd: Change: standard deviation per pixel—dark areas are largely stable, bright areas are highly variable. 3rd: Darkness: minimum value per pixel—brightness indicates areas that are never dark throughout the entire playthrough. (Visualization by Jeremy Douglass.)

the precision of our attention (by noting each change exactly at the pixel level). The z-projection is thus both complete and precise in ways that create interesting new possibilities for reading. For example, our machine reader could now take this image and measure it against every single moment in our montage, rating how "typical" it finds every other by comparison, and eventually selecting its perfect *Project* image in which the screen takes on its most archetypal form. While we earlier selected the "biohazard poppy" imagetext for interpretation in part by chance, the color projection already suggests new approaches to plucking significant moments out of streams of thousands of images and hold them up for close reading.

Our second projection creates an image of *change* and where it occurs on the screen by calculating the standard deviation of each pixel and then color-coding the results in a spectrum: static black, slow blue, active red, and hyperactive white. Once we understand how to read this visualization, we recognize the three zones of activity (edge, rim, and center) earlier discovered in the bands of our volume slice visualization. When we look closer, however, as if reading a medical X-ray of the work, this new image reveals two crucial details that complicate our understanding of the visual rim as a liminal zone. First, note how the white box corners extend outside the red circle. This indicates that the hyperactivity of the icons is not only framed within the rim, but also spills out of its moving boundary. Unlike the Pit, which consumes the safety rail in the course of its constant outward expansion, the visual rim both expands and contracts, continually shifting whether text and icons fall into or out of it. In the volume slice, we identified three distinct bands associated with different elements at different distances from the center of the screen—the text and icons at the center, the rim farther out, and the background beyond. Because the rim actually shifts in and out of the text area, this summary was not entirely accurate, yet on reflection, such inaccuracy is appropriate to the work's theme of uncertain distances.

Throughout *Project* we encounter individuals and groups who misjudge their distance from the Pit. Devon Little's home is "a vast distance from the Pit," and yet he finds that this is no defense against structural damage that leaves him sleeping in his car. The Beale Pike construction project has "a generous margin of safety" from the Pit, and yet it ends in seventy-three deaths when a new chasm appears. It is not enough to say that these were mistakes. *Project* narrates many more failures to account for distances. Each example emphasizes the ways in which we think of spatial relationships as fixed, yet the text makes manifest fact that they can and do change. Viewing *Project* subjects us to similar unpredictable displacements. We read inside the rim, yet may find ourselves reading outside of it at any time. Even as we focus our eyes ever more firmly onto a fixed space, the rim moves and the place of our attention shifts beneath our gaze.

The second notable detail in the change projection is a surprise coming on the heels of the first. The blackest areas of the image are the place of least change, but these do not occur at the "stable" edges of the screen, as our earlier visual readings might lead us to expect. Instead, a dark shadow falls around the outer edge of the rim. While the "distractions" move the background color through long periods of stability followed by sudden high-contrast changes, according to our algorithm this is not the most visually stable part of the screen. Instead, some portion of the light-colored, ever-shifting rim is almost always found hovering in about the same place, whether on dark backgrounds or bright, no matter the distractions. While we barely noted the rim in our earlier reading of the visual layers of a single imagetext, here, each new visual exploration of a complete playthrough suggests the rim as a central figure of both the visual presentation and the narrative.

Turning to our third projection, we consider an image of *darkness* and where it occurs on the screen by combining the minimum value of each pixel. This image reveals that indeed some places on the screen are never dark—in particular, the area of the rim. Even at its darkest, there is no instant when it is absent. The work *always* displays some form of rim or edge. From this perspective, it is not the background, but the rim that is the most enduring and dominant part of *Project*'s visual presentation. This finding has interpretative significance, for the rim can be understood to be a central organizing principle and formal device, but also a symbolic facet of *Project*. In a work that changes constantly—flowing, streaming, flashing, pulsing, distracting, etc.—and that constantly describes change, our discovery of the rim's stability is remarkable. There is calm not at the center of the storm, nor beyond its edge, but at the rim of the vortex. It is liminality itself that is stable. At every moment of every performance, *Project* visually and poetically enacts this point through the framing device of the rim. The rim is the figure of the work itself.

In this chapter we were drawn into the Pit, and considered it from many perspectives. We located and mapped it, read it as an allegory, and considered its relationship to the authoring software that created it. In readings of images, source code, and media history, one recurring theme has been *liminality*—the edge or limit (whether physical or psychological) that marks a place between two spaces, objects, images, words, or even frames of animation. In the next chapter, we move from the liminal to the subliminal, examining an equally important framing device and poetic element in *Project*: its use of subliminal messages.

■ ■ ■ Jeremy Sees the Unseen

It had seemed like such a simple question. *Project* flashed a sequence of words on-screen when the software ran. Were the words the same or different each time? They flickered so quickly that it was hard to determine.

I recorded the screen. When I reviewed different recordings I saw different white-flashing subliminal words in each one. I was *sure* these words were chosen at random each time. Meanwhile, Mark was tracing the lines of source code to see how each word was selected and displayed on the screen. He insisted the same words are selected every time, in the same order. I exported video at a high frame rate and went through the images by hand—but instead of seeing what Mark described, I saw a few subliminal words scattered throughout the text. After months, we couldn't agree. We both decided to take another look.

Then Jessica and I received an e-mail titled "a present for both of you." Mark had modified the software to record the sequence of displayed words into a text file. He ran his modified program twice, then shared the results. I opened the two text files and stared in disbelief at their contents—two identical word lists. Then I replied:

TO: Mark　　　　　　FROM: Jeremy
You were right, I was wrong. They are *exactly* the same!

I had been foolish to rely too much on my eyes, and I had been far too conservative in my "high frame rate" explorations—*Project*'s fixed sequence of words had been flickering by me the whole time, disappearing between video frames and hiding in low contrast black-on-black changes. On reflection, I realized that our conflicting viewpoints had led to a greater understanding. The software always generated the same word order, while simultaneously revealing different words each time because of how they were displayed. The results were neither random (as they appeared to me on-screen) nor perfectly ordered (as they appeared to Mark in the code), but both: a fixed sequence whose shifts in color and layout caused different words to rise into or fall out of perceptibility in unpredictable ways.

The entryscreens to *Project* overtly discuss its relationship to subliminal messaging, and I had been primed to perceive the work in a particular way. Because I could perceive brief flashes of words, I assumed that their role in the work was metaphorical: not truly subliminal, but instead a liminal performance, perceptibly prompting the audience to reflect on the idea of the subliminal. Yet, during months of careful study, I had still been seeing words and yet not seeing them.

SUBLIMINAL ADVERTISING AND DEPTH MARKETING (JESSICA)

Project presents subliminal messages in a Flash movie about a bottomless pit, and it does so in ways that remediate both the tachistoscope and also James Vicary's famous 1957 experiment in using that swift-viewing machine to present subliminal advertising. Regardless of whether or not Vicary actually projected "buy popcorn" and "drink Coca-Cola" onto selected frames of a screening of the 1955 movie *Picnic*, his purported use of subliminal advertising touched a cultural nerve in Cold War–era America and set off a firestorm of interest in (and fear of) subliminal messaging.[1] Vicary's stunt exacerbated paranoia about the possibility of outsiders, whether corporations or communists, infiltrating the minds and hearts of the American public through subtle subterfuge.[2] Vicary was not alone in exploring how the subconscious can be used to stimulate consumer desire. His experiment was an offshoot of the more mainstream branch of advertising that came to the fore in the mid-1950s called Motivation Research (MR).

MR sought to revolutionize advertising by harnessing techniques from the social sciences and, importantly for our exploration here, from Freudian psychoanalysis. MR deployed popularized theories about "depth psychology" in which the subject is understood to possess latent layers of desire and fear that manifest themselves in intentional and unconscious actions. Ernest Dichter, a student of Freud, applied depth psychology to marketing and, in 1947, founded the Institute for Motivation Research. In 1952, the Advertising Research Foundation (ARF) established the Committee on Motivation Research with the goal to assist advertisers in employing these new psychological methods toward the purpose of increasing consumerism. In the monograph report produced by the ARF, George Horsley Smith explains, "Motivation research is a phase of marketing research which attempts to answer the question, *'Why?'* *Why* do people behave as they do in relation to a particular advertising, marketing, or communication problem?"[3] Motivation Research "seeks to *relate* [consumer] *behavior to underlying processes*, such as people's desires, emotions, and intentions."[4] The connections to Freudian psychology are especially evident when Horsley Smith explains, "If a certain stratum of men do not like to drink milk, we [MR researchers] wonder about their childhood experiences."[5] In addition to adapting versions of psychoanalysis for practical applications, MR also harnessed studies in perception that sought to explain the relation between stimulus and response time. Horsley Smith states, "We might summarize by saying that motivation research *focuses on what happens inside the person between the time a stimulus is applied and a response is made.*"[6] The effort to measure the relation between stimulus and response was part of the initial reason the tachistoscope was invented and employed. This desire to explain perception inspires the early history of psychoanalysis (with its effort to locate the repressed trauma that stimulates later behaviors or responses) and, as we now see, the inception of modern advertising as well.

In 1957, the same year as Vicary's subliminal experiment, Vance Packard published his bestselling and hugely influential book on MR, *The Hidden Persuaders*. The book focused a spotlight on the shadowy world of advertising agencies and introduced the American public to "depth marketing," a type of applied MR. "The symbol manipulators and their research advisers," Packard writes, "have developed depth views of us by sitting at the feet of psychiatrists and social scientists."[7] By blending advertising design and psychoanalysis, these ad men pursued, in Packard's words, "subterranean operations."[8] Packard's book illuminated the machinations of motivation research whereby Madison Avenue advertising firms sought to manipulate consumer desire at the subliminal level. Packard states, "These depth manipulators are, in their operations beneath the surface of American life, starting to acquire a power of persuasion."[9] Packard found the underground and invisible nature of this advertising particularly threatening, and in the midst of the Cold War, so did most Americans.

Although it never gained widespread use (so far as we know), subliminal messaging remained in the American popular consciousness (and subconsciousness). Fifteen years after Vicary's experiment, Wilson Bryan Key stoked the fire of America's concern about subliminal messaging in his book *Subliminal Seduction: Ad Media's Manipulation of a Not So Innocent America* (1973). Key argued that Packard's exposé of advertising was on the right track but did not go far enough. Subliminal messaging, Key claimed, now pervaded American advertising. His book explores the covertly embedded messages (about, he claims, sex and death) in nearly everything we see or touch (advertisements, music, food, and even printed money). Though it has been widely criticized for its paranoid tone and lack of critical grounding, Key's book shared with Packard's the goal of alerting readers to the subliminal operations of advertising in order to inspire awareness as a form of defense. "To penetrate the illusions and trickery," Key writes, "we must take a close-up, almost molecular approach to media content analysis."[10] Key's book performs "close-up" readings of advertisements, and it does so with the conviction that such skills constitute an important cultural literacy. Key was, it should be noted, a student of Marshall McLuhan; indeed, McLuhan wrote the introduction to Key's book. When Key writes, "anyone who cannot read and understand the subliminal languages of symbolic illusion is functionally illiterate,"[11] he is reiterating a point McLuhan made twenty years earlier in *The Mechanical Bride: The Folklore of Industrial Man* (1951).

In McLuhan's first and largely unappreciated book, *The Mechanical Bride*, the pioneer of media studies argued that advertisements deserve to be closely analyzed and, indeed, closely read. McLuhan begins *The Mechanical Bride* by claiming, "Ours is the first age in which many thousands of the best-trained individual minds have made it a full-time business to get inside the collective public mind," so "why not assist the public to observe consciously the drama which is intended to operate upon it unconsciously?"[12] Though he does not use the word "subliminal," McLuhan identifies advertising as operating on the reader's unconscious, and his effort to model ways of analyzing the hidden messages of print advertising paved the way for others after him—including Packard and Key—to approach advertising with attention to its formal practices. It is vital to McLuhan, Packard, and Key that we learn to read and to close-read the layers of multimodal semiotics in everyday advertising and media that work on the mind, or that "work us over completely," as McLuhan argues in *The Medium Is the Massage: An Inventory of Effects* (1967).[13]

Project pursues the slippery slope between McLuhan and Key, between critical interpretation of consumer "texts" and paranoid obsession with finding manipulation everywhere. The work teases and tantalizes the reader with barely noticeable words that flicker throughout the play-through of a story about a bottomless pit, and it prompts questions about how readers are supposed to respond to the presence of this subliminal text. *Project* invites us to consider how we can read and analyze such text even as it intimates other instances of subliminal influence, thereby fostering larger questions about how we know what we know. *Project* inspires these questions through its formal presentation of subliminal text but also through its deliberate framing of this poetic practice of subliminal text: conjoining Vicary's cinematic experiment to concrete poetry.

COINCIDENCE: THE CONCRETE AND THE SUBLIMINAL (JESSICA AND JEREMY)

"The starting point of this piece," Poundstone writes, "is the historical coincidence that 'subliminal advertising' and 'concrete poetry' were introduced as concepts at nearly the same time."[14] He makes this claim about *Project*'s genesis in an author's statement included in *The Electronic Literature Collection*, volume 1. A different version of this text is also included in the work's paratextual entryscreens. There, he writes, "Subliminal advertising is coeval with concrete poetry." This statement is *Project*'s foundational premise, and it is now time for us to explore it.

Project dates the co-origin of subliminal advertising and concrete poetry to the 1950s. This is a decade that saw the establishment of advertising as an art, a science, and an industry. It is also the era of the Cold War and its culture of paranoia. Poundstone is even more specific in identifying a particular year as the origin point for this inspirational "coincidence": 1957, the year of Vicary's stunt in subliminal advertising. Although it remains uncertain whether or not (or in what capacity) Vicary actually produced subliminal messaging, the press conference and news blitz surrounding his subliminal experiment hit a nerve in Cold War America, stunning the American public and stimulating its imagination. As Jessica explained, 1957 was also the year Packard published *The Hidden Persuaders*, making visible and public latent fears about advertising's power. Nineteen fifty-seven is also the year of another important publication: *Plano-Pilôto para Poesía Concreta* (*Pilot-Plan for Concrete Poetry*), a manifesto for a visual poetics by Augusto

FIGURE 4.1: Décio Pignatari's "beba coca cola" as it appears in the Ubu-web version linked by *Project*. The Portuguese original (white-on-red, evoking the Coca-Cola brand) is accompanied by an English transla-tion (red-on-white) by Maria José de Queiroz and Mary Ellen Solt from *Concrete Poetry: A World View* (1968).

de Campos, Haroldo de Campos, and Décio Pignatari.[15] Although authors of the manifesto formed the Noigandres group in 1952, and they had been producing po-etry in a recognizably concrete style for several years, *Project* in-vokes the manifesto in order to mark an occasion—the public an-nouncement of "concrete poetry" as a named concept. *Project* is not directly concerned with *Pilot-Plan*, but it does rely upon a refer-ence to a specific poem published in that same year by one of the manifesto's authors: Pignatari's concrete poem "beba coca cola."[16]

By identifying the coevolution between concrete poetry and sublimi-nal advertising, Poundstone invites consideration of their similarities. In particular, it is worth comparing Pignatari's parody "beba coca cola" in his poem by that title and Vicary's provocation "Drink Coca-Cola" in his subliminal experiment. These are two very different types of language experiments that share certain distinct formal and medial points of intersections. Textually, both begin with a shared phrase. In the entryscreen "Concrete Poetry," *Project* points out that both works "masqueraded as authorized ads for an American soft drink." Yet both differ significantly from an actual advertisement for Coca-Cola, as both decompose the line into word units and thereby turn a slogan into poetry. Pignatari spreads his words in three columns across the page space, while Vicary (purportedly) spreads the same words out across the frames of a celluloid filmstrip. But both of these projects depend upon the specificities of their media format to make their point. Indeed, comparing Pignatari and Vicary's experiments exposes both to be decidedly about media and mediation.

In concrete poetry, the page is an interface that mediates meaning. The unmarked expanse of the page in a concrete poem is a negative space, which acts to define its form and composition. In the case of "beba coca cola," in particular, the poem exploits the interplay of presence-absence in its presentation of foreground-background of the page-space through a three-column arrangement of text. Vicary's purported experiment does something similar in its arrangement of text on celluloid, but it uses speed to create the meaningful interplay of presence and absence. Vicary supposedly added text stimulating thirst and hunger into a film using the speed of the projector to enable the words to appear but resist recognition. Vicary's subliminal stunt inspired MR to test the edges of perception across media formats, and so too were the techniques used in the print poetry of "beba coca cola" also adapted for subliminal advertising. The most famous example is the arrangement of negative space in a photograph's composition to suggest or spell out "sex" (such as in the iconic example of ice cubes in a glass used to sell liquor, which Wilson Bryan Key analyzes in *Subliminal Seduction*).[17] Regardless of the particular technology employed or the content projected in it, subliminal orchestrations are always exactingly dependent upon the specificities of their media formats. Like concrete poetry, subliminal advertising exploits the potential of voids and blank spaces to convey meaning.

Focusing on the textual poetics that conjoin Vicary and Pignatari's experiments obscures the ways in which their projects had distinct rhetorical purposes. *Project*'s conjunction of these two works is all the more striking considering that Pignatari's poem presents a critique of Coca-Cola (and, by extension, of consumer capitalism), while Vicary's operates as a stealth campaign to promote the very same product. Pignatari's poem adopts the famous marketing phrase and red-and-white logo only to twist the power of that brand's immediate recognition, thereby defamiliarizing it. The poem critiques the way that text, color, and image are used to sell—not only beverages—but also desires to the consumer. By contrast, Vicary's purported stunt is a tool to promote consumption, not just of the Coca-Cola product but also of advertising itself. These two experiments are drawn from very different genres, and they have diametrically opposed relationships to consumer capitalism. Yet, *Project* places them in dialogue with one another and, moreover, on equal footing, calling them "pivotal 1957 achievements." In so doing, the work invites interpretations of subliminal advertising as poetry, as well as interpretations of concrete poetry as both subliminal and advertising.

Project pursues this line of exploration by engaging with the poetic possibilities of covert, appropriative, and experimental media practices. *Project* makes apparent that some part of reading operates unconsciously and through our reading machines. Further, by foregrounding the role of the reading machine as a medium and a mediator in literary experience, *Project* suggests that these media techniques and strategies are elements of literature and of literary history more broadly.

READING THE "SPAM" VARIABLE (MARK)

Project tantalizes us with words that flicker at the edge of perception. What are these words, why are they there, and how should we describe them? And are they the subliminal content suggested by the paratextual entryscreens? Like subliminal advertising, these flashing words hint at invisible layers of meaning. They incite awareness and perhaps also anxiety about what we have seen and yet not consciously noticed. They reference a deeper agenda of the piece and of the cultural history it explores: hidden persuasion through technological means. On inspection of the code, it turns out that there is something hidden in *Project*, though not at all what we expected. There, hidden in plain sight in the code, is a powerfully charged conceptual metaphor, one that significantly changed the way we read the words and their relationship to the story. That metaphor: spam.

Thus far we have referred to the rapid-firing words that appear, barely perceptibly, as "subliminal" words. We use this language because we follow the suggestion (or perhaps psychological priming) that Poundstone provides in the paratextual entryscreens. However, another paratext offers a different conceptual framework for reading these fast-flashing words, "semantic primes."[18] The entryscreen labeled "Aporia" explains that *Project* "invokes one of the best established subliminal effects, 'subliminal priming,'" a practice whereby "subliminal words can affect perception of subsequent, conscious stimuli." Semantic priming works by briefly activating (or priming) closely related semantic concepts in the mind each time they are flashed, thereby influencing the direction of the cognitive flow. Within this framework, *Project* operates as a kind of literary experiment on cognition. However, the code reveals yet another paradigm.

When *Project* prepares its list of special words to be displayed using rapid flashes, it does so using a series of source code instructions that manipulate the data referred to not as subliminal or priming but as "spam." This term is invisible in a different way than subliminal words or semantic primes: it is clearly present behind the scenes where the programmer-artist works, while just as clearly absent in the presentation on-screen for the reader. Yet, the code level is important to the on-screen reader because it is here that the programmer-artist encodes his thoughts and reveals how he conceives of this processes. For those not familiar with computer programming, this act of giving a variable a significant name that is not revealed to the on-screen reader is worth unpacking. As noted in chapter 2, analyzing the source code of *Project* reveals that the work acts like a scope for encountering text—a reading machine that loads two long strings of text (story words and rapidly flashing words) from a file (BP.txt) into its Flash framework. In order to recognize, store, and manipulate these text strings, the code imports these contents in two distinct variables.[19] The text of the narrative is loaded into one variable and subsequently displayed on-screen, one word at a time. This variable for the narrative into which the narrative is loaded is named "storyVar". The remaining words, which appear to be the "subliminal words" mentioned by the paratexts, are loaded into another variable named "spamVar".

Calling this variable, and the words it contains, "spam" is completely unexpected and not suggested by anything in the paratexts or story narrative. To underscore its significance, let us clarify that these variables could just as easily have been named "subliminalVar" or "subliminalWords" or almost any string of characters, for that matter. Such a naming would have continued the framing metaphor that the paratexts present in their opening screens, bringing continuity from the screen to the code. Poundstone had the option to name his variables using other conventions. He might have chosen dichotomies such as "signal / noise," "treasure / trash," "text / subtext," and so on. Alternately, he might have used completely indifferent labels, such as "text1 / text2."

Instead, he introduces a word not found in the public presentation of the work, one that reconfigures our analysis of the narrative, the Pit, and the overall piece. Spam: that blight on correspondence, that bane of electronic messaging. Spam: the detritus that accumulates in digital public spaces such as message boards and wikis. Furthermore, the form that it takes—spamVar—reflects the system of naming conventions that Poundstone developed for his variables throughout *Project*. In the variable storyVar, for example, the prefix "story" represents the category or genre of the content. The suffix "Var" identifies the way that it is stored in memory as a variable—in this case, a simple string that happens to hold the story text. Elsewhere in the code, Poundstone uses "spamArray" (the content of the spam words, separated out into an array or list of individual words) and "spamLimit" (a counter for the number of words in the spam variable). This pattern of naming confirms that this choice of labeling all content as "spam" was not a momentary whim but a systematically planned nomenclature.

The evocative naming of variables is highly significant and yet deeply arbitrary, since code is read by both humans (the author of the source code) and machines (the software that compiles and runs it) in such decidedly different ways. For the machine, a variable name is arbitrary because it is of no consequence. No matter what name is used, whether spamVar or xyzzy, the resulting software will function in precisely the same way when it is compiled and run. Yet, recognizing the arbitrary nature of a variable name only exposes the textual significance of the name "spamVar." "Arbitrary" is a technical classification referring to how the machine readers process information; it does not refer to the meaning for potential human readers for whom the name "spam" will have poetic significance. Indeed, it is here, in the space of the "arbitrary" nature of the file's naming convention, that the programmer-author can add a layer of meaning into his code for other humans to read. Those humans might be other programmers, code-cracking readers with decompilers, or even the author himself at a later point in time.[20]

Our discovery in the source code of this specific name for what we came to call the "spam words" had a strong impact on the course of our research of *Project* and on our thinking about the work. The rapidly flashing words were no longer just technical instruments of manipulation. They also acquired a sense of poignancy and poetry. This idea exerted a strong gravitational force on our readings. We reconsidered the significance of the layers of discarded objects and cultural detritus that litters *Project*'s Pit, and we started to consider how spam might be a more central concept and appropriate descriptor of *Project*'s poetic than "the subliminal." In order to understand how the idea of spam and spamming constitute poetic acts in *Project*, we needed a conceptual framework for "spam."

SPAM: A SHORT HISTORY (JESSICA)

Spam interrupts. It is unwanted and abject, but it is a central part of digital communication and culture. Spam is unsolicited mass correspondence that, in our contemporary culture, is often automated: it is written, read, and filtered by machines. A recent statistic shows that as much of 40 percent of global e-mail traffic is spam, or unsolicited bulk e-mail; this means that some 12.4 billion spam e-mails are sent (and read, filtered, or parsed) daily.[21] That's a lot of spam. According to Brad Templeton, the term "spam" was applied to unwanted and iterative bulk electronic mail as early as 1990.[22] But "spam" is also the trademarked name of a processed, canned meat product (a portmanteau of "spiced ham") manufactured by Hormel Foods since 1937.[23] The popular appropriation of this name from a processed food product to the description of unwanted e-mail is probably due to a Monty Python comedy sketch (which premiered in 1970). In this skit, a couple sit down in a restaurant filled with Vikings (yes, Vikings) and inquire about the menu. They are told that everything on the menu is served with Spam, and the Vikings then burst into a song composed solely of the word "spam." The skit mocks the ubiquity of Spam and the difficulty of avoiding it. It also works at a semantic level to show how the repetition and proliferation of this mass cultural runoff—the word "spam"—creates a shared cultural experience and expectation. In the skit, the word "spam" sutures and supplements; it is the ingredient added to every item on the menu.[24] Similarly, in digital communication spam is the supplemental, added-on aspect that infiltrates nearly every electronic mailbox and thus requires filtering.

Though spam probably continues to deceive some Internet users into thinking they have won thousands of dollars, lira, or yen, a message is not called "spam" until it is identified as unwelcome and unrequested mail. What is spam for one person may be of value to someone else. Moreover, the "someone" that judges the value or level of interruption of a given piece of electronic mail is not always human. A computer program is usually the first to identify and label the content as undesired. What one does with and to spam (whether that reader is human or machine) is to filter it. Filtering is an interpretative act and part of the reading process, whereby a reader scans or skims to determine what counts as worthwhile reading material and whether or not further reading is necessary. *Project*'s formal flashing aesthetic of informational and sensory overload demands continual filtering on the part of the reader, at both conscious and unconscious levels. The work also promotes awareness to and a focus on these acts of filtering. In so doing, it illuminates the fact that much reading is neither close, deep, nor sustained but instead a kind of filtering or scanning. Thus, while spam may be abject, it has much to tell us about our reading practices and the values we ascribe to them.

Turning critical attention to spam means turning from reading any one message, an e-mail and its characteristics, to examining the wider network through which such correspondence happens. Over a century before the word "spam" brought to mind unwanted e-mails and pop-up windows or even canned lunch meat, unsolicited mass advertisements were a staple of an earlier networked communication system. Historian David Henkin identifies the American antebellum postal system as the first social network, a communications network that paralleled today's Internet (particularly after the postal reform acts of the 1840s). Unsolicited printed postings sent to strangers, known as "circulars," were central to this network, and Henkin describes circulars as "early purveyors of spam" because they were sent to numerous unsuspecting recipients.[25] Circulars advertised diverse content, including commodities, political causes, religious tracts, and social events. They were "cheap and interchangeable pieces of junk mail," Henkin writes, but they served an important function:[26] they helped established the postal network as a space for interpersonal and private communication. It might sound paradoxical, but this early spam provided an opportunity to filter out, identify, and desire intimate correspondence via the postal service. Henkin explains, "Circulars formed a ubiquitous model for impersonal mail against which mode intimate correspondence could be measured."[27] Circulars may have been an undesirable nuisance in nineteenth-century America, but they played an important function in the social development of the postal system and cultural communication around it. Though the communication network and message have become digital, the roll of the circular—or spam—remains the same: spam is unwanted but impactful in shaping social and communicative norms.

In *The Spam Book* (2011), editors Jussi Parikka and Tony D. Sampson approach digital culture by focusing on the supposed anomalies of web content, that which supposedly constitutes the dark underside of the Internet but is also vital to its success and proliferation: spam, pornography, and viruses. The editors explain that distinctions between "normal" and "abnormal" online are always unstable due to the fact that "anomalies are continuously processed and rechanneled back into the everyday of network culture."[28] Alexander Galloway and Eugene Thacker's essay in this volume provides an example of undesirable spam proving generative. They explain that at a certain point in Internet history, spam becomes something more than a nuisance—it becomes a literary genre. Galloway and Thacker argue that "spam" no longer designates just a genre of mail but also now designates a genre of poetic style. "Spam e-mails," they write, "with their generated misspellings and grammatical errors, appropriated key words and names, have actually become generative in their mode of signification."[29] Spam stylistics can intrude and annoy, but may also puzzle, provoke, and inspire. The literary potential of spam certainly inspires Poundstone, not only in *Project*, wherein he explores the recursive relationship between poetry and spam, but also in another digital work that addresses this theme more directly.

Poundstone's "Spam Poem: For Paul Graham" (published the same year as *Project*, in 2005) consists of a single black screen displaying colorful, revolving "found" text, presumably extracted from spam e-mails.[30] The poem appears in a peephole of sorts: the black background upon which its colored text twirls is confined to a circle whose rim merges into a white screen containing paratextual explanation that literally frames the short, combinatorial poem. On this screen, Poundstone explains that his poem is inspired by Paul Graham's online essay "A Plan for Spam" (2002) which proposes applying Bayesian filtering to e-mail in order to improve the detection of spam.[31] Bayes's Rule is used in probability theory to determine the odds of an event occurring, and Graham's essay describes how Bayesian filters could be used to screen the contents of incoming mail. The spam-filtering technique that interests both Graham and Poundstone operates by focusing on the content of spam, applying probability statistics to individual words or "tokens" based on their appearance in legitimate and illegitimate e-mail. This information is then used as a basis of comparison for evaluating new e-mail upon arrival. Poundstone explains, in the text surrounding and framing "Spam Poem," that the spam-filtering strategy is suggestive of a modernist understanding of language in which, as Poundstone writes, the "popular identification of disconnected words and phrases as poetry documents the lingering influence of the Imagist aesthetic in William Carlos Williams's dictum 'No ideas except in things.'"[32] In the case of Poundstone's poem, spam supplies content for an imagistic, or even concrete, poetry. For the spam filter, words are "things," and in the poem "Spam Poem," spam delivers the "things" that produce poetic "ideas." We might think of Poundstone's "Spam Poem" as a sketch for the more substantial *Project*, and considering the two works together prompts us to return to *Project* to carefully explore the intertwined relationships between spam and poetry.

READING THE SPAM (JEREMY)

Not only is the concept of spam text a vital component of *Project*, but the specific form that "spam" takes in the work is quite unusual, whether considered as poetry, as prose, or as spam found in an e-mail inbox. *Project*'s "spam" (the text of spamVar) does not resemble advertising language for cheap prescription drugs, promotions for dating services, promises of money from far-off banks, chain letters, or circulating urban legends.[33] Instead, spamVar presents us with 223 words separated by spaces. The text begins:

> *elongate radon crackpot mausoleum sassafras trend jetliner titular Valois arduous bombast Bellatrix taboo moneymaker offend panjandrum henbane psychotherapist reportorial IEEE judicial endomorphism . . .*

With these words, we confront an interpretive problem: a text sans grammar, syntax, or indeed any apparent order or organization, whether topical, alphabetical, or by part of speech. It is at first tempting to say that these appear to be words "chosen at random," but even if so, by what random process and from what source? The words do not look like the result of a surrealist cut-up process, or of an

Oulipian dictionary-based constraint.[34] Even an encyclopedia is an un-likely source for the acronym "IEEE."[35] Indeed, after reading just a few words, it is difficult to say if one source might have contained them all. In what other texts do radon, sassafras, and Valois all co-exist? Would that source be a library, the Internet, or simply the mind of the poet educing words through a process such as automatic writing? What kind of writing is this? How might we read this jumbled bag of words?

In order to frame our expectation of the spam words, we can re-turn to the paratextual entryscreens of *Project*. The "Requirements" en-tryscreen explains that the "rapidly flashed ('subliminal') words" will "complicate the perception" of this electronic text. As Mark discussed while reading the "spam" variable, the psychological technique of se-mantic priming is normally used to introduce a related word in order to color reader responses to later stimuli in predictable ways. By con-trast, the "Aporia" entryscreen instead describes *Project*'s strategy as us-ing "subliminal content unrelated to the words it precedes," in order to create an effect in which "each word is, at least subliminally, an aporia."

Poundstone invokes an aesthetic of subliminal "aporia," and we may already be familiar with this term from literature (an unresolv-able paradox in meaning) or rhetoric and philosophy (a question with-out answer). However, its meaning for *Project* is best understood in terms of the word's Greek etymology ("without passage") indicating a state of impasse or being at a loss. The cognitive process of semantic priming is normally used to facilitate the passage of a thought from one associated idea to another, as the mind is more likely to leap to a previously "primed" word than to an unprimed one. Rather than using subliminals to guide the mind along a chain of associations, however, Poundstone proposes priming a series of *unrelated* words—a cacoph-ony of pathways that trace through the mind like sheet-lightning, each path directing one's thoughts away from a word's normal neighbors and leading to failed associations. Semantic priming can shape how we complete or predict the next word in a sentence, and a successful prime will make our prediction predictable. By contrast, Poundstone's aporetic priming aspires to make it difficult for a reader to anticipate the next word. We are buffeted by the subliminal noise of neural path-ways that compete to distract us. This overabundance of pathways con-nected to subliminal words causes each story word to become disso-ciated from its normal contexts. Because anticipated associations are disrupted, the question "What story word might come next?" cannot be answered, and in that sense each story word becomes impassible—a subliminal aporia.

The disruptive aesthetic of the subliminal aporia suggests that we might investigate the relationships of story and spam to one another. Do the flickering spam words always disrupt the meanings in the main story text, as the paratexts propose, or do the two text sources ever resonate or reinforce each other, whether covertly or unintentionally? How do these sets of words compare in style, and what is their strategy for maintaining an aporetic difference? By adopting a broadly forensic approach—that is, a method concerned with the accumulation of specific evidence and particularly with what is unique[36]—our investigation seeks out qualities within the spam and story that will answer these questions. While we have previously considered evidence drawn from the particulars of digital source files and source code, here we draw our methods from slightly different intellectual traditions, those of forensic linguistics and specifically of literary stylometry—methods of approaching a text by identifying its patterns (i.e., style). In both literature and law, stylometry has traditionally been employed in order to identify a text's authorship, in the manner of a fingerprint, whether by considering if a contested play has qualities associated with Shakespeare or by considering if a mysterious ransom letter resembles the other writings of a man on trial.[37] Here, by contrast, we will use the methods of stylometry in a comparative fashion, investigating how the story text and the spam text relate to one another. In keeping with a forensic mode, stylometric reading begins in small, careful observations that become the seeds of bigger interpretations. Our method begins with simple questions such as: What unique words are in each text? Which appear most frequently? Which appear in both texts?

In order to count our two word lists, one of the simplest stylometric methods is to characterize two "bags of words" through a word frequency analysis (WFA). As its name suggests, this method counts the frequency of each word within a text and generates lists of literary data, which can then be analyzed.[38] While WFA finds exact repetitions of words, either within texts or between texts, we extend this basic approach by grouping together inexact matches of similar words through the computational linguistic technique of lemmatization. Words are grouped by rewriting each in its simplest base form (or "lemma"). For example, the lemma "go" is the base form that matches "goes," "going," and also "went"; "foot" is grouped with "feet." Finally, we eliminate a

TABLE 4.1: Word frequency analysis results for story words (left), spam words (center), and words shared between both (right). (Table by authors.)

Story words		Spam words		Shared words	
words	2483	words	200 (223)		
unique	1183	unique	199 (222)	unique matches	1 (2)
lemma	850	lemma	199 (222)	lemma matches	3 (4)

Story word duplicates		Spam word duplicates		Shared lemma matches	
Pit	59	ah	2	pressure	1 : 1 (exact)
subsidence	11			propel	1 : 1 (lemma)
area	10			move	1 : 1 (lemma)
foot	10			distant*	1 : 1 (exact)
report	10				
ground	9				
Kellogg	8				
people	7				
resident	7				
dream	6				
. . . and 840 more					

* Spam words past the 200th are never displayed.

list of common English words (e.g., "the," "and"); filtering these "stop words"[39] focuses our attention on what is distinctive about each text. After analyzing each and comparing for matches, the data in the table 4.1 summarizes our results.[40]

Our results are remarkable in a number of ways, beginning with the dramatic presence of repetition in the story and the equally dramatic absence of repetition in the spam words—which are each singular, even in base (lemma) form. This will be our starting point for exploring the work's aporetic strategy, in which repetitive words and singular words act together to create a field of difference in meaning, "priming" the reader's attention in new directions.

The word "Pit" is repeated fifty-nine times in the story text (table 4.1: column 1 "story words"). This prominence is unsurprising given that it is the work's title and topic, but even so, the word stands apart, occurring at least six times as often as any other. In addition, unlike the unstable boundaries of the Pit in the narrative, the word is almost completely unvarying. There are no "pits" or "pitfalls." There is only "the Pit."[41] Comparison with other writing offers a point of reference for understanding the significance of such repetition. Recall, for example, iterative prose poetry that adopts the form of a litany, such as Joe Brainard's *I Remember* (1970) and the many works it inspired[42]—in particular the strategy of constantly reiterating a word or phrase from the title. When considering the degree of repetition in *Project*, an even more relevant comparison is with Allen Ginsberg's "Howl" (1955), a poem famous for its relentless reuse of words and phrases to open each line. Those familiar with "Howl" will be unsurprised to learn that its most frequent word is "who": "who poverty . . . / who bared . . . / who passed . . . / who cowered . . . / who got busted. . . ."[43] While lack of parallel structure in *Project* makes its repetitions more subtle than "Howl," both works are of similar length, and both invoke their top word ("Pit" and "who") a similar number of times. In fact, *Project* is proportionally more repetitive than "Howl."[44]

Why is *Project* so repetitive? If the work is attempting to render each word an aporia, why is it more repetitive than one of the most recognizably repetitious works in American poetry?[45] One part of the answer may be that the Pit recurs because it is not only a word, but also a name, and not merely the name of a place or thing, but of a character—the antagonist (or protagonist) of the story. Reflecting on our previous consideration of advertising, the name "Pit" is further a kind of name brand and operates as such at two levels. First, in the story, the Pit sometimes serves as a product in commodity culture, as when locals promote it to tourists or when developers use it as a site of venture capitalism (as discussed in our last chapter). Second, the word "Pit" circulates in a fashion that is aesthetically similar to the brand promotion of a product. Rather than reinforcing the word subliminally (as Vicary claims to have done in order to sell Coca-Cola), instead the Pit is overtly established using a technique of constant repetition that resembles a public ad campaign. Just as the widely recognized Coca-Cola brand is decomposed through the poetic process of Pignatari's "beba coca cola," the very familiarity of the Pit provides a ground that subliminal spam words work against.

Our analysis of the spam indeed emphasizes its contrast with the story (table 4.1, column 2, "spam words"). The spam text contains 223 words[46] with only a single repetition: the word "ah."[47] We do not see repetition, but instead its absence. Of the 221 words remaining, each is atypical in common English,[48] each is unique among spam, and, further, each has a unique lemma—no word shares a root, stem, or base form with any other word. Many complex words are also unique in every part. For example, "psychotherapist" is the only spam word beginning with "psych-" or "psy-," or containing "thera," or ending in "-ist." The word "endomorphism" likewise does not share "endo-," "morph," or "-ism" with any other spam word. Unlike the surprisingly repetitive key words in the story, spam words are systematically unique. The two sets emphasize the identities of their words through opposite methods. While the word "Pit" becomes recognizable through a branding technique (extreme repetition with little variation), each spam word appears singular (extreme variation with no repetition). Aporia in *Project* arises out of a synthesis of these two approaches to story and spam.

This aporetic strategy complicates our original idea of story word "repetition" in *Project*. Consider how different spam words "prime" the first few recurrences of the word "Pit":

> . . . *ferrous* Pit . . .
> . . . *hepatitis* Pit . . .
> . . . *equivocate* Pit . . .
> . . . *propel* Pit . . .

Like Pignatari's transformation of "coca cola" into a "cloaca," spam transforms the (ferrous) Pit into the (hepatitis) Pit—identical, and yet completely different in subliminal framing. Here, in the interstices between story words, spam words act as radically individual "things" in the sense of the Williams dictum "no ideas but in things." Together, these things generate a field of differences between every idea, "priming" the reader's attention in a new direction at each moment. Through this process, each story word likewise becomes a thing in itself, with spam separating story, word from word, and coloring each story word differently with its own repetitions. The Pit is a different Pit at every moment, and we can never read the same Pit twice. The spam words in *Project* isolate each story word, creating the semiotic equivalent of a field of static or a wall of white noise.

NOISE (MARK AND JESSICA)

We know from communication and information theory that noise is a vital component of communication. Most notably theorized by Claude Shannon and Warren Weaver, noise represents the fact that transmission is never direct and pure; it is always mediated. "The fundamental problem of communication," Shannon writes in his seminal paper "A Mathematical Theory of Communication" (1948), "is that of reproducing at one point either exactly or approximately a message selected at another point."[49] Information theory, a field that grew out of Shannon's work, identifies two elements in any channel for transmitting a message: a signal (the desired information) and noise (the unwanted information). Noise is the part of the message that enters in during transmission and needs to be filtered out, for noise gets in the way of the signal. Think of the aural static in radio communication, the smudged ink that blurs text on a printed page, pixilation in digital video, or the famous image of "white noise" that appeared on the television screen when an analog signal faltered. Noise is a byproduct of transmission, added to the message as it is filtered through a medium in the process of being transferred to the receiver. Shannon's interventions in information theory became guidelines for optimizing electronic communication for machine transmission. They inform, for example, the spam filters designed for e-mail (including the Bayesian filters that inspire Poundstone's "Spam Poem"). In contrast to noise, spam, in today's electronic communications, is created as a message by the sender and then designated as noise by the receiver (the human or computer reader) during the process of reception. The message itself (the signal) is determined to be unwanted and is filtered out in the process of assigning the direction and value of a received message. (If it is worth reading, it is allowed to enter the electronic inbox.) While noise attends every message as a function of the media channel, spam is an intentional signal transmitted with noise of its own (to help it elude detection). Nonetheless, noise and spam are both supplements that attend the digital communication process, and they both play an important poetic role in Poundstone's *Project*.

Project employs noise, distractions, and subliminal spam to trouble the reader's ability to privilege any one subset of information as "the signal" over another deemed "noise." If we identify the narrative story text as *Project*'s message, then the spam words are disruptions and noise. However, since this spam has been intentionally added as content that disrupts the message, spam in *Project* might also be considered a kind of signal. The spam text in *Project* is not a consequence of interference produced by the infidelity of the communication channel. Rather, it is intentionally produced. Its lack of linguistic patterns and connections to the story words is designed intentionally in order to, in Shannon's terms, increase the degree of noise and disruption. This is purposeful and poetic noise. Similar to the seven "distractions" that Mark discusses in chapter 2, spam does and does not function as visual noise, for it serves to distract the reader as an intentional and machine-enabled effort to control attention, all of which serves *Project*'s poetic purpose of illuminating the impact of our reading machines. The presence of these noisy distractions signifies intentional poetic effort, and the effect is to prompt readers to recognize how the multiple elements vying for attention serve to subvert the assumed centrality of the story as *Project*'s main message. In this way, *Project* employs metaphorical noise or, rather, depictions of noise (whether visual, aural, or textual) as a poetic device. To find a disturbance that actually qualifies as noise, therefore, we would have to examine not the carefully curated spam but the presumably unwanted technical glitches Jeremy identified in chapter 2, which appear while *Project* is computing in overdrive. Recognizing this distinction between purposeful and poetic noise and actual technical noise, we can say that where it has been intentionally authored, noise operates like spam in *Project*—as poetic message.

Of course, to talk about noise in a work of literature is to use the concept metaphorically. A certain amount of formal and poetic noise is precisely what turns a communicative utterance into a literary text. As William Paulson points out, there is no way of distinguishing between message and noise in literature because "literature is a noisy transmission channel that assumes its noise so as to become something other than a transmission channel."[50] Literature is never just message or signal; message and medium, content and form, are inseparable in literature in ways that turn noise, medium, and artifice into literary devices. Marjorie Perloff identifies the concept of "radical artifice" (a term she takes from Richard Lanham) as a defining aspect of contemporary poetry, which revels in and is, at heart, *about* its mediation. "The meaning of a given message," Perloff writes, "includes not only information (the message actually sent) but whatever modifies that message, whatever references become relevant, in the course of transmission."[51] *Project* exemplifies and extends Perloff's discussion, providing an example of how noise both inspires digital poetics and also becomes a poetic element in such work.

Recognizing the poetics of noise in *Project*, we are compelled to approach the spam words and distractions not as supplement or noise but as message and, moreover, as messages that deserve interpretation. *Project*'s provocative poetics turn noise into message, spam into subliminal message, and subliminal message into concrete poetry. In this way, *Project* exemplifies how the supplementary noise of technological mediation can actually serve to productively transform, distort, and inspire new ways of perceiving, communicating, and reading.

CONTEXTUALIZING THE SPAM (JEREMY)

Project's subliminal spam acts to disrupt meaning much like a field of static or a wall of white noise, and yet the spam is not an absolute barrier to poetic meaning-making. Although spam words act as boundaries between story words, they may also create continuities. We can complicate our reading of *Project*'s aporetic strategy by exploring how spam also provides a liminal space for meaning. Our discovery of shared words between story and spam first raised the possibility that spam words could act to create connections within the text. However, such possible continuities may also be found in other places, including in similar sounds and visual rhymes between the two types of text, as well as in the surprisingly circular nature of the spam itself, which is highly repetitious in its own fashion. While a spam word may achieve aporia by isolating a story word from its neighbors, through a variety of repetitions that same spam word may simultaneously create connections in the text, drawing disparate words closer together. By allowing the distinctions that spam creates to collapse, we can read spam alongside and indeed as part of the *Project* story.

Revisiting our word frequency table, we *do* find shared words between story and spam (table 4.1, column 3, "shared words"), and these overlaps are a surprising discovery given the rigor with which spam words are separated from one another. The three shared base words in our results are "move," "propel," and "pressure."[52] Whether by happenstance or design, these words share a dynamic theme, in which motion or force results in difference or change. By contrast, top story words focus on two comparatively static themes: places and people: geography ("Pit," "subsidence," "area," "foot," "ground") and community ("Kellogg," "people," "resident"). The static words repeat overtly (within the story), while the dynamic words echo subliminally, bouncing between spam and story.

We can interpret a shared word by tracing the dynamic interplay of its appearances. Consider the word "pressure." At the outset, the story text describes how construction piles are sunk in order to "anchor highway margins." Subliminal spam renders this: "anchor *pressure* highway *formatting* margins." Spam words are typically non sequiturs—for example, the piles are made of "steel-reinforced *rabbi* concrete." Yet using the spam "pressure" to semantically prime the story word "highway" is strangely apropos in two ways. When "pressure" is flashed, it reads as a reinforcement of the current topic, underscoring how the piles were just described as anchored and "supported by native soil friction." Yet shortly thereafter, this topic reads as a form of foreshadowing. Highway construction is exerting pressure on the ground, which will shortly collapse into a great chasm. Attempts to anchor it in place have instead stressed it, increasing its instability. Whether the word placement is planned or accidental, this moment of subliminal "pressure" is notable because it primes the word for when it will recur later in the story text, in the phrase "air pressure creates mirages." That overt repetition of "pressure" recalls its earlier subliminal introduction, collapsing two scenes together and joining the later depths of the Pit with the earlier construction site that vainly sought to maintain a safe distance.

Spam words may color our perception of story words that they precisely match—or our perceptions of story words that they merely resemble in sound or shape. For example, our initial formal analysis of roots, stems, and lemma indicated that the spam text contains no words that are related to the word "Pit" at the level of meaning. Nevertheless, there are two spam words that contain similar sounds or partial eye rhymes: "*pitch*blende" and "*epi*taxial." Etymologically, these fragments are each unrelated. "Pit" descends from the Latin *puteus* (well, shaft); "pitch" descends from the Latin *pix* (resin, tar); "epi-" signifies "upon." In meaning, however, the full words are obscure, but rather more related to pits: "pitchblende" is a term for mined ore that contains uranium,[53] while "epitaxial" describes crystalline formations on a rock face. To what extent are such word flashes experienced in terms of meaning (if a meaning is even known to the reader, and if it can be recalled at speed)? To what extent do they instead impact us like the fragments of a concrete poem, with recognizable particles such as "pit" appearing within a shifting field of reconfigured letterforms? Whatever the case, *any* recognitions or associations hold a potential to suddenly collapse the distances between meanings which are maintained by the aporetic strategy. When echoes arise between what we perceive consciously and subliminally, spam may not only separate neighboring words from each other, but at the same time bring distant words together.

Our reading of repetitions and echoes in spam has so far explored a handful of overlaps. It may appear that these exceptions still prove the rule of spam's singular nature, and that these words largely remain a long series of chaotically unique signs. However, we arrive at a final reversal. There is another sense in which *all* spam words are as repetitious as story words, if not more so. Just as visualizing the montage forced us to deal with the looping, never-ending quality of *Project*, here we must again recall that while our spam source loads a finite two hundred words, these words then proceed in an infinite loop. Given the small number of spam words and the much larger story text, every spam word will reappear at least one dozen times per story cycle—that is, every spam word recurs more often than any word in the story with the exception of "Pit" itself.

Understanding the significance of this spam repetition hinges on examining the precise manner in which it repeats. Some spam words will repeat twelve times during a story cycle, others thirteen. Because the story length is not a precise multiple of the spam, and because the spam does not "start over" each time, each story word is paired with a new spam word on the second story cycle. Each pairing changes again on the third cycle and again on the fourth, following a perfect tour of two hundred new and different combinatorial alignments between story and spam, until at last the 201st playthrough returns us to the initial arrangement.[54] Paradoxically, spam's repetitive cycle is perfectly nonrepetitive. *Every* story word will eventually be primed by *every* spam in an exploration of maximal variation without repetition. Strangely, the reasons for this behavior are nowhere specified in code—although Mark's investigation of the source code reveals facts that are crucial to computing it. This perfect "tour" of spam combinations emerges out of a peculiar numerical detail: the remainder of spam words that have been displayed after each story cycle is eighty-three. Eighty-three is a prime number, and specifically one that shares no factors with two hundred, the total number of loaded spam words.[55] The importance of this awkward spam remainder to producing the work's perfectly combinatorial poetics cannot be overstated.

Had the story text of *Project* been only a single word shorter or longer, the spam would explore only a fraction of these variations. Three story words less would produce only five different spam cycles, while a few words more would produce only two cycles, rather than two hundred. Had the story length been a perfect multiple of two hundred, then spam words would always be canonically aligned with the story, paired in exactly the same way every time. Instead, the result is quite the opposite. While "elongate" will appear over a dozen times in the first story cycle, *Project* will run through exactly two hundred story cycles over about thirty hours before the opening words "*elongate* Sinkholes" are repeated. This thirty-hour period, while inconceivable as a single viewing session, is nevertheless the true full duration of the complete text. Of course, *Project* runs ever onward—as with our discovery of the eight-second beat or the nine-minute story cycle. Marking this true full duration is an act of imagination. We are metaphorically marking the moment when the last page of an enormous, nearly one million word typescript ends, and we then return from the 4,000th page to the first—and keep reading.[56]

Having unpacked spam's short cycle of repetition and its longer cycle of shifting nonrepetitions, what are the implications for interpreting specific spam conjunctions as poetic language? On the one hand, every first viewing of *Project* will begin with the same spam words occurring in the same place.[57] This stable initial form should describe the experience of most viewers. It is difficult to imagine a viewer sitting with *Project* through three full story cycles, let alone two hundred, and focusing solely on the progression of words. Given this, we might say that the first story cycle presents a canonical form of our shared experience of the work. On the other hand, due to repetition, the spam words will not only shift across story cycles but also repeat many times within any one cycle. These repetitions raise serious questions about the possibility of meaningful alignments between spam and story. If the spam words will not keep still, is it possible that they were never carefully arranged by the author in the first place? Might the spam story alignments be arbitrary—either in their alignments after the story cycle repeats, or in their pairings after the spam words repeat (beyond the first two hundred story words), or perhaps even altogether arbitrary? If they were arbitrary, then interpreting the specifics of spam and story together could be a kind of Dada or Surrealist game, like a cut-up:[58] a poetically productive exploration of a shared experience, but divorced from any authorship or intentional word craft beyond the initial selection of sources. However, this is not the case—spam and story may be meaningfully aligned even in their repetitions, and these alignments are worth interpreting because they reflect thoughtful poetic craft.

In order to illustrate how alignments between spam and story can emerge in a rich and deep way, we will explore the multiple appearances of one spam word. That spam word is the eighty-third in the spam list, "commodious"—and as the eighty-third word, it marks the last word before the "remainder" spam words that will overlap after the first story cycle and set the spam and story texts spinning into different alignments in each cycle thereafter. "Commodious" appears thirteen times in the first story cycle, priming each of the following evenly spaced story words in order: "holes," "who," "disappearance," "after," "spirits," "in," "and," "down," "confusing," "isolated," "denial," "had," "deeper." Some of these conjunctions appear poetically productive ("*commodious* spirits"), while others are less noteworthy ("*commodious* and"). However, before inspecting each pair for poetic potential, we should first examine the spam word itself. "Commodious" means both spacious and convenient, and this sense of convenience descends from the Latin *commodus*. That word also gave rise to its closely related euphemism, the "commode," or the convenience of a chair containing a chamber pot (later a toilet).[59] "Commodious" denotes a pleasant space, while the related word "commode" indicates a hole for human waste. In this context the most striking and poetically productive pairing of "commodious" with a story word is its very first appearance, when it primes the "holes" on the Beale Pike in a way that colors them as accommodating and perhaps wasteful: "test commodious holes designed to detect unstable areas." If our reading ended here, then the fact that "commodious" is most obviously matched with its very first pairing would at first seem to be evidence for spam alignments only being poetically intentional (that is, specifically authored) during the first two hundred words of the work.

Yet the first appearance of "commodious" is not where our reading ends. Because it is the eighty-third word, the thirteen appearances of commodious (as the 2,483rd spam word) is thus the last spam word in the cycle, appearing just before the final story word, "deeper." What is most striking when we consider this late repetition is not the thematic resonance of the word pairing but its positional significance. As discussed earlier, "deeper / Sinkholes" is the moment when *Project* returns to its beginning, and this eternal return recalls the structure of experimental circular texts, in particular *Finnegans Wake* (1939) by James Joyce. In *Finnegans Wake,* the last line and first line of that work connect as follows: "A way a lone a last a loved a long the / riverrun, past Eve and Adam's, from swerve of shore to bend of bay, brings us by a commodius vicus of recirculation back to Howth Castle and Environs." Joyce opens his circular experiment by describing a "commodius vicus," and this phrase finds an intertextual echo in the *"commodious* deeper Sinkholes" which end and renew the circular *Project.* In Joyce, the etymological jesting and scatological humor that permeates *Finnegans Wake* is on display in its spelling of "commodious," which underscores the presence of "commode" in the word. In *Project,* we find a similar conjunction of spacious and scatological ideas at the ending and beginning of the text. Here, the end of the story cycle acts as an anatomical "bottom" to the text—although it does not reveal a geological bottom to the Bottomless Pit.

Instead of terminating our reading, the final words at the bottom of the text act as a terminal opening—a cloaca, in the sense of that word as found in Pignatari's poem "beba coca cola" (which *Project* references). Recall that "cloaca" is not only a word meaning "sewer, cesspool, or place of waste." "Cloaca" also denotes an avian orifice with a dual nature—a passage that is a place of both excretion *and* reproduction, of endings and beginnings. When it appears as the final spam word of the story cycle, "commodious" is not only wasteful but also welcoming. It signifies a nidificatory moment when waste is used to build a makeshift nest, within which is nestled an egg: the imminent renewal of the work.

GARDEN PATH SENTENCES (ALL)

Project's narrative begins with the sentence: "Sinkholes and unstable soil characteristic of the karstland around Bluefields long plagued construction of the Beale Pike between Breezewood and Roanoke Park."

This sentence is challenging to parse, particularly when one reads it one word at a time, as *Project*'s formal presentation demands. We want to consider the reason for and the significance of this difficulty.

Reading *Project* is an act of parsing. One must constantly filter out content in the process of attempting to retain a meaningful focal point in the midst of an onslaught of multimodal content, and all of this must be done on the fly in the speed of the tachistoscopic flash. But the work's first sentence does not unfold in a simple and immediate subject-verb order; it instead contains a series of phrases. The reader searches for the sentence's subject but encounters instead "Sinkholes and unstable soil characteristic." The last word appears to be the start of an adjectival phrase, so one might hold the first four words as the subject while pursuing or, in computational terms, caching what follows in the adjectival phrase: "characteristic of the karstland around Bluefields long plagued construction of the Beale Pike between Breezewood and Roanoke Park." It in turn contains its own prepositional phrase, beginning "around." If we miss the lack of an apostrophe (Bluefields, not Bluefield's) then the karstland apparently surrounds a construction site owned by a company or person named Bluefield. In that parsing, the sentence appears to end without a predicate. We know where the soil is, but what has the soil done? If it has a predicate, it must be that the soil has "long plagued" the construction. The adjectival phrase that begins with "characteristic" should have ended at "Bluefields." The sentence takes a strange turn, and leads us down a garden path.

A "garden path sentence" is a grammatically correct sentence whose syntax defies the ability to parse it, particularly to understand its meaning by reading one word at a time. Famous examples include, "The old man the boat," and, "The horse raced past the barn fell." Such sentences often appear to end too soon or too late, although the fact that they are already grammatically correct is apparent with a small change ("The old people man the boat," and, "The horse that was raced past the barn fell"). Such sentences start out in one direction and imply a logical progression, but they mislead the reader and take her down an unexpected path toward an unintelligible conclusion. Steven Pinker explains that garden path sentences are not only grammatical situations but are also linguistic opportunities to see how human brains function. In particular, he uses the garden path sentence as an opportunity to contrast the functioning of the human brain with that of the computer. "Most people process contentedly through the sentence up to a certain point," Pinker writes, "then hit a wall and frantically look back to earlier words and try to figure out where they went wrong."[60] He concludes, "people, unlike computers, do not build all possible trees as they go along" in their cognitive reading process but, instead, read by "picking an analysis that seems to be working and pursuing it as long as possible. If they come across words that cannot be fitted into the tree, they backtrack and start over with a different tree."[61] Humans read by building a mental model of a sentence's structure through a linear, word-by-word composition. When that linearity fails to produce meaning, they rewind and rebuild. "[T]he human parser," Pinker writes, "gambles at each step about the alternative most likely to be true and then plows ahead with the single interpretation as far as possible."[62] Garden path sentences challenge this cognitive strategy by tempting the reader to derail the linear progression of meaning-making. The beginning of *Project* presents a parallel challenge: a series of words that lead us down the garden path.

Project's flashing aesthetic supports the confusion, forcing the reader to constantly "gamble" (Pinker's term) in order to produce meaning. Because the work's formal poetic presents flashing single words in a rapid succession, it refuses its reader the ability to look back at what preceded, let alone to pause to consider the context for the content. As a result, the reader must determine whether or not to stop and dissect the sentence. Choosing to stop means running the risk of missing what comes next in the flashing animation; neglecting to stop means that the work will proceed without the reader being able to identify a clear subject for the action. There is no way to go back in *Project*, no way to return to the beginning of the sentence and begin climbing a new cognitive tree. This experience poetically illuminates how reading is always an act of parsing and filtering information with and through machines.

To begin a work of digital literature with a garden path sentence is to introduce the intention of challenging and even misleading its reader. Such stress on the reader's parsing is, of course, further exacerbated by a poetic that intersperses seemingly irrelevant spam words into syntactically complex sentences alongside various other distractions at a fast-flashing pace. In fact, we can now claim that this garden path sentence reads much like the hidden subliminal spamVar list. Just as those words seem to disrupt by their lack of coherence and continuity, word choice and sentence construction in the storyVar also serve to complicate the prose. As a result, the story text itself seems to read like spam. Spam is thus, in a way, formalized into the narrative and made poetic on-screen through a formal strategy of intentional obfuscation. This strategy turns reading into parsing and draws attention to this fact.

Our detour into garden path sentences via *Project*'s first sentence allows us to weave together a few threads of our interpretation in this book so far. When Pinker identifies the use of garden path sentences in psycholinguistic laboratory studies, he describes how research subjects bite on a bar to keep their heads still, and they are then presented sentences to read on a computer screen. While sitting completely still, reading the on-screen text, their eye movements are recorded.[63] The situation echoes traditional laboratory uses of the tachistoscope wherein a seated, staring viewer is subjected to a slew of visual images in an effort to track and study human vision, cognition, and memory. *Project* adopts the performance of the tachistoscope, encouraging its reader to sit still and stare straight ahead, but it opens with a garden path sentence that makes the reader want to move her eyes back and forth across the sentence to identify its subject and verb. The fast-flashing, one-word-at-a-time presentation of the garden path sentence produces dissonance, and this complex relationship between form (tachistoscopic) and content (garden path) registers how reading situations, techniques, and technologies shape (and complicate) a reader's perception and comprehension.

In his analysis of Milton's *Paradise Lost*, Stanley Fish explores how Milton uses garden path sentences to lead his reader down winding poetic paths. The effect, Fish writes, is that "by encouraging and then blocking the construction of sequential relationships [Milton] can lead the reader to accept the necessity of, and perhaps even apprehend, negatively, a time that is ultimately unavailable to him because of his limitations."[64] Garden path sentences thus serve a poetic and pedagogical purpose in the poem by formally describing and mirroring the loss described therein. Fish's point can help explain how garden path sentences work in *Project*: they turn the reader's awareness to the way literature operates in a kind of diegetic doubling. *Project*'s garden path sentence— along with it Bottomless Pit of attention, distractions, and spam—create challenges for the reader, who learns to recognizes that all of this content is only accessible due to mediating techniques and technologies.

CODE ANALYSIS (MARK)

Although *Project* seems to begin with a garden path sentence, this sentence is preceded by the very first word, which is actually a spam word. We can see as much from a transcript of the story's output with the spam words included (see Appendix C). As this transcript shows, the very first word of the piece is not "Sinkholes" but the spam word "elongate." On the one hand, it is tempting, in light of Jeremy's analysis of the lack of similarities between the spam and story words, to situate the spam words as something outside the piece, as something secondary, since they are literally stored in a variable separate from the storyVar. Furthermore, loading those values into a variable named "spam" suggests that the content is ancillary, delivered without being desired, interference in a communication circuit. Jeremy's reading of the spam words also demonstrates the lack of internal similarity in the spam words: a quick perusal of them suggests that no one rule accounts for the relationship between the spam words and the story text. However, on the code side, the words are inextricably linked to the story, or to put it another way, the display of the spam words is inextricably intertwined with the display of the story words. In fact, the spam is not something secondary that the code will add on to the primary text of the story. Instead, we find in the code that the spam function is primary. By "primary," here, I mean both that it is called *before* the call to the story function and that the story words would not be called without this first call to the spam function. In the course of updating the spam array and bringing forth the next spam word, it also calls a function that displays the next story word. This procedure, which we can describe as displaying a list of spam words with regular interruption by story words, structurally inverts our assumed hierarchy of the two texts.

To illustrate the interconnections between the function that calls the story and the function that calls the spam words, allow me to step through the code. The first portion of the code on the main file (Appendix D) defines functions and assigns variables, notably establishing the process for displaying the seven distractions. The actual instructions for the ActionScript code, as a result, are relatively few, and they come near the end of the list of instructions. In that section, we find a function called "mainInterval."

```
mainInterval = setInterval(updateWords, textMilliseconds);
```

In ActionScript 2, "setInterval" is a timed function, essentially a loop. In this declaration, mainInterval begins a loop of the function "updateWords" that takes place every "textMilliseconds," which has already been assigned to 0.2. So this first call in the code that displays words begins a loop at a regular interval. "updateWords" is another function call that performs two operations: to advance the spam array[65] and to call another loop: killInterval. Note that updateWords does not update the story words but instead the spam words, which is why the first word of the story is a spam word.

```
killInterval = setInterval(killSubliminal, subliminalMilliseconds);
```

Like mainInterval, killInterval begins a loop that calls the function killSubliminal at an interval of subliminalMilliseconds, which is 0.017 seconds. At one point "kill" was a term that, in Unix and other languages, indicated the termination of a process. In this case, rather than ending a process, it begins another process that will kill the subliminal (or spam) word by replacing it with the next word in the story. So that first call to mainInterval has essentially started two subroutines—one updating the spam words, and the other updating the story words. But the spam words are updated first. Meanwhile, the call to update the story, which kills the subliminal words by erasing them from the display, is subordinated, technically speaking. Since the call to update the story words happens on a shorter interval, the erasure of the spam word it replaces happens much faster. This is what accounts for the flickering of the spam words.

The calls to update spam and text words are thus imbricated in a way that does not easily sustain the distinction of main and subordinate. Progress through the spam words and story words occurs as two interlocking processes, given equal value in terms of the structural hierarchies of the program. More importantly, there cannot be story text without spam text. The story would not move on to the next word if the spam had not been first called forth. The history of spam, as Jessica summarized it, seems to indicate that "legitimate" communication calls forth the parasite of opportunistic, unwanted messaging (spam). However, this piece, through its encoding, situates the spam as primary, as calling forth the story and being no less significant for the speed of its flickering. The fact that the spam call precedes and leads to the story call does not mean that the spam is more important; rather, the two are inseparable, and in effect, their relationship is the *conditio sine qua non* of the story. Interestingly, Jessica and I have reached this same conclusion on the spam though she entered through the history of spam, and I through the code.

At this point, it is easy to argue that the chain of function calls makes no difference to the computer that implements them. What is key to this reading of *Project* through its code is that the programmer designed these calls not in a hierarchy or as separate calls but as intertwined and, indeed, inseparable. Thus, though the content of the spam and story variables are separable and easily changed, the spam is not so easily separated from the story text—it is an equal and indeed causal part of the "mainInterval."

When viewed with an emphasis on the narrative text, *Project* appears to be a story that gets interrupted by rapidly flashing words. When viewed from the perspective of the code, *Project* is a machine that calls forth and then braids words from two sequences: a narrative sequence and a nonnarrative sequence. However, rather than the system presenting a story and then interrupting that story, the code reveals that the software presents an array of spam and then interrupts that array with story. Put another way, the calling forth of spam words gives rise to the calling forth of subsequent narrated words. Also, as noted in chapter 2, even though the spam words appear to be displaying a random set of interruptions that arrive in bursts, the code reveals (and the output file confirms) that spam words and story words regularly alternate throughout the run of the Flash file. Additionally, the placement of the spam words is not accidental or random.

The main reason they cannot be perceived is that in one of the distractions they appear as white and, as we explained in chapter 2, the priming of the fixation crosses helps readers to perceive their presence. What this means for our reading is that the placement of the spam words has been authored. Poundstone determined when and in what order the spam words would appear in relation to the text. This unordered list, therefore, has been assembled with just as much ordering as the story and so warrants being closely read, not as interruptions but as fundamental contributors to the poetic system. Just as we have read the story in sequence, we can revisit the spam word list, reading and interpreting it in sequence:

elongate radon crackpot mausoleum sassafras trend jetliner titular Valois arduous bombast Bellatrix taboo moneymaker offend panjandrum henbane psychotherapist reportorial IEEE judicial endomorphism Nicholas punch wiry

Some of these words are strange and add an element of estrangement to the narrative (arduous, elongate, endomorphism). Other words seem to mock the content presented on-screen (crackpot and sassafras). Most of these spam words are multisyllabic, a fact further at odds with *Project's* fast-flashing aesthetic. These longer words slow down and even throw a wrench in our reading practice. Still other spam words (like the acronym "IEEE") are not really words at all. No doubt this presents another bottomless pit, enticing us into schematic analysis while defying any attempt at taxonomy.

Having turned the flashing, nearly illegible spam words into visible text, we can now compare them to the story text and put them into dialogue with that narrative content. If we insert the spam words where they are displayed in sequence with the story text (but italicize them to mark their identities), we encounter passages such as the following rendering of the opening sentence:

elongate Sinkholes *radon* and *crackpot* unstable *mausoleum* soil *sassafras* characteristic *trend* of *jetliner* the *titular* karstland *Valois* around *arduous* Bluefields *bombast* long *Bellatrix* plagued *taboo* construction *moneymaker* of *offend* the *panjandrum* Beale *henbane* Pike *psychotherapist* between *reportorial* Breezewood *IEEE* and *judicial* Roanoke *endomorphism* Park.

In his section on reading the spam, Jeremy considered the way individual spam and story word pairs act to prime the reader. Here we take that process further by interpreting long series of priming words as they shape the poetic line. Even before sinkholes appear, "elongate" casts a shadow of lengthening and widening. "Radon" adds another potential hazard to home life. "Unstable" is shaded with the slang term of mental instability, "crackpot," a word which may refer to readers of the Pit to be introduced later, while "mausoleum" introduces the pall of death. "Sassafras" lightens up the list, while later on "bombast" will complete an alliterative chain of "Bluefields" and "Bellatrix," as the spam envelops the story in sound poetry. "Plague taboo construction moneymaker offend" evokes a string critical of boondoggles, perhaps implicating the disrupted road project, and this sensible string both culminates in and is disrupted by "panjandrum." This nonsense term for a pompous official was first popularized by Samuel Foote when he extemporized a passage of non sequiturs as a challenge to any orator claiming to be capable of memorizing a speech upon hearing it once.[66] It signifies both foolish authority and meaningless language itself. Having passed into English usage, the term took on a third meaning as the name of an experimental explosive siege-cart for barrier-busting, developed by the British during World War II.[67] This sense invokes the military-industrial complex and its legacy of Cold War paranoia that gives context to Vicary's subliminal hoax. Continuing on, "psychotherapist" stirs up the realm of the subliminal, while "reportorial" and "judicial" bring the fourth estate and third branch of government into the mix. It is perhaps too limiting to assign any one meaning to these words, as it detracts from their power as primers. Nonetheless, our study of the code has established that this list of words, appearing in the same order each time *Project* begins, has been hand curated and ordered. Thus, it can be read with an eye toward human intentionality, as Jeremy has done, rather than the randomness, or pseudo-randomness, of the machine.

These two bodies of text—the spam words and the story text—share a similar aesthetic of semantic obfuscation, discontinuity, and disorientation. Trochaic and dactylic rhythms combined with the lack of a clear pattern conspire to discourage reading these words as part of a sentence. Content complicates form, not just the other way around. As a result, from the very beginning of the story, Poundstone's parade of words challenge and complicate our desire to establish order in the flow of information. But opening and reading the spam words enables us to see how the subliminal words contained and projected in *Project* promote a critical paradigm that challenges the hierarchical order of meaning in the text registers. In *Project*, spam is not the unwanted or unimportant; instead, the hidden and incomprehensible serve to destabilize the legible. Focusing on the spam in *Project* challenges the system of signifieds usually associated with the signifiers "spam" and "story" or "message." In this case, "spam" is essential to *Project*'s story; the two "Vars" are inseparable. Like the trash that flows into the Pit, the spam in this work provides the elementary building blocks that construct the flashing vortex and the effect it produces. In the logic of *Project*, sinkholes of spam precede and bring forth the roadways of communication.

APORIA AS CRITICAL ANALYSIS (JESSICA)

In this chapter we showed that the subliminal spam is a literal, figurative, and programmatic text that rewards reading. *Project*'s spam is not just a distraction from the main narrative, not just a formal enactment of the disposable detritus in and around the Pit. This subliminal text, the text named "spam," is a rich and relevant part of *Project*. But our focus on the subliminal spam also leads us to larger questions about *Project* and digital literature more generally: namely, what content constitutes its narrative? What noise and detritus is actually meaningful message? These questions prompt us to return to the prefatory entryscreens—to move full-circle—as a way of concluding our examination of Poundstone's digital work.

On the entryscreen titled "Aporia," Poundstone describes his ambition for *Project* and his use of subliminal words to achieve it. "The intent," he writes, "is to create a text in which each word is, at least subliminally, an aporia." Whether Poundstone is describing as aporetic "text" the subliminal text file or the entire narrative in *Project* remains unclear, but the concept of his "intent" deserves analysis. How is *Project* an aporia? Why, at this stage in our examination of the work, should this question matter? We can address these questions formally by recognizing how Poundstone creates a poetic effect of aporia by using Flash to present the subliminal spam words interspersed as interruptions in the main story text. He defines the effect as "semantic priming," which he explains by way of example on the "Aporia" entryscreen: "When the word ANGRY is flashed subliminally, subjects asked to read a passage and describe a person in it are more likely to do so in hostile terms than those receiving no subliminal cue." In contrast with this example, however, *Project*'s Flash-based techno-poetics don't use subliminal words to intentionally color the subsequent content. Instead, *Project*'s "Aporia" entryscreen states that its "subliminal content is unrelated to the word it precedes." Poundstone uses Flash to splice the narrative and insert discrete, autonomous words into it. Flash is employed not to create a seamless stream, as one would expect from a program based on the tween, but instead to create cognitive discon-nection. The result is a conceptual and concrete poem created from subliminal spam.

Project's subliminal concrete poetry is visible but not necessarily leg-ible. It can be seen but not fully perceived; it is in some sense sub-liminal. Whereas subliminal advertising seeks to be received but not perceived, Poundstone's text seeks to create a poetic dissonance that demands observation. Moreover, the digital subliminal concrete poetry elicits hybrid reading practices that creatively involve human and ma-chine readers. *Project* makes apparent that part of reading always op-erates unconsciously, mediated through machines: and, in so doing, *Project* promotes exploration of the ways technologies assist in sutur-ing conscious and unconscious attention toward that action that we call "reading."

Aporias are contradictions, blockages, or gaps that challenge logic and call out for analysis. In other words, aporias demand to be read. Most famously, Jacques Derrida employed the term "aporia" to indicate a place in a text or in logic (particularly as made manifest in ethics and law) that reflexively calls attention to its own incongruities in ways that invite interpretation. The aporia is "the nonpassage, or rather from the experience of the nonpassage," Derrida writes, and it has the effect of "paralyzing us in this separation in a way that is not necessarily nega-tive: before a door, a threshold, a border, a line."[68] The aporia, in other words (and in the language we have been employing throughout this book), is positioned at the liminal (think "subliminal"), the in-between (think Flash's tween), or the rim (of the Pit or Flash layer). For Derrida, the aporia marks the space where the seemingly impossible situation becomes an opportunity and opening; "far from paralyzing," Derrida writes, the aporia "sets in motion a new thinking of the possible."[69] *Project*'s poetic onslaught could certainly induce paralysis. The reader is induced into physical immobility before the tachistoscopic remedia-tion and the work's fast-flashing stream of words, garden path sen-tences, and visual distractions—all of which are interrupted by ordered and meaningful subliminal spam—could bring any critical ambition to a halt. Yet, as we argued, the combination also produces an invita-tion to new kinds of analysis, to "new thinking of the possible." In liter-ary criticism, the aporia maps onto the trope of the paradox (a central term in New Criticism) or the symptom (in Fredric Jameson's terms), concepts that signify and promote deep, careful, close, and excavatory reading.[70] If *Project* is an aporetic text, and the aporia promotes "new thinking" (as Derrida suggests), then our efforts to read and interpret *Project* and its subliminal text bring us full circle—back to the beginning of our book and to our stated intention therein to explore and model new ways of critically analyzing digital literature.

Pursuing our analysis of the poetic aporia that is *Project*, we forged a collaboration between scholarly partners, critical reading practices, and digital technologies. In the process of reading this text together, we revamped close reading practices to consider code, visualizations, data-mapping, and more. In this final chapter, we showed how reading the subliminal spam text—the hidden and seemingly secondary or sup-plementary text—served to transform our assumptions about *Project*'s main narrative. Focusing on the subliminal spam illuminated how the work deliberately and reflexively challenges attention and draws atten-tion to this challenge. Because the spam text possesses an intentional order and arrangement, and because it produces specific poetic effects, this text can (and should) be interpreted. But because it appears in-between the main story text and flashes too fast to be read, it requires a reading practice that uses the computer as collaborator . . . and other human collaborators as well.

The terrain of digital poetics is emergent and unstable, and it cer-tainly abounds with great opportunities to experiment in adapting and reforming traditional reading practices. But grand, sweeping gestures might stimulate a sinkhole, so we must take small steps and proceed with continual reflection. We move now toward this kind of reflection in our conclusion.

CONCLUSION

OUR READING PROJECT used Poundstone's work as an opportunity to experiment with a method of collective criticism. Reading the work as we did—collaboratively, recursively, and through a hybrid of digitally informed reading methods—taught us how born-digital literature rewards combining creative and critical approaches. Rather than merely implementing a variety of readings and then compiling them into a single book, we pursued a different strategy. Our mutual and interdependent inquiry pushed us to develop as readers and expand our critical practices. Specifically, we worked toward a media archaeology that is as attentive to content and poetics as to the media it studies, toward a Critical Code Studies that interprets the divergence and intersections of the code and the poetics the code produces, and toward a cultural analytics whose large data sets and "distant" visualizations lead to nuanced interpretation in close readings. Our most significant intervention might not be any specific argument about *Project* or digital poetics, but our documentation of and reflection on our interpretative collaborative process as scholarly labor.

As its title implies, and as we have shown, *Project* is a "project"—not just a final product but also an experiment in remediating technopoetics from tachistoscopes into Flash. We remix the work's title in our own to suggest that our reading of *Project* is also an experiment in the critical process. If the story of the Bottomless Pit is an allegory, showing the foundations of reading shifting beneath our feet in this digital age, and if its performance is a poetic experiment in programmed distractions and subliminal words that render each moment an aporia, then reading *Project* is an occasion to meditate on the methods and machines we use to read. *Project* makes apparent that some part of reading always operates unconsciously and through machines and, thus, promotes exploration of the ways technologies assist in suturing conscious and unconscious attention toward that action that we call "reading." Defining what reading is, in other words, is a continual project. The work teaches us that we need to read our reading machines in order to understand how they inform our perception, comprehension, and resulting interpretations. As we learned, such efforts require coordination with other readers. Consequently, we offer *Reading* Project as a demonstration of the potential for collaborative scholarship.

AN INTERVENTION

To read *Project* is to confront the changing terrain of digital textuality. Digital texts are not fixed or stable. They perform through a complex interplay of codes and operations, some of which are hidden and even remotely distributed. Born-digital literature like *Project* exploits this technical fact of digital textuality and makes it poetic. As readers, we are challenged in our ability to even locate "the text," let alone plumb its depths. For these reasons, the specific question, "How do we read born-digital poetics?" has broad significance for our digital culture, for it metonymically represents the challenges of approaching and understanding digital textuality.

Such challenges can prove significant to readers trained in traditional literary criticism. Readers may be skilled at performing close readings of text, sound, or images, but dynamically generated content, interactivity, or animation present new possibilities and poetics. Critics in new media and digital literature have proposed many approaches to this situation and have formed scholarly communities around specific methods (including Critical Code Studies, software studies, platform studies, digital forensics, media archaeology, and cultural analytics, among others). These reading methods can provide access to a unique glimpse of the digital work (the transcript, the screenshot, the montage, the source file, etc.), but if used in isolation they may also be limiting. Debates about critical methodology have often hinged on a reader's primary approach to the born-digital artwork: should one closely engage the screenic content, the source code, the operating processes of a work, the platform upon which the work appears, the material history of its medium, or the software culture within which it circulates? Most readers cannot assume the skill sets necessary to perform critical interpretation of a multimodal digital work from all of these angles—indeed, the inner workings of software and hardware are foreign worlds to many of us. Thus, for an individual reader, engagement with any one aspect of digital hermeneutics must come at the expense of others. Confronted with zero-sum choices and finite limits of attention and personal expertise, what's a reader to do? Our answer: collaborate.

Born-digital literary objects require not only new critical approaches but also new understandings of how criticism happens: a focus on how we read, interpret, and communicate. Engaging in collaboration can shift not only the practices but also the emphases of scholarly work. A collaborative model enables us to imagine the complexities of digital works not as barriers but as expansive horizons that beckon us. Entering collaboration requires an acknowledgement that a solitary reader can only do so much. There are limits to expertise, and engaging in collaboration can actually support specialization by supplementing it. Collaboration can produce understandings that are greater than the sum of their parts. Conversely, collaboration can foster new ways of understanding what we do as critics, scholars, and readers. Such reflection and innovation is vital not only to literary criticism but also to the future of the humanities more generally.

Currently, much discussion about the future of the humanities occurs under the heading of "Digital Humanities," a term that describes a multitude of practices and ambitions—scholarly, pedagogical, and institutional. Some digital humanities projects apply new digital methods to traditional humanities subjects. Examples include developing or making use of digital tools such as online archives, text-encoding, database-driven research, or computational visualizations, and then applying those tools to the understanding of collections of sonnets, ballads, letters, or novels. A different type of digital humanities project applies traditional humanities methods to new digital objects, for example, analyzing a digital corpus of social media poetry or cell-phone novels while using humanities interpretive methods such as formalism, historicism, or cultural criticism. Collaboration is central to both types of projects and to the networked nature of digital humanities. Our reading project is a digital humanities effort in that it is a collaboration that employs digital computing practices in order to analyze a text from the perspective of humanistic hermeneutics. At the same time, we realize that "digital humanities" is a placeholder term that may someday melt away, leaving a renewed "humanities" whose practices are broadly inflected by digital media and culture. Our intervention in this book is to show how digital-based practices can enable literary interpretation while also providing new models of how interpersonal collaboration works. Toward that point, let us now reflect on our personal collaborative process.

Our reading project had two goals: (1) to produce a multi-perspective, critical interpretation of a complex literary work, and (2) to model collaborative, digital-based literary criticism. As our chapter openings recount, our writing process was one of surprise and discovery, assertion and correction, progress and retreat. During this process we learned a lot about each other and about ourselves. Writing together proved to be more challenging—and more work!—than writing alone. Rewriting involved not just rewording sentences but true re-vision—viewing *Project* anew, informed by each other's insights and propelled by our intersecting investigations.

Discoveries rerouted our individual interpretative efforts and led to group epiphanies. Here are some of the epiphanies that determined the course of our interpretations, examples of a few of our favorite intellectual exchanges—from Mark to Jeremy, Jeremy to Jessica, and Jessica to Mark. Without question, the signal finding in "Chapter 4: Subliminal Spam" was the presence and centrality of spam in *Project*. Although we knew from the outset that the work contained hidden, subliminal words, it was not until Mark looked into *Project's* files (and more specifically the ActionScript code and the BP.txt file) that we could read all those words, categorized as "spam," in their entirety—and even in more than their entirety, for the files included words that are never displayed on-screen. Their availability inspired Jeremy to study the makeup of these spam words using word frequency analysis, and from there to argue that the systematically unique spam words such as "commodius" make meaning through their poetic interplay with repetitious story words such as "Pit."

Or recall the diagram of the depths of the Pit that appears in "Chapter 3: Bottomless Pit." To create that visualization, Jeremy compiled a list of information about the Pit's depth from the narrative and then mapped the depth of the Pit according to markers from both the diegetic world and our real world. The resulting image had a great impact for our interpretative process, as it highlighted a detail from the narrative that none of us had previously found significant: the nidificatory limit. This detail, he claimed, exposed how the narrative of the Pit actually described larger ontological efforts to map meaning onto unfathomable depths. This point inspired Jessica to consider the relation between bird nest symbolism in the digital narrative and in medieval mnemonics. That connection became a foundation on which to mount an interpretation of *Project* as allegory.

Not all discoveries made interpretation easier. Some were productive for precisely the opposite reason. In "Chapter 2: Tachistoscope," Jessica's media archaeological exploration of the tachistoscope prompted her to delve into the numerous patents on devices called "tachistoscopes," and this research turned up far more information than we bargained for. Rather than finding one basic prototype for all tachistoscopes, we unearthed a whole host of machines with a wide variety of purposes—from speed-reading and military identification training to advertising and behavioral and cognitive psychology. Where Mark was hoping for a tidy profile of the device that he could use to compare and contrast with the workings of *Project*'s code, we found the opposite and had to revise our approaches accordingly. Being open to revising previous conceptions and being willing to change the course of our inquiry and interpretation was vital to this collaborative process.

In each of these three examples, one of us enabled or inspired another to move in a new interpretative direction and changed the course of our overall understanding of the work. However, the form of these intellectual exchanges (and the many more throughout this book) varied widely. Mark's methods made basic materials available that enabled Jeremy's analysis. Jeremy's methods illuminated a detail that then became a significant starting point for Jessica's investigation. Jessica's methods led Mark to ask new basic questions based on a more complex understanding of the subject of the work. These exchanges were neither planned nor predictable. Sometimes, one of us would make an observation off-the-cuff or in passing that greatly excited and inspired a coauthor. Other times, someone would conduct an investigation with the express intention of "handing off" our insights to a collaborator, only to have the results fall flat and the conversation fizzle. Over time we learned that the paths of interpretive discovery were not something we could map out in advance. Such learning required openness and patience. Ironically, analyzing *Project*'s fast-flashing poetics took us a long time (years longer than we anticipated); or perhaps more accurately, our collaborative writing process was incredibly time-consuming.

But collaboration is not just about scholarly questions and their pursuit, and digital collaboration is not just about digital tools. Collaboration is also about interpersonal relationships and communication skills—about not only rationality, but also personality. It requires vulnerability, which can be extremely challenging and even a little frightening. But, we believe that collaboration is not just a trendy practice but a powerful sea change in academic knowledge work, and in the hopes that it will encourage future collaborators and inspire future experiments, let us briefly share and reflect on some specific learning experiences from this particular collaboration, our own reading project.

In composing this book, we had to work across geographic locations, different working schedules, and multiple media formats. Our ongoing conversations—sometimes from different time zones or continents—proceeded over phone and video calls, chat streams, e-mail threads, and in-person meetings. We each had very different writing practices, as well as different concepts of what research is and how one does it. Unlike recent models for collaborative writing, wherein multiple people write under one cumulative, shared voice,[1] we strove from the beginning to maintain a sense of writerly autonomy that emphasized our individual contributions but still allowed (and even encouraged) all authors to participate in revising all sections of the manuscript. Rather than trying to erase our individual contributions and proclivities, we chose to perform individual voices and write a braided dialogue with them. Our intention was to show how performing collaboration is a personal and personality-driven activity as much as it is an exercise in practicing critical method. To emphasize that aspect, we worked to produce prose that retained the distinct flavors of our scholarly practices, intellectual styles, and personal voices. We aimed to create something cohesive while preserving the very differences that propelled our collaboration in the first place. This was hard. And this manner of presenting our contributions was not altogether honest, since that format obscured both the work we did on each other's sections and, in particular, the persistent and extensive feedback and revisions Jessica contributed throughout the process to keep the book project moving forward and on track.

We chose a writing platform, Google Docs, that allowed us to compose in online documents.[2] Instead of each drafting our own documents and then sharing, collating, or merging them, we wrote together in a small set of shared documents: one document per chapter, many differently authored sections per document. Writing in a single, shared, real-time location proved dramatic, both in the sense of being significant and also reflecting a sense of contestation, correction, and challenge. Like a stage or an arena, we came to speak of "the documents" as a place, a proving ground, and met each other weekly "in the documents." During these writing sessions we logged in simultaneously, and could see and feel the copresence of other invisible bodies writing and working beside us in real time (represented on the screen by color-coded cursors that appeared labeled with our names). The documents retained the traces of our individual writerly processes and the history of our revisions. The patterns in this revision history itself evolved through different stages as we learned how to work together.

For example, we communicated via the "comment" function, leaving marginal notes attached to specific passages in the document. These timestamped comment boxes appeared in the margins, labeled with our names and photos, and contained questions, suggestions, and critiques. They signified a readerly community—or sometimes a lack of one, in instances when we neglected to provide feedback on someone's new prose. These comments, each delivered also to our e-mail inboxes with attendant pings on our mobile phones, incited anxiety (oh, no! more work to do) and also relief (oh, yes! someone agrees with me), gratitude (oh yes! someone else is working!) and also guilt (oh, no! someone else is working!)—but they always represented the recursive work of reading and writing. When the margins of a paragraph were littered with comments, we knew reading and writing was happening; we felt ourselves building an argument. When we clicked the "Resolve" button on a comment, we felt a sweet sense of satisfaction as the little box disappeared in a sweeping movement, leaving the margins clear once again. Our most productive course was to maximize our exposure to each other's work, and this meant engaging in dialogue through cowriting—a process of recursive writing and revision—rather than dividing up the writing into individually owned sections.

Sharing meant not only sharing writing but also the materials that inspired the writing. Sometimes a new idea might be sparked by a peek into each other's source code, sketches, screenshots, or research notes. At other times, we needed to share more than just the "raw resources" in order to start a group conversation. A directory of images, a file full of code, or a bibliography of references might be announced and available, yet it would often remain undiscussed until the creator drafted a description of what it was, an explanation of why it was important or interesting, and even an example of how he/she planned to work with the material. The more access we had to each other's resources, work, and workspaces, the greater our shared understanding and the better our chances of happy accidents.

As we looked back on all we had done (and looked forward to what came next), we found ourselves repeatedly asking what kind of tools we could have used to better facilitate our project. If we were to imagine an online working space that would support and promote collaborative multimodal analysis of born-digital objects, what would it look like? That question prompted the next phase of our collaboration.

YOUR INVITATION

Throughout the process of our reading project we often longed for a virtual "workbench" for collaboration, a place of visibility (where the materials of work-in-progress could be shared [or displayed]) and a place of actual work—including investigations, experiments, commentaries, and the creation of new arguments. We agree with Kathleen Fitzpatrick that "the greatest value added by the scholarly publishing process of the future, likely will lie not in the content itself, but in the tools that enable authors to produce and readers to interact with that content, and with one another via that content."[3] Toward that end, we wanted to take what we learned about multimodal collaboration and translate it into a tool for others to use.

Our writing process required us to improvise the creation of a cloud of small shared spaces in any way we could—in documents and e-mailed attachments, on whiteboards and websites, through chat channels and discussion threads. Consequently, our online working spaces proliferated. Some spaces were better suited to viewing materials, others to editing or annotating. Not only that, our different critical modes tended to have different digital objects. We used whatever mechanisms were available, but the result was often disorganization and confusion. Word-processing documents offered too primitive a space for many of our materials. Similarly, merely posting the files online only solved the problem of creating a central repository for our objects of study—code, images, audio, and text—but no way to engage with them. We needed a location that would allow us to pool our resources, annotate them, and then work these materials into appropriate formats for presenting scholarly arguments.

Writing the book forced us to synthesize our discoveries into a coordinated linear argument. However, when we chose the form of a book to present those arguments, we realized that not all of these digital materials would fit into its material confines. Still, we wanted to make them available, to share them with our readers as we had shared them with each other. These video clips, visualizations, annotations, interviews, and source files supported our interpretations. They are part of our "text." But, a web companion or included disc containing them just wouldn't cut it.

We wanted to extend the collaboration via a shared "workbench" that could reach beyond the three of us to include our imagined readers. We envisioned our reader—you—curious to see how we hacked the Flash files, how we made the montage visualization, and what our annotation process for reading these elements looked like. At the same time, we wanted to allow you to use those assets in your own interpretations. We needed a platform that would support collaborative analysis of digital literature and other genres of interactive media that would extend beyond we three readers and serve a larger community. So, we embarked on a second, related, collaborative critical venture.

We developed an online platform for building collaborative scholarly arguments. We call this site "ACLS Workbench" (http://scalar.usc.edu/aclsworkbench/).

With the generous support of an ACLS Collaborative Research Fellowship, we built an online space for readers to gather and build arguments, collaboratively and digitally.[4] Our site, ACLS Workbench, offers a platform for humanities scholars, especially those exploring born-digital literary art, to read, produce, and publish. Built upon the ANVC Scalar[5] platform, and in collaboration with Lucas Miller, Craig Dietrich, and Erik Loyer, our workbench is a place where discoveries can be explored, shared, used, and saved. The system supports online editing and publishing spaces, online collections that in Scalar parlance are called "books." Fundamental to the system is making the critical exploration of texts *multimodal* through collections that are *joinable* and *cloneable*.

ACLS Workbench serves many of the needs and desires we had while writing this book. We needed to build a site that could serve as holding bin for content that was multimodal. As you can see, our Workbench collection "Reading *Project*"[6] contains all the materials we collected and created during the process of writing this book, including

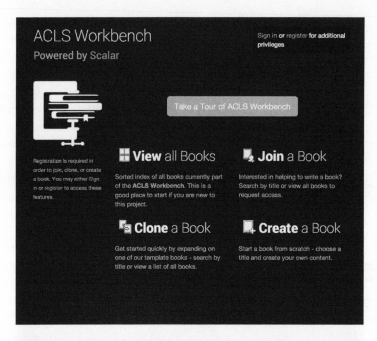

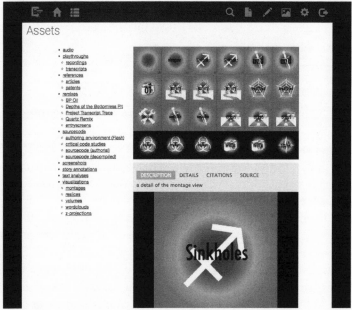

FIGURE 5.1: Screenshots of the ACLS Workbench website, http://scalar
.usc.edu/aclsworkbench/. (Screenshots by authors.)

recordings of the animation's playthrough, the decompiled Flash files, screenshots from *Project* that motivated our close readings, the text from the BP.txt file, and our visualizations. The underlying framework of Scalar provided an excellent multimedia platform for collecting and connecting all of the materials we generated in writing this book.

In addition to a website to contain the digital elements we were analyzing, we also needed a way to make these collections of materials *joinable*. As we have narrated through this book, our frequent interactions, shared discoveries, disagreements, and detours determined the evolution of our understanding of *Project*. As a result, we wanted ACLS Workbench to be a site where scholars were encouraged (and technologically supported) to collaborate directly with other scholars on new readings by sharing their collections. The sticking point for many discussions of digital objects is the lack of shared resources. However, many assets and computational analytics of digital objects are not readily available. To reproduce Jeremy's visualizations, for example, a reader would need to use the software and the same source assets that we do. We realize that it would be very difficult for another scholar or group of readers to respond to our assertions unless they had access to the same or similar materials—to see, understand, disagree, and build upon. Hence, we have made the Workbench collection cloneable— new authors may create their own editable copy at any time. When an author or a group of authors choose to clone a Workbench "book," they can build their argument upon the already gathered materials. We like the image of cloning (with all its overdetermined meanings) as a representation of the process of duplicating our materials for remix and reuse, and for purposes that we (the originators) cannot determine. Sharing knowledge is a form of producing knowledge, and we hope that Workbench will invite scholars to share not just their conclusions but also the assets and practices that led them to those conclusions.

We envision our ACLS Workbench providing content along with tools and techniques for collaborative multimodal criticism. Workbench collections can serve as starter kits for readers, platforms for performing new interpretations of a work using the same materials as previous readers. We hope that, when used in conjunction with this book, the site will inspire new interpretive approaches to Poundstone's *Project* as well as many other works of electronic literature. The primary goal is to support and to strengthen emerging modes of collaborative, born-digital scholarship.

Avowing a desire to foster new collaborations and pathways for analyzing digital poetics, we now conclude by refusing to end. Following in the poetic of *Project*'s programmatic loop and its visual design of never-ending circular ripples, we now loop back to the beginning of *Project*'s narrative about the Bottomless Pit to render it in our own way: sinkholes that have opened near the construction site of our critical reading practices have identified some fault lines and general instability in contemporary humanities scholarship. Our project in analyzing *Project* has been to respond, not by proceeding as normal with traditional critical methods or by pretending that the transformation is not upon us, but by seeking new routes and platforms for collaborative and critical analysis. We hope you'll join us in exploring this shifting terrain.

APPENDIX A: BP.txt

&storyVar=Sinkholes and unstable soil characteristic of the karstland around Bluefields long plagued construction of the Beale Pike between Breezewood and Roanoke Park. The route was selected for its distance from the Bottomless Pit and the perceived need to allow a generous margin of safety mandated not by necessity but by the psychology of the people in this region, whose conceptions of the Pit and its supposed hazards are not easily dispelled by the best scientific testimony. Engineers supervised the drilling of test holes designed to detect unstable areas in a 30 foot grid extending 200 feet on either side of the intended highway's shoulders. Workers pulled up core samples revealing a subsoil of finely compacted kaolin silica and gabbro. 200 foot piles of steel-reinforced concrete supported by native soil friction were sunk to anchor highway margins against a substrate judged to be sandy and suffering from lack of compaction. The soil problems were not considered serious. No subsidence incidents of any importance were reported in the first 58 days of construction. The 59th day began unseasonably warm and cloudless. Towards mid morning highway workers began hearing sounds like distant gunfire detonations or firecrackers. Several strong bursts each a cluster of reports lasting a few seconds occurred in the hour before noon. Not all workers were able to hear the sounds which some ascribed to the backfire of pavement machinery. At 12:56 or 12:57 they felt the ground rocking beneath their feet. Those who could run to safety did. Behind them a great chasm opened in the earth. 73 workers and nearly four million dollars worth of government equipment disappeared into a cavity of unknown depth. The state brought in geologist Nelson Playfair who had experience with deep wells. Playfair's attempts to measure the depth of the Pit by triangulation failed owing to poor visibility at the lower levels. The Pit is not an isolated phenomenon. It is only an extreme case of what has been happening all along in this region where integration of geologic layers has become compromised. The forces that maintain the Pit remain a puzzle to geologists. The soil in the entire area is sandy friable and loose. Playfair explained: You're really not on solid ground anywhere in this region. The Pit's early history is sketchy. In the nineteenth century Chandler Moody described as a sign painter inventor libertine and atheist collected all that had been written about the Pit. An heir of Moody's established the New Lebanon Historical Society which preserved maps newspapers books paintings relating not only to the Pit (which was much smaller and shallower at that time) but to the entire region and its people.

Among the items on display was Church's famous unfinished painting of the Bottomless Pit. Moody complained that maps of the Pit are of limited and at best temporary value. Walls and ledges are subject to sudden settling rearrangement and complete disappearance. The Historical Society was long housed in Hoar House the first substantial dwelling built in the area; and unfortunately Hoar House was pulled apart in the ground stress accompanying the 1993 subsidence its timbers and foundation stones being scattered in the characteristic rhomboid pattern. The debris was pulled into the Pit during a relatively minor subsidence event the following night. A number of residents attested to the former existence of books and clippings in the Society library alluding to earlier similar events in the past; i.e. to incidents in which all or nearly all existing records of the Bottomless Pit's history were effaced by its own unpredictable expansion. The lost records were themselves reputed to have contained accounts of similar catastrophes and irretrievable losses of history in past times yet more remote. Government psychologists have noted the self-validating elements of these stories. At least one of the persons making these claims was judged by a psychologist to be a woman capable [of] doing or saying anything in order to draw attention to herself and her emotional problems. Daring men have attempted to attain great depths in the Pit. Kellogg the astronomer, described as being in an erratic mental state after having quarreled with a colleague with whom he shared a house, descended to the 14,000 foot level, where he believed that he would be able to view extra-galactic nebulae at midday. Kellogg claimed in the caption of a once-popular lithograph that that stars were visible during the daytime when viewed from the bottom of deep wells or chimneys. The fact is that Kellogg was unable to see anything below 22000 feet, even his own lamp held inches from his eyes. Visibility in the Pit is a complex matter. Haze and shadow permit little visibility below the 4 mile depth. Dense fogs have been reported at lower levels. At still lower depths air pressure creates mirages. Other reported mirages may be psychological in nature. Much depends on angle of the sun and atmospheric conditions. Kellogg was the first to describe many famed optical phenomena of the Pit. Weather permitting a viewer standing at the Pit's rim at sunrise or sunset may see weird shadows cast on a bank of fog miles away haloed by a prismatic effect of light producing a famous illusion of Our Lady. Kellogg described the odd lights seen on moonless nights, locally supposed to be the spirits of brigands or lost men. A theme of Kellogg's writing was that the Pit was related to the Pit of Conklin or more often the Well of Conklin, a subject of local legend held to contain malign influences lethal to travelers. Others believe this pit was only a well poisoned out of spite by a man named Conklin, over disappointment in a legal matter.

Kellogg wrote articles for such popular publications as Enigma Strange and Libido. He suggested the Pit to be the lair of vortices and fantastic beings whose description varied with his reading popular tastes and motion pictures and television programs he had seen. In 1962 Kellogg perished when an ambitious two-man winch broke at the 54,000 foot level sending his gondola tumbling downward. Thermal expansion of chain and an unusual ratchet mechanism for drawing out the chain were blamed for the accident. The Pit has become an integral part of life in the region. Children are told to behave lest Father Christmas throw them into the Pit. Children and to some extent the adults of the area are subject to recurring dreams and nightmares about the Pit. Dreams of falling into the Pit are common. Often in the dream the Pit is ever widening and threatens the dreamer's home and familiar surroundings. In another locally common class of dream the dreamer finds him or herself already in the Pit and unable to scale its walls. Feelings of anxiety despair fear abandonment and anomie are frequently reported. Even when dream content is not manifestly about the Pit residents dream of falling off cliffs or being stranded in crevices. The Pit was long popular with church groups. Chartered buses brought church members who proof of the literal reality of Hell. Some brought telescopes and cameras and many have reported success in viewing hell fires or demonic beings. More often they fail (as have geologists with more sophisticated equipment) to see any evidence of a fiery inner layer. For many years Miltown Evangelical Church presented a passion play at a pavilion on the south rim. Sermons invoked the Pit as an allegory. The performance began with a costumed angel trumpeting followed by the meteoric appearance of a magnesium flare star that fell from the sky into the Pit remaining visible up to 4 minutes. The Pit was symbolically opened with a golden key. There issued great billows of smoke and a plague of locusts enacted by the release of 600 horned lizards caged in concealed locations on the perimeter of the Pit. The play's elaborate costumes and sets were made by local people. Families rehearsed many months for a short season in midsummer. A lawsuit brought by the family of a woman who fell into the Pit while trying to get a better view brought an end to the production. The Pit remains an attraction to travelers. Devil's boiling pots are a natural formation as are calcite spars sold at roadside stands as devil horns or Satan's jewel boxes. Locusts sold in bamboo cages as souvenirs are actually the local 17-year cicada. Compasses and dip needles act erratically near the Pit. Normally reliable water witches fail. Tame animals turn hostile. It has been reported that dogs refuse to approach the Pit or act strangely in its vicinity. A common behavior is to hunker down and crawl across the ground propelled by the hind legs while emitting low gurgling sounds. Flocks of birds are sometimes observed flying down into the Pit. The flocking behavior may be an instinct triggered by the absence of a ground sense. Nests have been found down to 3,340 feet. Near the so-called nidificatory limit nests become disorganized irregular composed of bizarre elements (wire debris pebbles hard candy chewing gum religious tracts). Fleas have been found down to the 18,000 foot level. A blind midge first discovered in the Pit (Cinea horribilis) has since been found in stagnant waste pools from the brewing industry worldwide. It has become popular to throw small or valueless objects into the Pit. People talk of casting something into the Pit when they mean to get rid of it with certainty. Metaphor has become reality: People literally cast into the Pit last packs of cigarettes photographs of ex-husbands images of the disgraced bad cars marriage certificates household junk. One commercial enterprise throws unwanted objects into the Pit for a fee. An expedition to the ledge on the southeast rim found its bottom lined with a layer of coins smooth stones beverage containers fast food wrappers, and feral cats. It is such a frequent practice to throw unwanted kittens in the Pit that an animal rights group patrols the perimeter on a selective basis. At least 23 people have attempted suicide by jumping into the Pit and all but one have succeeded. Confusing the matter is a reported tendency to jump involuntarily into the Pit. It is possible to lose all sense of direction in the vicinity of the Pit for obscure reasons that are under investigation. One individual questioned by police reported the illusion of transposing the sky and the Pit. Thus some suicides may have been the result of reflex actions hallucinations or magnetic anomalies while others are the consequence of depression grief and loss of emotional affect. Motel owners in the area have agreed to an informal system of psychological screening. The subsidence has devastated the local real estate market in an area extending far beyond that where measurable subsidence has occurred. Homeowners in this marginal zone find disaster coverage impossible to obtain or prohibitively priced or available only with exclusions for damage owing to further ground subsidence. Cracks in pavements sidewalks driveways breezeways patios and interior and exterior walls are a universal sight. Doors will not open or are impossible to shut. Windows shatter explosively. Makeshift repairs have made shantytowns of formerly fine neighborhoods. Authorities warn that areas once viewed as remote from the Pit are in fact slowly sliding inward. The few remaining residents of Carbondale sit isolated in their homes surrounded by houses their neighbors have long abandoned. At night the community is pitch black. Ground stress has snapped power lines water pipes sewer connections and television cables. Squatters are unaware of developments in the outside world; some show signs of derangement. When Carbondale resident Devon Little moved here, this neighborhood was considered to be a vast distance from the Pit. This was not considered to be a risky area. Like many residents Little sleeps in his car. His modest amenities (a satellite dish a construction crew's portable toilet and a microwave oven and cooler plugged into a portable generator) are steps away. I am comfortable living outside now. Little's home has been on the market for nearly two years finding few lookers and no buyers. One potential buyer backed out after discovering that the area had landslide problems. In an attempt to secure the house's foundation Little nailed plywood over the studs to form a cripple wall. Local handymen report a brisk trade in such work yet these very measures have been ineffective against major subsidence events in the past. Residents are moody and fearful about the future, yet there is also an element of denial. Mentions of the Pit are conspicuously absent from area real estate brochures and Chamber of Commerce publications. If the Pit is mentioned at all it is only via such circumlocutions as describing the general region as a geological wonderland. It is not uncommon to hear residents talk animatedly of potholes or sinkholes they saw on a vacation or business trip concluding with evident satisfaction that subsidence is a problem wherever you go in the world! We're actually luckier than a lot of people! Things could be much worse! A common theme of conversations is that the Pit is filling up and will eventually stabilize. Geologists deny any basis for this hope. A 3,000-room Indian casino was once planned for the Bottomless Pit's south rim. It was to have featured a spectacular glass ballroom cantilevered over the Pit. Guests would have viewed the glorious abyss opening beneath their feet according to promotional literature. Financing fell apart when it was discovered that an engineer had been tampering with survey markers in order to conceal progressive subsidence. The shift was less than one half of an inch according to documents filed with the Gaming Board but it was ominous nonetheless for it had occurred within a five-month period. A state engineer told the Board that such subsidence transmitted as a torque [force] to the glass floor could cause it to shatter unpredictably. The casino's backers responded with a plan to measure the deformation of the glass floor through sensors. In the event of dangerous stress alarms would sound and the projecting ballroom would be evacuated. The Building Safety Commission rejected this plan. Glass, though possessing a greater tensile strength than steel, does not undergo a plastic deformation and may fail without any warning of the magnitude contemplated [by the engineer] as the basis of a mass evacuation. A portion of the northeast corner of the casino lot has since fallen into the Pit. Test pilings for the projecting ballroom are still visible as is the construction firm's temporary office whose walls are now several inches out of plumb. Large cracks parallel to the Pit's rim have appeared in the ground where construction was to have begun and this pattern of ground deformation has preceded past subsidence events. The Pit has swallowed part of the safety rail system encircling the Pit's perimeter. In recent years the Pit has both widened and gotten alarmingly deeper.&spamVar=elongate radon crackpot mausoleum sassafras trend jetliner titular Valois arduous bombast Bellatrix taboo moneymaker offend panjandrum henbane psychotherapist reportorial IEEE judicial endomorphism Nicholas punch wiry woven beck Mackinac neutron exploration Kathleen alterman ferrous Heidelberg quadruple Inca gorse move dominate urbanite cabana exogenous glycerin mold twinkle craftsperson softball turtle cauldron Arlington morsel Brennan electrocardiograph hermitian retribution TV parliamentary rapacious RCA Morton hepatica snag hepatitis cash CUNY Jesse squid informative moneymake pharmaceutic congressional Chinatown mite equivocate ah audiovisual legible pitchblende calla sulfonamide John swag commodious ah sheriff Cameron propel normative Masonic progress landfill Roger diagram Rollins sacrosanct leap curvilinear pilferage Cerberus utopian purslane cotman Stanhope levee Rasmussen Acapulco bullish airmass ant algorithm Cushman therefrom discrepant showy acropolis Hitachi retinue penna difluoride armchair Nile Rico ravage paid rabbi shrugging anatomy gauleiter philanthropic corundum formulate operand cup gallberry pressure formatting Chomsky Elinor Bloch pear horseman cupric lion separate terrible Brisbane hereafter fogy gallus songful virtuoso diathermy petroleum tombstone erect Dietz screenplay depreciable epitaxial king sea silicon volatile impale Barnet schoolteacher mandrake Kampala tropopause combine alumna Icelandic corruptible Mouton forswear Zan dashboard Fogarty vocate compelling Mollie monarch contour creek adoptive complicate junketeer synapses scrooge caprice hatchway fresh retail lament eliminate patriarchal crawlspace Kuwait klaxon Johanson nuclear earthshaking covariate wrongful dogfish physiochemical edict registrable soliloquy escape Evans Kowalski know distant amiss Adelia Conway mayor impute convolute Henrietta successful semantic&done=1

APPENDIX B: Subliminal Word List

The complete subliminal word list in the order displayed on-screen, top to bottom, left to right.

elongate
radon
crackpot
mausoleum
sassafras
trend
jetliner
titular
Valois
arduous
bombast
Bellatrix
taboo
moneymaker
offend
panjandrum
henbane
psychotherapist
reportorial
IEEE
judicial
endomorphism
Nicholas
punch
wiry
woven
beck
Mackinac
neutron
exploration
Kathleen
alterman
ferrous
Heidelberg
quadruple
Inca
gorse
move
dominate
urbanite
cabana
exogenous
glycerin
mold
twinkle

craftsperson
softball
turtle
cauldron
Arlington
morsel
Brennan
electrocardiograph
hermitian
retribution
TV
parliamentary
rapacious
RCA
Morton
hepatica
snag
hepatitis
cash
CUNY
Jesse
squid
informative
moneymake
pharmaceutic
congressional
Chinatown
mite
equivocate
ah
audiovisual
legible
pitchblende
calla
sulfonamide
John
swag
commodious
ah
sheriff
Cameron
propel
normative
Masonic
progress

landfill
Roger
diagram
Rollins
sacrosanct
leap
curvilinear
pilferage
Cerberus
utopian
purslane
cotman
Stanhope
levee
Rasmussen
Acapulco
bullish
airmass
ant
algorithm
Cushman
therefrom
discrepant
showy
acropolis
Hitachi
retinue
penna
difluoride
armchair
Nile
Rico
ravage
paid
rabbi
shrugging
anatomy
gauleiter
philanthropic
corundum
formulate
operand
cup
gallberry
pressure

formatting
Chomsky
Elinor
Bloch
pear
horseman
cupric
lion
separate
terrible
Brisbane
hereafter
fogy
gallus
songful
virtuoso
diathermy
petroleum
tombstone
erect
Dietz
screenplay
depreciable
epitaxial
king
sea
silicon
volatile
impale
Barnet
schoolteacher
mandrake
Kampala
tropopause
combine
alumna
Icelandic
corruptible
Mouton
forswear
Zan
dashboard
Fogarty
vocate
compelling

Mollie
monarch
contour
creek
adoptive
complicate
junketeer
synapses
scrooge
caprice
hatchway
fresh
retail
lament
eliminate
patriarchal
crawlspace
Kuwait
klaxon
Johanson
nuclear
earthshaking
covariate
wrongful
dogfish
physiochemical
edict
registrable
soliloquy
escape
Evans
Kowalski
know
distant
amiss
Adelia
Conway
mayor
impute
convolute
Henrietta
successful
semantic

elongate Sinkholes radon and crackpot unstable mausoleum soil sassafras characteristic trend of jetliner the titular karstland Valois around arduous Bluefields bombast long Bellatrix plagued taboo construction moneymaker of offend the panjandrum Beale henbane Pike psychotherapist between reportorial Breezewood IEEE and judicial Roanoke endomorphism Park. Nicholas The punch route wiry was woven selected beck for Mackinac its neutron distance exploration from Kathleen the alterman Bottomless ferrous Pit Heidelberg and quadruple the Inca perceived gorse need move to dominate allow urbanite a cabana generous exogenous margin glycerin of mold safety twinkle mandated craftsperson not softball by turtle necessity cauldron but Arlington by morsel the Brennan psychology electrocardiograph of hermitian the retribution people TV in parliamentary this rapacious region, RCA whose Morton conceptions hepatica of snag the hepatitis Pit cash and CUNY its Jesse supposed squid hazards informative are moneymake not pharmaceutic easily congressional dispelled Chinatown by mite the equivocate best ah scientific audiovisual testimony. legible Engineers pitchblende supervised calla the sulfonamide drilling John of swag test commodious holes ah designed sheriff to Cameron detect propel unstable normative areas Masonic in progress a landfill 30 Roger foot diagram grid Rollins extending sacrosanct 200 leap feet curvilinear on pilferage either Cerberus side utopian of purslane the cotman intended Stanhope highway's levee shoulders. Rasmussen Workers Acapulco pulled bullish up airmass core ant samples algorithm revealing Cushman a therefrom subsoil discrepant of showy finely acropolis compacted Hitachi kaolin retinue silica penna and difluoride gabbro. armchair 200 Nile foot Rico piles ravage of paid steel-reinforced rabbi concrete shrugging supported anatomy by gauleiter native philanthropic soil corundum friction formulate were operand sunk cup to gallberry anchor pressure highway formatting margins Chomsky against Elinor a Bloch substrate pear judged horseman to cupric be lion sandy separate and terrible suffering Brisbane from hereafter lack fogy of gallus compaction. songful The virtuoso soil diathermy problems petroleum were tombstone not erect considered Dietz serious. screenplay No depreciable subsidence epitaxial incidents king of sea any silicon importance volatile were impale reported Barnet in schoolteacher the mandrake first Kampala 58 tropopause days combine of alumna construction. Icelandic The corruptible 59th Mouton day forswear began Zan unseasonably dashboard warm Fogarty and vocate cloudless. compelling Towards Mollie mid monarch morning contour highway creek workers adoptive began complicate hearing junketeer sounds synapses like scrooge distant caprice gunfire hatchway detonations fresh or retail firecrackers. lament Several eliminate strong patriarchal bursts crawlspace each Kuwait a klaxon cluster Johanson of elongate reports radon lasting crackpot a mausoleum few sassafras seconds trend occurred jetliner in titular the Valois hour arduous before bombast noon. Bellatrix Not taboo all moneymaker workers offend were panjandrum able henbane to psychotherapist hear reportorial the IEEE sounds judicial which endomorphism some Nicholas ascribed punch to wiry the woven backfire beck of Mackinac pavement neutron machinery. exploration At Kathleen 12:56 alterman or ferrous 12:57 Heidelberg they quadruple felt Inca the gorse ground move rocking dominate beneath urbanite their cabana feet. exogenous Those glycerin who mold could twinkle run craftsperson to softball safety turtle did. cauldron Behind Arlington them morsel a Brennan great electrocardiograph chasm hermitian opened retribution in TV the parliamentary earth. rapacious 73 RCA workers Morton and hepatica nearly snag four hepatitis million cash dollars CUNY worth Jesse of squid government informative equipment moneymake disappeared pharmaceutic into congressional a Chinatown cavity mite of equivocate unknown ah depth. audiovisual The legible state pitchblende brought calla in sulfonamide geologist John Nelson swag Playfair commodious who ah had sheriff experience Cameron with propel deep normative wells. Masonic Playfair's progress attempts landfill to Roger measure diagram the Rollins depth sacrosanct of leap the curvilinear Pit pilferage by Cerberus triangulation utopian failed purslane owing cotman to Stanhope poor levee visibility Rasmussen at Acapulco the bullish lower airmass levels. ant The algorithm Pit Cushman is therefrom not discrepant an showy isolated acropolis phenomenon. Hitachi It retinue is penna only difluoride an armchair extreme Nile case Rico of ravage what paid has rabbi been shrugging happening anatomy all gauleiter along philanthropic in corundum this formulate region operand where cup integration gallberry of pressure geologic formatting layers Chomsky has Elinor become Bloch compromised. pear The horseman forces cupric that lion maintain separate the terrible Pit Brisbane remain hereafter a fogy puzzle gallus to songful geologists. virtuoso The diathermy soil petroleum in tombstone the erect entire Dietz area screenplay is depreciable sandy epitaxial friable king and sea loose. silicon Playfair volatile explained: impale You're Barnet really schoolteacher not mandrake on Kampala solid tropopause ground combine anywhere alumna in Icelandic this corruptible region. Mouton The forswear Pit's Zan early dashboard history Fogarty is vocate sketchy. compelling In Mollie the monarch nineteenth contour century creek

Chandler adoptive Moody complicate described junketeer as synapses a scrooge sign caprice painter hatchway inventor fresh libertine retail and lament atheist eliminate collected patriarchal all crawlspace that Kuwait had klaxon been Johanson written elongate about radon the crackpot Pit. mausoleum An sassafras heir trend of jetliner Moody's titular established Valois the arduous New bombast Lebanon Bellatrix Historical taboo Society moneymaker which offend preserved panjandrum maps henbane newspapers psychotherapist books reportorial paintings IEEE relating judicial not endomorphism only Nicholas to punch the wiry Pit woven (which beck was Mackinac much neutron smaller exploration and Kathleen shallower alterman at ferrous that Heidelberg time) quadruple but Inca to gorse the move entire dominate region urbanite and cabana its exogenous people. glycerin Among mold the twinkle items craftsperson on softball display turtle was cauldron Church's Arlington famous morsel unfinished Brennan painting electrocardiograph of hermitian the retribution Bottomless TV Pit. parliamentary Moody rapacious complained RCA that Morton maps hepatica of snag the hepatitis Pit cash are CUNY of Jesse limited squid and informative at moneymake best pharmaceutic temporary congressional value. Chinatown Walls mite and equivocate ledges ah are audiovisual subject legible to pitchblende sudden calla settling sulfonamide rearrangement John and swag complete commodious disappearance. ah The sheriff Historical Cameron Society propel was normative long Masonic housed progress in landfill Hoar Roger House diagram the Rollins first sacrosant substantial leap dwelling curvilinear built pilferage in Cerberus the utopian area; purslane and cotman unfortunately Stanhope Hoar levee House Rasmussen was Acapulco pulled bullish apart airmass in ant the algorithm ground Cushman stress therefrom accompanying discrepant the showy 1993 acropolis subsidence Hitachi its retinue timbers penna and difluoride foundation armchair stones Nile being Rico scattered ravage in paid the rabbi characteristic shrugging rhomboid anatomy pattern. gauleiter The philanthropic debris corundum was formulate pulled operand into cup the gallberry Pit pressure during formatting a Chomsky relatively Elinor minor Bloch subsidence pear event horseman the cupric following lion night. separate A terrible number Brisbane of hereafter residents fogy attested gallus to songful the virtuoso former diathermy existence petroleum of tombstone books erect and Dietz clippings screenplay in depreciable the epitaxial Society king library sea alluding silicon to volatile earlier impale similar Barnet events schoolteacher in mandrake the Kampala past; tropopause i.e. combine to alumna incidents Icelandic in corruptible which Mouton all forswear or Zan nearly dashboard all Fogarty existing vocate records compelling of Mollie the monarch Bottomless contour Pit's creek history adoptive were complicate effaced junketeer by synapses its scrooge own caprice unpredictable hatchway expansion. fresh The retail lost lament records eliminate were patriarchal themselves crawlspace reputed Kuwait to klaxon have Johanson contained elongate accounts radon of crackpot similar mausoleum catastrophes sassafras and trend irretrievable jetliner losses titular of Valois history arduous in bombast past Bellatrix times taboo yet moneymaker more offend remote. panjandrum Government henbane psychologists psychotherapist have reportorial noted IEEE the judicial self-validating endomorphism elements Nicholas of punch these wiry stories. woven At beck least Mackinac one neutron of exploration the Kathleen persons alterman making ferrous these Heidelberg claims quadruple was Inca judged gorse by move a dominate psychologist urbanite to cabana be exogenous a glycerin woman mold capable twinkle [of] craftsperson doing softball or turtle saying cauldron anything Arlington in morsel order Brennan to electrocardiograph draw hermitian attention retribution to TV herself parliamentary and rapacious her RCA emotional Morton problems. hepatica Daring snag men hepatitis have cash attempted CUNY to Jesse attain squid great informative depths moneymake in pharmaceutic the congressional Pit. Chinatown Kellogg mite the equivocate astronomer, ah described audiovisual as legible being pitchblende in calla an sulfonamide erratic John mental swag state commodious after ah having sheriff quarreled Cameron with propel a normative colleague Masonic with progress whom landfill he Roger shared diagram a Rollins house, sacrosanct descended leap to curvilinear the pilferage 14,000 Cerberus foot utopian level, purslane where cotman he Stanhope believed levee that Rasmussen he Acapulco would bullish be airmass able ant to algorithm view Cushman extra-galactic therefrom nebulae discrepant at showy midday. acropolis Kellogg Hitachi claimed retinue in penna the difluoride caption armchair of Nile a Rico once-popular ravage lithograph paid that rabbi that shrugging stars anatomy were gauleiter visible philanthropic during corundum the formulate daytime operand when cup viewed gallberry from pressure the formatting bottom Chomsky of Elinor deep Bloch wells pear or horseman chimneys. cupric The lion fact separate is terrible that Brisbane Kellogg hereafter was fogy unable gallus to songful see virtuoso anything diathermy below petroleum 22000 tombstone feet, erect even Dietz his screenplay own depreciable lamp epitaxial held king inches sea from silicon his volatile eyes. impale Visibility Barnet in schoolteacher the mandrake Pit Kampala is tropopause a combine complex alumna matter. Icelandic Haze corruptible and Mouton shadow forswear permit Zan little dashboard visibility Fogarty below vocate the compelling 4 Mollie mile monarch depth. contour Dense creek fogs adoptive have complicate been junketeer reported synapses at scrooge lower caprice levels. hatchway At fresh still retail lower lament depths eliminate air patriarchal pressure crawlspace creates Kuwait mirages. klaxon Other Johanson reported elongate mirages radon may crackpot be mausoleum psychological sassafras in trend nature. jetliner Much titular depends Valois on arduous angle bombast of Bellatrix the taboo sun moneymaker and offend atmospheric panjandrum conditions. henbane Kellogg psychotherapist was reportorial the IEEE first judicial to endomorphism describe Nicholas many punch famed wiry optical woven phenomena beck of Mackinac the neutron Pit. exploration Weather Kathleen permitting alterman a ferrous viewer Heidelberg standing quadruple at Inca the gorse Pit's move rim dominate at urbanite sunrise cabana or exogenous sunset glycerin may mold see twinkle weird craftsperson shadows softball cast turtle on cauldron a Arlington bank morsel of Brennan fog electrocardiograph miles hermitian away retribution haloed TV by parliamentary a rapacious prismatic RCA effect Morton of hepatica light snag producing hepatitis a cash famous CUNY illusion Jesse of squid Our informative Lady. moneymake Kellogg pharmaceutic described congressional the Chinatown odd mite lights equivocate seen ah on audiovisual moonless legible nights, pitchblende locally calla supposed sulfonamide to John be swag the commodious spirits ah of sheriff brigands Cameron or propel lost normative men. Masonic A progress theme landfill of Roger Kellogg's diagram writing Rollins was sacrosanct that leap the curvilinear Pit pilferage was Cerberus related utopian to purslane the cotman Pit Stanhope of levee Conklin Rasmussen or Acapulco more bullish often airmass the ant Well algorithm of Cushman Conklin, therefrom a discrepant subject showy of acropolis local Hitachi legend retinue held penna to difluoride contain armchair malign Nile influences Rico lethal ravage to paid travelers. rabbi Others shrugging believe anatomy this gauleiter pit philanthropic was corundum only formulate a operand well cup poisoned gallberry out pressure of formatting spite Chomsky by Elinor a Bloch man pear named horseman Conklin, cupric over lion disappointment separate in terrible a Brisbane legal hereafter matter. fogy Kellogg gallus wrote songful articles virtuoso for diathermy such petroleum popular tombstone publications erect as Dietz Enigma screenplay Strange depreciable and epitaxial Libido. king He sea suggested silicon the volatile Pit impale to Barnet be schoolteacher the mandrake lair Kampala of tropopause vortices combine and alumna fantastic Icelandic beings corruptible whose Mouton description forswear varied Zan with dashboard his Fogarty reading vocate popular compelling tastes Mollie and monarch motion contour pictures creek and adoptive television complicate programs junketeer he synapses had scrooge seen. caprice In hatchway 1962 fresh Kellogg retail perished lament when eliminate an patriarchal ambitious crawlspace two-man Kuwait winch klaxon broke Johanson at elongate the radon 54,000 crackpot foot mausoleum level sassafras sending trend his jetliner gondola titular tumbling Valois downward. arduous Thermal bombast expansion Bellatrix of taboo chain moneymaker and offend an panjandrum unusual henbane ratchet psychotherapist mechanism reportorial for IEEE drawing judicial out endomorphism the Nicholas chain punch were wiry blamed woven for beck the Mackinac accident. neutron The exploration Pit Kathleen has alterman become ferrous an Heidelberg integral quadruple part Inca of gorse life move in dominate the urbanite region. cabana Children exogenous are glycerin told mold to twinkle behave craftsperson lest softball Father turtle Christmas cauldron throw Arlington them morsel into Brennan the electrocardiograph Pit. hermitian Children retribution and TV to parliamentary some rapacious extent RCA the Morton adults hepatica of snag the hepatitis area cash are CUNY subject Jesse to squid recurring informative dreams moneymake and pharmaceutic nightmares congressional about Chinatown the mite Pit. equivocate Dreams ah of audiovisual falling legible into pitchblende the calla Pit sulfonamide are John common. swag Often commodious in ah the sheriff dream Cameron the propel Pit normative is Masonic ever progress widening landfill and Roger threatens diagram the Rollins dreamer's sacrosanct home leap and curvilinear familiar pilferage surroundings. Cerberus In utopian another purslane locally cotman common Stanhope class levee of Rasmussen dream Acapulco the bullish dreamer airmass finds ant him algorithm or Cushman herself therefrom already discrepant in showy the acropolis Pit Hitachi and retinue unable penna to difluoride scale armchair its Nile walls. Rico Feelings ravage of paid anxiety rabbi despair shrugging fear anatomy abandonment gauleiter and philanthropic anomie corundum are formulate frequently operand reported. cup Even gallberry when pressure dream formatting content Chomsky is Elinor not Bloch manifestly pear about horseman the cupric Pit lion residents separate dream terrible of Brisbane falling hereafter off fogy cliffs gallus or songful being virtuoso stranded diathermy in petroleum crevices. tombstone The erect Pit Dietz was screenplay long depreciable popular epitaxial with king church sea groups. silicon Chartered volatile buses impale brought Barnet church schoolteacher members mandrake who Kampala proof tropopause of combine the alumna literal Icelandic reality corruptible of Mouton Hell. forswear Some Zan brought dashboard telescopes Fogarty and vocate cameras compelling and Mollie many monarch have contour reported creek success adoptive in complicate viewing junketeer hell synapses fires scrooge or caprice demonic hatchway beings. fresh More retail often lament they eliminate fail patriarchal (as crawlspace have Kuwait geologists klaxon with Johanson more elongate sophisticated radon equipment) crackpot to mausoleum see sassafras any trend evidence jetliner of titular a Valois fiery arduous inner bombast layer. Bellatrix For taboo many moneymaker years offend Miltown panjandrum Evangelical henbane Church psychotherapist presented reportorial a IEEE passion judicial play endomorphism at Nicholas a punch pavilion wiry on woven the beck south Mackinac rim. neutron Sermons exploration invoked Kathleen the alterman Pit ferrous as Heidelberg an quadruple allegory. Inca The gorse performance move began dominate with urbanite a cabana costumed exogenous angel glycerin trumpeting mold followed twinkle by craftsperson the softball meteoric turtle appearance cauldron of Arlington a morsel magnesium Brennan flare electrocardiograph star hermitian that retribution fell TV from parliamentary the rapacious sky RCA into Morton the hepatica Pit snag remaining hepatitis visible cash up CUNY to Jesse 4 squid minutes. informative The moneymake Pit pharmaceutic was congressional symbolically Chinatown opened mite with equivocate a ah golden audiovisual key. legible There pitchblende issued calla great sulfonamide billows John of swag smoke commodious and ah a sheriff plague Cameron of propel locusts normative enacted Masonic by progress the landfill release Roger of diagram 600 Rollins horned sacrosanct lizards leap caged curvilinear in pilferage concealed Cerberus locations utopian on purslane the cotman perimeter Stanhope of levee the Rasmussen Pit. Acapulco The bullish play's airmass elaborate ant costumes algorithm and Cushman sets therefrom were discrepant made showy by acropolis local Hitachi people. retinue Families penna rehearsed difluoride many armchair months Nile for Rico a ravage short paid season rabbi in shrugging midsummer. anatomy A gauleiter lawsuit philanthropic brought corundum by formulate the operand family cup of gallberry a pressure woman formatting who Chomsky fell Elinor into Bloch the pear Pit horseman while cupric trying lion to separate get terrible a Brisbane better hereafter view fogy brought gallus an songful end virtuoso to diathermy the petroleum production. tombstone The erect Pit Dietz remains screenplay an depreciable attraction epitaxial to king travelers. sea Devil's silicon boiling volatile pots impale are Barnet a schoolteacher natural mandrake formation Kampala as tropopause are combine calcite alumna spars Icelandic sold corruptible at Mouton roadside forswear stands Zan as dashboard devil Fogarty horns vocate or compelling Satan's Mollie jewel monarch boxes. contour Locusts creek sold adoptive in complicate bamboo junketeer cages synapses as scrooge souvenirs caprice are hatchway actually fresh the retail local lament 17-year eliminate cicada. patriarchal Compasses crawlspace and Kuwait dip klaxon needles Johanson act elongate erratically radon near crackpot the mausoleum Pit. sassafras Normally trend reliable jetliner water titular witches Valois fail. arduous Tame bombast animals Bellatrix turn taboo hostile. moneymaker It offend has panjandrum been henbane reported psychotherapist that reportorial dogs IEEE refuse judicial to endomorphism approach Nicholas the punch Pit wiry or woven act beck strangely Mackinac in neutron its exploration vicinity. Kathleen A alterman common ferrous behavior Heidelberg is quadruple to Inca hunker gorse down move and dominate crawl urbanite across cabana the exogenous ground glycerin propelled mold by twinkle the craftsperson hind softball legs turtle while cauldron emitting Arlington low morsel gurgling Brennan sounds. electrocardiograph Flocks hermitian of retribution birds TV are parliamentary sometimes rapacious observed RCA flying Morton down hepatica into snag the hepatitis Pit. cash The CUNY flocking Jesse behavior squid may informative be moneymake an pharmaceutic instinct congressional triggered Chinatown by mite the equivocate absence ah of audiovisual a legible ground pitchblende sense. calla Nests sulfonamide have John been swag found commodious down ah to sheriff 3,340 Cameron feet. propel Near normative the Masonic so-called progress nidificatory landfill limit Roger nests diagram become Rollins disorganized sacrosanct irregular leap composed curvilinear of pilferage bizarre Cerberus elements utopian (wire purslane debris cotman pebbles Stanhope hard levee candy Rasmussen chewing Acapulco gum bullish religious airmass tracts). ant Fleas algorithm have Cushman been therefrom found discrepant down showy to acropolis the Hitachi 18,000 retinue foot penna level. difluoride A armchair blind Nile midge Rico first ravage discovered paid in rabbi the shrugging Pit anatomy (Cinea gauleiter horribilis) philanthropic has corundum since formulate been operand found cup in gallberry stagnant pressure waste formatting pools Chomsky from Elinor the Bloch brewing pear industry horseman worldwide. cupric It lion has separate become terrible popular Brisbane to hereafter throw fogy small gallus or songful valueless virtuoso objects diathermy into petroleum the tombstone Pit. erect People Dietz talk screenplay of depreciable casting epitaxial something king into sea the silicon Pit volatile when impale they Barnet mean schoolteacher to mandrake get Kampala rid tropopause of combine it alumna with Icelandic certainty. corruptible Metaphor Mouton has forswear become Zan reality: dashboard People Fogarty literally vocate cast compelling into Mollie the monarch Pit contour last creek packs adoptive of complicate cigarettes junketeer photographs synapses of scrooge ex-husbands caprice images hatchway of fresh the retail disgraced lament bad eliminate cars patriarchal marriage crawlspace certificates Kuwait household klaxon junk. Johanson One elongate commercial radon enterprise crackpot throws mausoleum unwanted sassafras objects trend into jetliner the titular Pit Valois for arduous a bombast fee. Bellatrix An taboo expedition moneymaker to offend the panjandrum ledge henbane on psychotherapist the reportorial southeast IEEE rim judicial found endomorphism its Nicholas bottom punch lined wiry with woven a beck layer Mackinac of neutron coins exploration smooth Kathleen stones alterman beverage ferrous containers Heidelberg fast quadruple food Inca wrappers, gorse and move feral dominate cats. urbanite It cabana is exogenous such glycerin a mold frequent twinkle practice craftsperson to softball throw turtle unwanted cauldron kittens Arlington in morsel the Brennan Pit electrocardiograph that hermitian an retribution animal TV rights parliamentary group rapacious patrols RCA the Morton perimeter hepatica on snag a hepatitis selective cash basis. CUNY At Jesse least squid 23 informative people moneymake have pharmaceutic attempted congressional suicide Chinatown by mite jumping equivocate into ah the audiovisual Pit legible and pitchblende all calla but sulfonamide one John have swag succeeded. commodious Confusing ah the sheriff matter Cameron is propel a normative reported Masonic tendency progress to landfill jump Roger involuntarily diagram into Rollins the sacrosanct Pit. leap It curvilinear is pilferage possible Cerberus to utopian lose purslane all cotman sense Stanhope of levee direction Rasmussen in Acapulco the bullish vicinity airmass of ant the algorithm Pit Cushman for therefrom obscure discrepant reasons showy that acropolis are Hitachi under retinue investigation. penna One difluoride individual armchair questioned Nile by Rico police ravage reported paid the rabbi illusion shrugging of anatomy transposing gauleiter the philanthropic sky corundum and formulate the operand Pit. cup Thus gallberry some pressure suicides formatting may Chomsky have Elinor been Bloch the pear result horseman of cupric reflex lion actions separate hallucinations terrible or Brisbane magnetic hereafter anomalies fogy while gallus others songful are virtuoso the diathermy consequence petroleum of tombstone depression erect grief Dietz and screenplay loss depreciable of epitaxial emotional king affect. sea Motel silicon owners volatile in impale the Barnet area schoolteacher have mandrake agreed Kampala to tropopause an combine informal alumna system Icelandic of corruptible psychological Mouton screening. forswear The Zan subsidence dashboard has Fogarty devastated vocate the compelling local Mollie real monarch estate contour market creek in adoptive an complicate area junketeer extending synapses far scrooge beyond caprice that hatchway where fresh measurable retail subsidence lament has eliminate occurred. patriarchal Homeowners crawlspace in Kuwait this klaxon marginal Johanson zone elongate find radon disaster crackpot coverage mausoleum impossible sassafras to trend obtain jetliner or titular prohibitively Valois priced arduous or bombast available Bellatrix only taboo with moneymaker exclusions offend for panjandrum damage henbane owing psychotherapist to reportorial further IEEE ground judicial subsidence. endomorphism Cracks Nicholas in punch pavements wiry sidewalks woven driveways beck breezeways Mackinac patios neutron and exploration interior Kathleen and alterman exterior ferrous walls Heidelberg are quadruple a Inca universal gorse sight. move Doors dominate will urbanite not cabana open exogenous or glycerin are mold impossible twinkle to craftsperson shut. softball Windows turtle shatter cauldron explosively. Arlington Makeshift morsel repairs Brennan have electrocardiograph made hermitian shantytowns retribution of TV formerly parliamentary fine rapacious neighborhoods. RCA Authorities Morton warn hepatica that snag areas hepatitis once cash viewed CUNY as Jesse remote squid from informative the moneymake Pit pharmaceutic are congressional in Chinatown fact mite slowly equivocate sliding ah inward. audiovisual The legible few pitchblende remaining calla residents sulfonamide of John Carbondale swag sit commodious isolated ah in sheriff their Cameron homes propel surrounded normative by Masonic houses progress their landfill neighbors Roger have diagram long Rollins abandoned. sacrosanct At leap night curvilinear the pilferage community Cerberus is utopian pitch purslane black. cotman Ground Stanhope stress levee has Rasmussen snapped Acapulco power bullish lines airmass water ant pipes algorithm sewer Cushman connections therefrom and discrepant television showy cables. acropolis Squatters Hitachi are retinue unaware penna of difluoride developments armchair in Nile the Rico outside ravage world; paid some rabbi show shrugging signs anatomy of gauleiter derangement. philanthropic When corundum Carbondale formulate resident operand Devon cup Little gallberry moved pressure here, formatting this Chomsky neighborhood Elinor was Bloch considered pear to horseman be cupric a lion vast separate distance terrible from Brisbane the hereafter Pit. fogy This gallus was songful not virtuoso considered diathermy to petroleum be tombstone a erect risky Dietz area. screenplay Like depreciable many epitaxial residents king Little sea sleeps silicon in volatile his impale car. Barnet His schoolteacher modest mandrake amenities Kampala (a tropopause satellite combine dish alumna a Icelandic construction corruptible crew's Mouton portable forswear toilet Zan and dashboard a Fogarty microwave vocate oven compelling and Mollie cooler monarch plugged contour into creek a adoptive portable complicate generator) junketeer are synapses steps scrooge away. caprice I hatchway am fresh comfortable retail living lament outside eliminate now. patriarchal Little's crawlspace home Kuwait has klaxon been Johanson on elongate the radon market crackpot for mausoleum nearly sassafras two trend years jetliner finding titular few Valois lookers arduous and bombast no Bellatrix buyers. taboo One moneymaker potential offend buyer panjandrum backed henbane out psychotherapist after reportorial discovering IEEE that judicial the endomorphism area Nicholas had punch landslide wiry problems. woven In beck an Mackinac attempt neutron to exploration secure Kathleen the alterman house's ferrous foundation Heidelberg Little quadruple nailed Inca plywood gorse over move the dominate studs urbanite to cabana form exogenous a glycerin cripple mold wall. twinkle Local craftsperson handymen softball report turtle a cauldron brisk Arlington trade morsel in Brennan such electrocardiograph work hermitian yet retribution these TV very parliamentary measures rapacious have RCA been Morton ineffective hepatica against snag major hepatitis subsidence cash events CUNY in Jesse the squid past. informative Residents moneymake are pharmaceutic moody congressional and Chinatown fearful mite about equivocate the ah future, audiovisual yet legible there pitchblende is calla also sulfonamide an John element swag of commodious denial. ah Mentions sheriff of Cameron the propel Pit normative are Masonic conspicuously progress absent landfill from Roger area diagram real Rollins estate sacrosanct brochures leap and curvilinear Chamber pilferage of Cerberus Commerce utopian publications. purslane If cotman the Stanhope Pit levee is Rasmussen mentioned Acapulco at bullish all airmass it ant is algorithm only Cushman via therefrom such discrepant circumlocutions showy as acropolis describing Hitachi the retinue general penna region difluoride as armchair a Nile geological Rico wonderland. ravage It paid is rabbi not shrugging uncommon anatomy to gauleiter hear philanthropic residents corundum talk formulate animatedly operand of cup potholes gallberry or pressure sinkholes formatting they Chomsky saw Elinor on Bloch a pear vacation horseman or cupric business lion trip separate concluding terrible with Brisbane evident hereafter satisfaction fogy that gallus subsidence songful is virtuoso a diathermy problem petroleum wherever tombstone you erect go Dietz in screenplay the depreciable world! epitaxial We're king actually sea luckier silicon than volatile a impale lot Barnet of schoolteacher people! mandrake Things Kampala could tropopause be combine much alumna worse! Icelandic A corruptible common Mouton theme forswear of Zan conversations dashboard is Fogarty that vocate the compelling Pit Mollie is monarch filling contour up creek and adoptive will complicate eventually junketeer stabilize. synapses Geologists scrooge deny caprice any hatchway basis fresh for retail this lament hope. eliminate A patriarchal 3,000-room crawlspace Indian Kuwait casino klaxon was Johanson once elongate planned radon for crackpot the mausoleum Bottomless sassafras Pit's trend south jetliner rim. titular It Valois was arduous to bombast have Bellatrix featured taboo a moneymaker spectacular offend glass panjandrum ballroom henbane cantilevered psychotherapist over reportorial the IEEE Pit. judicial Guests endomorphism would Nicholas have punch viewed wiry the woven glorious beck abyss Mackinac opening neutron beneath exploration their Kathleen feet alterman according ferrous to Heidelberg promotional quadruple literature. Inca Financing gorse fell move apart dominate when urbanite it cabana was exogenous discovered glycerin that mold an twinkle engineer craftsperson had softball been turtle tampering cauldron with Arlington survey morsel markers Brennan in electrocardiograph order hermitian to retribution conceal TV progressive parliamentary subsidence. rapacious The RCA shift Morton was hepatica less snag than hepatitis one cash half CUNY of Jesse an squid inch informative according moneymake to pharmaceutic documents congressional filed Chinatown with mite the equivocate Gaming ah Board audiovisual but legible it pitchblende was calla ominous sulfonamide nonetheless John for swag it commodious had ah occurred sheriff within Cameron a propel five-month normative period. Masonic A progress state landfill engineer Roger told diagram the Rollins Board sacrosanct that leap such curvilinear subsidence pilferage transmitted Cerberus as utopian a purslane torque cotman [force] Stanhope to levee the Rasmussen glass Acapulco floor bullish could airmass cause ant it algorithm to Cushman shatter therefrom unpredictably. discrepant The showy casino's acropolis backers Hitachi responded retinue with penna a difluoride plan armchair to Nile measure Rico the ravage deformation paid of rabbi the shrugging glass anatomy floor gauleiter through philanthropic sensors. corundum In formulate the operand event cup of gallberry dangerous pressure stress formatting alarms Chomsky would Elinor sound Bloch and pear the horseman projecting cupric ballroom lion would separate be terrible evacuated. Brisbane The hereafter Building fogy Safety gallus Commission songful rejected virtuoso this diathermy plan. petroleum Glass, tombstone though erect possessing Dietz a screenplay greater depreciable tensile epitaxial strength king than sea steel, silicon does volatile not impale undergo Barnet a schoolteacher plastic mandrake deformation Kampala and tropopause may combine fail alumna without Icelandic any corruptible warning Mouton of forswear the Zan magnitude dashboard contemplated Fogarty [by vocate the compelling engineer] Mollie as monarch the contour basis creek of adoptive a complicate mass junketeer evacuation. synapses A scrooge portion caprice of hatchway the fresh northeast retail corner lament of eliminate the patriarchal casino crawlspace lot Kuwait has klaxon since Johanson fallen elongate into radon the crackpot Pit. mausoleum Test sassafras pilings trend for jetliner the titular projecting Valois ballroom arduous are bombast still Bellatrix visible taboo as moneymaker is offend the panjandrum construction henbane firm's psychotherapist temporary reportorial office IEEE whose judicial walls endomorphism are Nicholas now punch several wiry inches woven out beck of Mackinac plumb. neutron Large exploration cracks Kathleen parallel alterman to ferrous the Heidelberg Pit's quadruple rim Inca have gorse appeared move in dominate the urbanite ground cabana where exogenous construction glycerin was mold to twinkle have craftsperson begun softball and turtle this cauldron pattern Arlington of morsel ground Brennan deformation electrocardiograph has hermitian preceded retribution past TV subsidence parliamentary events. rapacious The RCA Pit Morton has hepatica swallowed snag part hepatitis of cash the CUNY safety Jesse rail squid system informative encircling moneymake the pharmaceutic Pit's congressional perimeter. Chinatown In mite recent equivocate years ah the audiovisual Pit legible has pitchblende both calla widened sulfonamide and John gotten swag alarmingly commodious deeper.

[The text continues:]

ah Sinkholes radon and crackpot unstable mausoleum soil sassafras characteristic trend of jetliner the titular karstland Valois around arduous Bluefields bombast long Bellatrix plagued taboo construction moneymaker of offend the panjandrum Beale henbane Pike psychotherapist between reportorial Breezewood IEEE and judicial Roanoke endomorphism Park . . .

APPENDIX D: Poundstone's Code

The following code is reproduced from the original precompiled code for *Project for Tachistoscope {Bottomless Pit}* as provided by the author, William Poundstone. When loaded in the Flash editing environment, this original code reveals that there are forty-nine named layers in the piece. In order from highest to lowest, these are:

> Actions, Exit from SR, Void Note, Aporia Note, Link to Coca Cola, Concrete Note, Sources Note, Monitor Note, Vicary Note, SR Text, Text background, Void button, Aporia button, Concrete Button, Colophon Button, Monitor Button, Vicary Button, SR Button, Exit Button, Void, Aporia, Omega, Computer, Colophon, The Subliminal Con, System requirement, Start, Date, William, Title, Fixation Crosses, storyMovie, Icons, Center point, Gleam, Loader Percent, Sphere, Backdrop, Inaudible10, Inaudible9, Inaudible8, Inaudible6, Inaudible5, Inaudible4, Inaudible3, Inaudible2, Inaudible1, Invisible Assets

The ActionScript code snippets reproduced below are attached to different frames and to objects through the Flash authoring interface. Poundstone's comments are indicated with //. Labels and commentary by Mark Marino are indicated with ///. The source frame/object is indicated at the top of each code section (e.g. "/// Frame 57"). When assigned, the name of that frame or button is placed after a colon in quotation marks (e.g. "loaderFrame"). **Functions** are bold; data is underlined, *comments* are italicized.

/// Frame 1: "loaderFrame"
```
totalBytes = Math.round(getBytesTotal() / 1024);
enoughBytes = .90*totalBytes;
loadedBytes = Math.round(getBytesLoaded() / 1024);
percentDone = Math.round((loadedBytes / enoughBytes) * 100);
if (percentDone >= 100) {
gotoAndPlay("doneLoadingFrame");
}
```

/// Frame 2
```
gotoAndPlay(1);
```

/// Frame 3
```
// this scene never plays. It contains images and sound so that they will load.
// this avoids having to link "export in first frame"
```

```
/// Frame 4: "doneLoadingFrame"

/// Frame 5: Tween 8: [Project for]
stop();

/// Frame 5: Tween 32
stop();

/// Frame 30
// Load the text
myStoryMovie.loadVariables("BP.txt");
//Swonk, then fill the arrays
myStoryMovie.onData = function() {
        this.storyArray = this.storyVar.split("_");
        this.spamArray = this.spamVar.split("_", 200);
        this.limit = this.storyArray.length;
        spamLimit = this.spamArray.length;
        this.i = 0;
        this.k = 1;
        // tells which picture to flash
        noOfPictures = 13;
        // number of pictures in rotation
        noOfIcons = 41;
        myColor = new Color(myBackgroundColor);
        mySubliminalColor = new Color(myStoryMovie.box2);
};
fixationArray = new Array("icon35", "icon31", "icon17", "icon43", "icon31",
"icon42");
noOfColors = 10;
palette = new Array("0x410001", "0x410001", "0x410001", "0xFFCCCC",
"0x99FF00", "0x990066", "0xFF9900", "0xFFCCFF", "0xF4F4F4", "0xEFEEDE");
// test computer speed and use score (lagTime) to adjust timing
i = 0;
countNum = 10000;
startTime = getTimer()/1000;
while (!lagTime) {
        i++;
        if (i == countNum) {
                stopTime = getTimer()/1000;
                lagTime = 10*(stopTime-startTime);
        }
```

```
}
if (lagTime<0.75) { lagTime = 0.75; }
handicap = Math.floor((lagTime-0.75)*6);
if (handicap>40) { handicap = 40; }


/// Frame 40: title_mc: (frame with preloaded icons)
stop();


/// Frame 54: "statFrame"
stop();
// this is for the button sounds. For some reason putting the sounds in the buttons
// (enclosed in movies) didn't work
myButtonSound = new Sound();
myButtonSound.setVolume(20);
showIcons = false;
mySRMovie.onEnterFrame = function() {
        x_pos = _root._xmouse-300;
        y_pos = _root._ymouse-300;
        if (x_pos*x_pos+y_pos*y_pos<60000) {
                showIcons = true;
        } else {
                showIcons = false;
        }
        if (showIcons) {
                this._x = this._x+.3*(209-this._x);
                this._y = this._y+.3*(158-this._y);
        } else {
                this._x = this._x+.3*(-50-this._x);
                this._y = this._y+.3*(-150-this._y);
        }
};
mySRMovie.onRollOver = function() {
        myButtonSound.attachSound("Note0.mp3");
        myButtonSound.start();
};
mySRMovie.onRelease = function() {
        gotoAndPlay("SRFrame");
};
myBrazilMovie.onEnterFrame = function() {
        if (showIcons) {
                this._x = this._x+.3*(386-this._x);
                this._y = this._y+.3*(156-this._y);
```

```
            } else {
                    this._x = this._x+.3*(500-this._x);
                    this._y = this._y+.3*(-200-this._y);
            }
};
myBrazilMovie.onRollOver = function() {
        myButtonSound.attachSound("Note1.mp3");
        myButtonSound.start();
};
myBrazilMovie.onRelease = function() {
        gotoAndPlay("concreteFrame");
};
myAporiaMovie.onEnterFrame = function() {
        if (showIcons) {
                    this._x = this._x+.3*(472-this._x);
                    this._y = this._y+.3*(276-this._y);
        } else {
                    this._x = this._x+.3*(700-this._x);
                    this._y = this._y+.3*(100-this._y);
        }
};
myAporiaMovie.onRollOver = function() {
        myButtonSound.attachSound("Note2.mp3");
        myButtonSound.start();
};
myAporiaMovie.onRelease = function() {
        gotoAndPlay("aporiaFrame");
};
myConMovie.onEnterFrame = function() {
        if (showIcons) {
                    this._x = this._x+.3*(436-this._x);
                    this._y = this._y+.3*(393-this._y);
        } else {
                    this._x = this._x+.3*(700-this._x);
                    this._y = this._y+.3*(600-this._y);
        }
};
myConMovie.onRollOver = function() {
        myButtonSound.attachSound("Note0.mp3");
        myButtonSound.start();
};
myConMovie.onRelease = function() {
        gotoAndPlay("vicaryFrame");
```

```
};
myQuotesMovie.onEnterFrame = function() {
        if (showIcons) {
                this._x = this._x+.3*(300-this._x);
                this._y = this._y+.3*(451-this._y);
        } else {
                this._x = this._x+.3*(254-this._x);
                this._y = this._y+.3*(700-this._y);
        }
};
myQuotesMovie.onRollOver = function() {
        myButtonSound.attachSound("Note1.mp3");
        myButtonSound.start();
};
myQuotesMovie.onRelease = function() {
        gotoAndPlay("sourcesFrame");
};
mySkullMovie.onEnterFrame = function() {
        if (showIcons) {
                this._x = this._x+.3*(131-this._x);
                this._y = this._y+.3*(259-this._y);
        } else {
                this._x = this._x+.3*(-200-this._x);
                this._y = this._y+.3*(100-this._y);
        }
};
mySkullMovie.onRollOver = function() {
        myButtonSound.attachSound("Note1.mp3");
        myButtonSound.start();
};
mySkullMovie.onRelease = function() {
        gotoAndPlay("monitorFrame");
};
myVoidMovie.onEnterFrame = function() {
        if (showIcons) {
                this._x = this._x+.3*(170-this._x);
                this._y = this._y+.3*(385-this._y);
        } else {
                this._x = this._x+.3*(-150-this._x);
                this._y = this._y+.3*(600-this._y);
        }
};
```

```
myVoidMovie.onRollOver = function() {
        myButtonSound.attachSound("Note2.mp3");
        myButtonSound.start();
};
myVoidMovie.onRelease = function() {
        gotoAndPlay("voidFrame");
};


/// Frame 54: Symbol 31 [START]
on (release) {
  showIcons=FALSE
  gotoAndPlay("segueFrame");
}


/// Frame 55: "segueFrame" Symbol 31 [START – smaller -- tween]
on (release) { gotoAndPlay("segueFrame"); }


/// Frame 56: Symbol 31
on (release) {
        gotoAndPlay("segueFrame");
        }


/// Frame 57: "mainFrame"
// refresh screen because we might be coming from a "system requirements" page
updateAfterEvent();
// start the "level" at 0
// 0 is default, just text with basic music loop
// 1 shows pictures and adds musical flourish
// 2 has orange and yellow background effect and frantic music
// 3 has zooming purple circle
level = 0;
// delete
count = 0;
mainTime = 0;
subTime = 0;
mainClick = 0;
spamClick = 0;
// play sound loops
my_sound = new Sound(this);
my_extraSound = new Sound(this);
my_sound.attachSound("mainLoop");
my_sound.start();
my_sound.onSoundComplete = function() {
```

```
my_sound.attachSound("mainLoop");
// the 0.05 second offset prevents a looping glitch
my_sound.start(0.05, 1);
// this randomly sets the "level"
var index = math.random();
if (index>.875) {
    level = 0;
    // the level always purges added backgrounds
    _level0.centerPoint.level2Effect_mc.unloadMovie();
    _level0.centerPoint.level3Effect_mc.unloadMovie();
    // set blue background color
    myColor.setRGB(0x0099CC);
    mySubliminalColor.setRGB(0x000000);
} else {
    if (index>.75) {
        level = 1;
        my_extraSound.attachSound("My Song26.mp3");
        my_extraSound.start();
        // get rid of purple background but allow orange-yellow if playing
        centerPoint.attachMovie("inwardGradient", "level4Effect_mc", 111);
        _level0.centerPoint.level3Effect_mc.unloadMovie();
        // set blue background color
        myColor.setRGB(0x0099CC);
        mySubliminalColor.setRGB(0x000000);
    } else {
        if (index>.625) {
            level = 2;
            my_extraSound.attachSound("My Song5.mp3");
            my_extraSound.start();
            // allow purple if playing
            centerPoint.attachMovie("level2Effect", "level2Effect_mc", 100);
            myColor.setRGB(0x0099CC);
            mySubliminalColor.setRGB(0x000000);
        } else {
            if (index>.50) {
                level = 3;
                _level0.centerPoint.level2Effect_mc.unloadMovie();
                var hue = Math.floor(Math.random()*(noOfColors+1));
                myColor.setRGB(palette[hue]);
                mySubliminalColor.setRGB(0xFFFFFF);
                fixation_mc.attachMovie("fixationCrosses",
                    "myFixationCrosses", 300);
            } else {
```

```
if (index>.375) {
    level = 4;
    _level0.centerPoint.level2Effect_mc.unloadMovie();
    centerPoint.attachMovie("inwardGradient",
        "level4Effect_mc", 111);
    mySubliminalColor.setRGB(0x000000);
    myColor.setRGB(0x000000);
    my_extraSound.attachSound("Tweak effect.mp3");
    my_extraSound.start();
} else {
    if (index>.25) {
        level = 5;
        my_extraSound.attachSound("My Song18.mp3");
        my_extraSound.start();
        mySubliminalColor.setRGB(0x000000);
        centerPoint.attachMovie("level3Effect",
            "level3Effect_mc", 110);
    } else {
        if (index>.125) {
            level = 6;
            my_extraSound.attachSound("My Song21.mp3");
            my_extraSound.start();
            myColor.setRGB(0x0099CC);
            mySubliminalColor.setRGB(0x000000);
            centerPoint.attachMovie("level6Effect",
                "myLevel6Effect", 299);
        } else {
            level = 7;
            my_extraSound.attachSound("My Song22.mp3");
            my_extraSound.start();
            myColor.setRGB(0x0099CC);
            mySubliminalColor.setRGB(0x000000);
            _level0.centerPoint.level3Effect_mc.unloadMovie();
            centerPoint.attachMovie("level5Effect",
                "myLevel5Effect", 301);
        }
    }
}
}
}
}
}
```

```
};
// three main values
subliminalMilliseconds = 13+handicap;
textMilliseconds = 200;
cuePicture = 2;
// picture is flashed one in cuePicture passes
// scale word to fill screen
scaleBox = function (myBox, myWord) {
    var l = myWord.length;
    switch (l) {
    case 1 :
        myBox._xscale = 600;
        myBox._yscale = 600;
        myBox._y = -390;
        myBox._x = -2520;
        break;
    case 2 :
        myBox._xscale = 500;
        myBox._yscale = 500;
        myBox._y = -300;
        myBox._x = -2100;
        break;
    case 3 :
        myBox._xscale = 400;
        myBox._yscale = 400;
        myBox._y = -260;
        myBox._x = -1700;
        break;
    case 4 :
        myBox._xscale = 300;
        myBox._yscale = 300;
        myBox._y = -210;
        myBox._x = -1270;
        break;
    case 5 :
        myBox._xscale = 250;
        myBox._yscale = 250;
        myBox._y = -180;
        myBox._x = -1040;
        break;
    case 6 :
        myBox._xscale = 240;
```

```
            myBox._yscale = 240;
            myBox._y = -180;
            myBox._x = -1000;
            break;
    case 7 :
            myBox._xscale = 200;
            myBox._yscale = 200;
            myBox._y = -150;
            myBox._x = -820;
            break;
    case 8 :
            myBox._xscale = 200;
            myBox._yscale = 200;
            myBox._y = -150;
            myBox._x = -850;
            break;
    case 9 :
            myBox._xscale = 200;
            myBox._yscale = 200;
            myBox._y = -150;
            myBox._x = -830;
            break;
    case 10 :
            myBox._xscale = 170;
            myBox._yscale = 170;
            myBox._y = -120;
            myBox._x = -720;
            break;
    case 11 :
            myBox._xscale = 160;
            myBox._yscale = 160;
            myBox._y = -120;
            myBox._x = -650;
            break;
    case 12 :
            myBox._xscale = 150;
            myBox._yscale = 150;
            myBox._y = -110;
            myBox._x = -620;
            break;
    default :
            myBox._xscale = 130;
```

```
            myBox._yscale = 130;
            myBox._y = -95;
            myBox._x = -540;
            break;
    }
};
// subliminal loop
killSubliminal = function () {
    myStoryMovie.box2.text = "";
    updateAfterEvent();
    _root.myPicture.unloadMovie();
    updateAfterEvent();
    // scale story box
    scaleBox(myStoryMovie.box3, myStoryMovie.storyArray[myStoryMovie.i]);
    // show story word and icon
    if (level != 3) {
        myIcon.attachMovie("icon"+Math.floor(1+Math.random()*
    noOfIcons), "icon", 3);
        myIcon.icon._xscale = 110;
        myIcon.icon._yscale = 110;
    } else {
        myIcon.icon.unloadMovie();
    }
    myStoryMovie.box3.text = myStoryMovie.storyArray[myStoryMovie.i];
    updateAfterEvent();
    clearInterval(killInterval);
    // increment word counter
    myStoryMovie.i++;
};
// Main loop, now a setInterval
updateWords = function () {
    // erase old words
    myStoryMovie.box3.text = "";
    updateAfterEvent();
    // scale spam box
    scaleBox(myStoryMovie.box2, myStoryMovie.spamArray[myStoryMovie.i]);
    // flash spam word
    myStoryMovie.box2.text = myStoryMovie.spamArray[myStoryMovie.i%
        spamLimit];
    updateAfterEvent();
    // flash picture if level = 1
    if (level == 1) {
```

```
            if (myStoryMovie.i%cuePicture == 0) {
                _root.attachMovie("imageMovie"+k, "myPicture", 200);
                myPicture._x = 300;
                myPicture._y = 300;
                updateAfterEvent();
                k++;
                if (k>noOfPictures) {
                    k = 1;
                }
            }
        }
        killInterval = setInterval(killSubliminal, subliminalMilliseconds);
        // loop back when it reaches the last word in the story file
        if (myStoryMovie.i == myStoryMovie.limit) {
            myStoryMovie.i = 0;
        }
};
mainInterval = setInterval(updateWords, textMilliseconds);
/// Here's the call to update the words
stop();
// code for EXIT button
myExitButton.onRelease = function() {
    clearInterval(killInterval);
    clearInterval(mainInterval);
    _root.myPicture.unloadMovie();
    myIcon.icon.unloadMovie();
    myStoryMovie.box2.text = "";
    myStoryMovie.box3.text = "";
    my_sound.stop();
    myColor.setRGB(0x0099CC);
    gotoAndPlay("startFrame");
};


/// Frame 58: "SRFrame"
stop();
// code for EXIT button
myExitFromSRButton.onRelease = function() {
        gotoAndPlay("startFrame");
        clearInterval(killInterval);
        clearInterval(mainInterval);
        _root.myPicture.unloadMovie();
        myStoryMovie.box1.text = "";
```

```
        myStoryMovie.box2.text = "";
        myStoryMovie.box3.text = "";
        my_sound.stop();
};
if (lagTime<2) {
} else {
}
```

/// The following buttons were positioned on Frame 58 and held till 64 to provide consistent navigation through
/// the entryscreens.

/// Frames 58-64: Aporia Button: [Aporia] <myAporiaButton>
```
on (release) { gotoAndStop("aporiaFrame"); }
```

/// Frames 58-64: Concrete Poetry Button: [Concrete Poetry]
```
on (release) { gotoAndStop("concreteFrame"); }
```

/// Frames 58-64: Monitor Button: <myMonitorButton> [via WWW]
```
on (release) { gotoAndStop("monitorFrame"); }
```

/// Frames 58-64: Sources Button: mySourcesButton [Colophon]
```
on (release) { gotoAndStop("sourcesFrame"); }
```

/// Frames 58-64: SR Button: <mySRButton>
```
on (release) { gotoAndStop("SRFrame"); }
```

/// Frames 58-64: steadyExitButton: [EXIT]
```
on (release) { gotoAndPlay("startFrame"); }
```

/// Frames 58-64: Vicary Button: <myVicaryButton> [Subliminal Con]
```
on (release) { gotoAndStop(vicaryFrame); }
```

/// Frames 58-64: voidTextButton [The Void]
```
on (release) { gotoAndStop("voidFrame"); }
```

/// Frame 59: "vicaryFrame"
```
stop();
```

/// Frame 60: "monitorFrame"
```
stop();
```

```
/// Frame 61: "sourcesFrame"
stop();

/// Frame 62: "concreteFrame"
stop();

/// Frame 62: Invisible Coca Cola Link ["bebe coca cola"]
on (release) { getURL("http://www.ubu.com/historical/pignatari/pignatari1.
html", "_blank"); }

/// Frame 63: "aporiaFrame"
stop();

/// Frame 64: "voidFrame"
stop();
```

APPENDIX E: The Decompiled Code (Selection)

The following ActionScript code was decompiled from the publicly available .swf file of *Project for Tachistoscope {Bottomless Pit}* using the Flash forensic analysis software Trillix. No author comments are present, as this process cannot recover them. Labels and commentary by Mark Marino are indicated with ///. Shown here is only *selected* code, taken from frames 57.

```
/// Frame 57
\updateAfterEvent();
level = 0;
count = 0;
mainTime = 0;
subTime = 0;
mainClick = 0;
spamClick = 0;
/// setting variables
my_sound = new Sound(this);
/// creating new instance of sound
my_extraSound = new Sound(this);
/// creating new instance of sound
my_sound.attachSound("mainLoop");
/// creates a new instance of sound file "mainLoop"
my_sound.start();
/// plays mainLoop
my_sound.onSoundComplete = function ()
/// when mainLoop finishes playing, do this
{
    my_sound.attachSound("mainLoop");
creates another instance of "mainLoop" -Mark Marino 5/26/10 10:49 PM
    my_sound.start(0.05, 1);
/// the parenthesis shows where in the loop to begin, so not quite at the start, and 1
means loop once
    var index = math.random();
/// getting a random number 0-1
    if (index > 0.875)
/// if it is greater than .875
    {
        level = 0;
        _level0.centerPoint.level2Effect_mc.unloadMovie();
/// unloads the level2effect of centerpoint
```

```
      _levelo.centerPoint.level3Effect_mc.unloadMovie();
/// same with level3 effect
      myColor.setRGB(39372);
/// sets color
      mySubliminalColor.setRGB(0);
/// sets color for subliminal to 0, or black
      return;
   }
   if (index > 0.75)
   {
      level = 1;
      my_extraSound.attachSound("My Song26.mp3");
/// or we switch to this song
      my_extraSound.start();
      centerPoint.attachMovie("inwardGradient", "level4Effect_mc", 111);
/// we add the inward gradiant movie
      _levelo.centerPoint.level3Effect_mc.unloadMovie();
/// turn off this movie
      myColor.setRGB(39372);
/// keep color at background?
      mySubliminalColor.setRGB(0);
/// set subliminal to 0 color
      return;
   }
   if (index > 0.625)
   {
      level = 2;
      my_extraSound.attachSound("My Song5.mp3");
/// or attach this song
      my_extraSound.start();
      centerPoint.attachMovie("level2Effect", "level2Effect_mc", 100);
/// attaches the movie and sets depth to 100 -Mark Marino 5/26/10 11:14 PM
      myColor.setRGB(39372);
      mySubliminalColor.setRGB(0);
      return;
   }
   if (index > 0.5)
   {
      level = 3;
      _levelo.centerPoint.level2Effect_mc.unloadMovie();
/// again, turns off level 2 effect
      var hue = Math.floor(Math.random() * (noOfColors + 1));
/// randomly
```

```
      myColor.setRGB(palette[hue]);
/// sets color to a randomly selected color
      mySubliminalColor.setRGB(16777215);
/// integer for the hexidecimal color "white" (FFFFFF)
      fixation_mc.attachMovie("fixationCrosses", "myFixationCrosses", 300);
      return;
   }
   if (index > 0.375)
   {
      level = 4;
      _level0.centerPoint.level2Effect_mc.unloadMovie();
      centerPoint.attachMovie("inwardGradient", "level4Effect_mc", 111);
      mySubliminalColor.setRGB(0);
/// both get set to 0
      myColor.setRGB(0);
      my_extraSound.attachSound("Tweak effect.mp3");
      my_extraSound.start();
      return;
   }
   if (index > 0.25)
   {
      level = 5;
      my_extraSound.attachSound("My Song18.mp3");
      my_extraSound.start();
      mySubliminalColor.setRGB(0);
      centerPoint.attachMovie("level3Effect", "level3Effect_mc", 110);
      return;
   }
   if (index > 0.125)
   {
      level = 6;
      my_extraSound.attachSound("My Song21.mp3");
      my_extraSound.start();
      myColor.setRGB(39372);
      mySubliminalColor.setRGB(0);
      centerPoint.attachMovie("level6Effect", "myLevel6Effect", 299);
      return;
   }
   level = 7;
   my_extraSound.attachSound("My Song22.mp3");
   my_extraSound.start();
   myColor.setRGB(39372);
   mySubliminalColor.setRGB(0);
```

```
    _levelo.centerPoint.level3Effect_mc.unloadMovie();
    centerPoint.attachMovie("level5Effect", "myLevel5Effect", 301);
}
;
subliminalMilliseconds = 13 + handicap;
textMilliseconds = 200;
cuePicture = 2;
scaleBox = function (myBox, myWord)
{
   var l = myWord.length;
   if (l === 1)
   {
      myBox._xscale = 600;
      myBox._yscale = 600;
      myBox._y = 0 - 390;
      myBox._x = 0 - 2520;
      return;
   }
   else
   {
      if (l === 2)
      {
         myBox._xscale = 500;
         myBox._yscale = 500;
         myBox._y = 0 - 300;
         myBox._x = 0 - 2100;
         return;
      }
      else
      {
         if (l === 3)
         {
            myBox._xscale = 400;
            myBox._yscale = 400;
            myBox._y = 0 - 260;
            myBox._x = 0 - 1700;
            return;
         }
         else
         {
            if (l === 4)
            {
               myBox._xscale = 300;
```

```
          myBox._yscale = 300;
          myBox._y = 0 - 210;
          myBox._x = 0 - 1270;
          return;
       }
       else
       {
          if (I === 5)
          {
             myBox._xscale = 250;
             myBox._yscale = 250;
             myBox._y = 0 - 180;
             myBox._x = 0 - 1040;
             return;
          }
          else
          {
             if (I === 6)
             {
                myBox._xscale = 240;
                myBox._yscale = 240;
                myBox._y = 0 - 180;
                myBox._x = 0 - 1000;
                return;
             }
             else
             {
                if (I === 7)
                {
                   myBox._xscale = 200;
                   myBox._yscale = 200;
                   myBox._y = 0 - 150;
                   myBox._x = 0 - 820;
                   return;
                }
                else
                {
                   if (I === 8)
                   {
                      myBox._xscale = 200;
                      myBox._yscale = 200;
                      myBox._y = 0 - 150;
                      myBox._x = 0 - 850;
```

```
          return;
    }
    else
    {
        if (l === 9)
        {
            myBox._xscale = 200;
            myBox._yscale = 200;
            myBox._y = 0 - 150;
            myBox._x = 0 - 830;
            return;
        }
        else
        {
            if (l === 10)
            {
                myBox._xscale = 170;
                myBox._yscale = 170;
                myBox._y = 0 - 120;
                myBox._x = 0 - 720;
                return;
            }
            else
            {
                if (l === 11)
                {
                    myBox._xscale = 160;
                    myBox._yscale = 160;
                    myBox._y = 0 - 120;
                    myBox._x = 0 - 650;
                    return;
                }
                else
                {
                    if (l === 12)
                    {
                        myBox._xscale = 150;
                        myBox._yscale = 150;
                        myBox._y = 0 - 110;
                        myBox._x = 0 - 620;
                        return;
                    }
                }
```

```
                    }
                  }
                }
              }
            }
          }
        }
      }
    }
  }
  myBox._xscale = 130;
  myBox._yscale = 130;
  myBox._y = 0 - 95;
  myBox._x = 0 - 540;
  return;
}
;
killSubliminal = function ()
{
  myStoryMovie.box2.text = "";
  updateAfterEvent();
  _root.myPicture.unloadMovie();
  updateAfterEvent();
  scaleBox(myStoryMovie.box3, myStoryMovie.storyArray[myStoryMovie.i]);
  if (level == 3)
  {
    myIcon.icon.unloadMovie();
  }
  else
  {
    myIcon.attachMovie("icon" + Math.floor(1 + Math.random() * noOfI-
cons), "icon", 3);
    myIcon.icon._xscale = 110;
    myIcon.icon._yscale = 110;
  }
  myStoryMovie.box3.text = myStoryMovie.storyArray[myStoryMovie.i];
  updateAfterEvent();
  clearInterval(killInterval);
  ++myStoryMovie.i;
}
;
updateWords = function ()
{
```

```
myStoryMovie.box3.text = "";
updateAfterEvent();
scaleBox(myStoryMovie.box2, myStoryMovie.spamArray[myStoryMovie.i]);
myStoryMovie.box2.text = myStoryMovie.spamArray[myStoryMovie.i %
spamLimit];
updateAfterEvent();
if (level == 1)
{
   if (myStoryMovie.i % cuePicture == 0)
   {
      _root.attachMovie("imageMovie" + k, "myPicture", 200);
      myPicture._x = 300;
      myPicture._y = 300;
      updateAfterEvent();
      ++k;
      if (k > noOfPictures)
      {
         k = 1;
      }
   }
}
killInterval = setInterval(killSubliminal, subliminalMilliseconds);
if (myStoryMovie.i == myStoryMovie.limit)
{
   myStoryMovie.i = 0;
}
}
;
mainInterval = setInterval(updateWords, textMilliseconds);
stop();
myExitButton.onRelease = function ()
{
   clearInterval(killInterval);
   clearInterval(mainInterval);
   _root.myPicture.unloadMovie();
   myIcon.icon.unloadMovie();
   myStoryMovie.box2.text = "";
   myStoryMovie.box3.text = "";
   my_sound.stop();
   myColor.setRGB(39372);
   gotoAndPlay(54);
}
;
```

NOTES

1. The work is available on the author's personal website, http://www.william poundstone.net/Tachistoscope/index.html, and at http://collection.eliterature.org /1/works/poundstone_project_for_tachistoscope_bottomless_pit.html. The Electronic Literature Collection (ELC) is an online digital anthology published by the Electronic Literature Organization, a nonprofit network for electronic literature publishing and scholarship. Volumes 1 and 2 of the ELC are invaluable resources for anyone interested in digital literature.

2. For the sake of brevity, *Project for Tachistoscope {Bottomless Pit}* will hereafter be identified as *Project*.

3. We use the backslashes here to emphasize the poetic structure of the one-word-at-a-time presentation of text. Subsequent quotations from the text will not use this notation system and, for the sake of ease, will instead present the text as prose.

4. For more on word-pictures combined in the form of "imagetexts," see W.J.T. Mitchell's *Picture Theory: Essays on Verbal and Visual Representation* (1994), 89 in particular.

CHAPTER ONE: *PROJECT*

1. "Lexia" is a key term in literary structuralism and hypertext criticism. In the contemporary sense signifying "a unit of text" the term was popularized by George Landow in *Hypertext: The Convergence of Contemporary Critical Theory and Technology* (Baltimore: Johns Hopkins University Press, 1991). Previously Roland Barthes used "lexias" to describe "units of reading" in *S/Z* (New York: Hill and Wang, 1974, 13). For a more general overview of the vocabulary of electronic literature, see N. Katherine Hayles "Electronic Literature: What Is It?" (The Electronic Literature Organization, 2007).

2. http://www.yhchang.com.

3. See chapter 3 of Jessica Pressman's *Digital Modernism: Making It New in New Media* (New York: Oxford University Press, 2014), wherein I read Young-hae Chang Heavy Industries's Dakota in relation to its inspiration, Ezra Pound's "Canto I" and "Canto II."

4. N. Katherine Hayles, "Deeper into the Machine: The Future of Electronic Literature," Culture Machine 5 (2003): http://svr91.edns1.com/~culturem/index .php/cm/article/viewArticle/245/241.

5. In the 1980s, early consumer animation software like Director (1985) coexisted with early hypertext tools like Hypercard (1985), and creators of electronic

literature often worked in both programs. Hypertext came to the fore of public attention around 1993 (the date of Robert Coover's provocative article in *The New York Times*, "The End of Books"), but scripted animation arguably took five years longer to reach the public. When it did, however, the impact was dramatic. Of course, hypertext continued to exist even after the advent of these tools, but the trend toward multimodal animation-based poetics informed even the most traditionally text-based linked narratives.

6. The ELC (there are currently 2 volumes) is an invaluable resources for anyone interested in digital literature, in part because it provides anthologies of important work in the field and in part because it archives literature with an otherwise a short "shelf life." For these reasons, ELC volumes are taught on course syllabi worldwide and serve as standard editions for many scholarly projects. For ELC 1, see http://collection.eliterature.org/1/. For more information, see The Electronic Literature Organization, http://eliterature.org—a nonprofit, grassroots network for the field of electronic literature.

7. This effect was designed for keyboard-and-mouse personal computers. *Project*'s design predates widespread use of touchscreen devices, whose users would tap "START" rather than moving a cursor toward it.

8. Gerard Genette, *Paratexts: Thresholds of Interpretation*, trans. Jane E. Lewin (Cambridge: Cambridge University Press, 1997).

9. For more on prehistories of electronic literature and digital poetics, see C.T. Funkhouser's *Prehistoric Digital Poetry: An Archaeology of Forms*, 1959–1995 (Tuscaloosa: University of Alabama Press, 2007).

10. We explore the relationship between subliminal advertising and concrete poetry in depth in chapter 4.

11. Poundstone makes this claim in the "author description" of the *Project* in the Electronic Literature Collection, vol. 1. http://collection.eliterature.org/1/works/poundstone__project_for_tachistoscope_bottomless_pit.html.

12. Describing these visual poetic elements as "layers" here is a media-specific metaphor. As Mark will explain, the Flash environment in which *Project* was created uses "layers" in its authoring user interface. Depth here is heuristic rather than material, as the physical arrangement of pixels on a display remain flat—unlike, for example, either layered pigments as painted on canvas or a physical stack of acetate animation cels.

13. See Mitchell's *Picture Theory: Essays on Verbal and Visual Representation*, p. 89 in particular.

14. Like "START," "EXIT" is also reactive—becoming visible whenever the reader's mouse pointer enters its space.

15. In the fourth cycle of the story, the word "psychologists" directly precedes the subliminal word "psychotherapist," underscoring *Project*'s interest in professional decryption of the psyche. We discuss the subliminal text and the interpretation of such word alignments in more detail in chapter 4.

16. "Unikko" was created by Maiji Isola in 1964 for the Finnish design firm

Marimekko (Aav, 2003) and has been in production for almost five decades. In addition to its resonance with 1960s counterculture, the pattern signaled a defiant reclamation of low culture (the tradition of floral prints) as populist art/design.

17. Poundstone's interest in emblems is also visible in his work *New Digital Emblems* (2000). Also see his informative interview with Brian Kim Stefans for *The Iowa Review Web* (2002).

18. These marks may be deceptive, for they do not indicate the only place code has been added to a frame. ActionScript can also be attached to an object placed anywhere on the timeline. For example, code can be attached to a button and not triggered until that button is pressed. Furthermore, that code may affect the appearance or functioning of other frames than the one in which the button is located.

19. Matthew Kirschenbaum originally mentioned this as a panel respondent at "Close Reading the Digital" (Los Angeles, 2011). Later, he discussed the ideas further as part of the HASTAC Scholars online forum "Critical Code Studies" in his post "<!—opening thoughts—>" (1/28/2011).

20. Chun develops this argument in her essay "On 'Sourcery,' or Code as Fetish" in *Configurations* 16.3 (2008) and in her book *Programmed Visions: Software and Memory* (Cambridge, MA: MIT Press, 2011).

21. For more on the role of metaphors in interface design, see Steven Johnson's *Interface Culture: How New Technology Transforms the Way We Create and Communicate* (New York: Basic Books, 1999).

CHAPTER TWO: TACHISTOSCOPE

1. Ruth Benschop, "What Is a Tachistoscope?: Historical Explorations of an Instrument," *Science in Context* 11.1 (1998): 26, emphasis in original.

2. Guy Montrose Whipple, *Manual of Mental and Physical Tests: A Book of Directions Compiled with Special Reference to the Experimental Study of School Children in the Laboratory or Classroom* (Baltimore: Warwick & York, 1910), 222.

3. U.S. Patent Office, patent no. 1526781, date Feb. 17, 1925, p. 1.

4. U.S. Patent Office, patent no. 2410237, Samuel Renshaw, filing date April 6, 1944, p. 1.

5. U.S. Patent Office, patent no. 2157058, Joseph Ray, filing date September 2, 1937.

6. Jonathan Crary, *Suspensions of Perception: Attention, Spectacle, and Modern Culture* (Cambridge, MA: MIT Press, 1999), 304.

7. Friedrich Kittler, *Discourse Networks, 1800/1900*, trans. Michael Metteer with Chris Cullens (Stanford: Stanford University Press, 1990), 223.

8. Kittler writes, "Tachistoscopes measure the automatic response, not synthetic judgments" (*Discourse Networks*, 223). This fact has signal ramifications for his epistemological history. Namely, while the earlier discourse network of 1800 "pretended," Kittler writes, "to be the inwardness and voice of Man," the discourse

network of 1900 "radicalizes the technology of writing in general" (212). The tachistoscope is part of this shift; it serves and represents the kind of cultural transition toward using machines to understand, teach, express, and record the self.

9. Charles Acland, *Swift Viewing: The Popular Life of Subliminal Influence* (Durham: Duke University Press, 2011), 66.

10. For more on media archaeology, see Erkki Huthamo and Jussi Parikka, "Introduction: An Archaeology of Media Archaeology" *in Media Archaeology: Approaches, Applications, and Implications*, eds. Erkki Huhtamo and Jussi Parikka (Berkeley: University of California Press, 2011); indeed, the entire volume is a valuable introduction to the field. For exemplary instances of media archaeology, see Matthew Kirschenbaum's *Mechanisms: New Media and the Forensic Imagination* (Cambridge, MA: MIT Press, 2008); Cornelia Vismann's *Files: Law and Media Technology*, trans. Geoffrey Winthrop-Young (Palo Alto: Stanford University Press, 2008); and Lisa Gitelman's *Scripts, Grooves, and Writing Machines: Representing Technology in the Edison Era* (Palo Alto: Stanford University Press, 1999).

11. Wendy Hui Kyong Chun, "Introduction: Did Somebody Say New Media?" in *New Media, Old Media: A History and Theory Reader*, ed. Wendy Hui Kyong Chun and Thomas Keenan (New York: Routledge, 2006), 9.

12. Jay David Bolter and Richard Grusin, *Remediation: Understanding New Media* (Cambridge, MA: MIT Press, 1999), 45.

13. Marshall McLuhan, *Understanding Media: The Extensions of Man* (1964; Cambridge, MA: MIT Press, 2001), 8.

14. Bolter and Grusin, *Remediation*, 47.

15. A thorough and insightful exploration of Flash can be found in Anastasia Salter and John Murray's *Flash: Building the Interactive Web* (Cambridge, MA: MIT Press, 2014).

16. Charles Arthur describes how Flash "was regularly hated, principally because of corporate websites that would blow half the budget on a fancy animation on the opening page—with an apologetic link saying 'Skip Intro'—that would take you to the useful stuff." See "Flash Is the New Publishing Tool of the Century," *The Guardian*, April 4, 2007, http://www.guardian.co.uk/technology/2007/apr/05/adobe.newmedia. Meanwhile a representative Macromedia press release cited a survey by DoubleClick that found "Macromedia Flash increased branding metrics by 71 percent for three different-sized ads," citing the various Fortune 500 companies from Miller Brewing to Kmart that were boarding the Flash bandwagon. "Fortune 500 Companies Rally Around Macromedia Flash for Online Advertisements," *PR Newswire*, September 26, 2001.

17. Rick Waldron, "The Flash History: How It All Began," *Flash Magazine*, November 20, 2000, http://www.flashmagazine.com/news/detail/the_flash_history/.

18. Macromedia's news releases called Flash "the most distributed software in the history of the Web," claiming that 97 percent of computers operated the Flash Player plugin in 2001. This percentage reemerges fairly consistently, for example, in a 2005 post by Ian Bogost and in Arthur, "Flash Is the New Publishing Tool."

However, the numbers themselves seem to come from Macromedia and later Adobe. Bogost, "MAX 2005—Visual Programming in Macromedia Flash & SOAP Web Services," SYS-CON Media, October 17, 2005, http://events.sys-con.com/node/132935/print.

19. See Lev Manovich, "Generation Flash," in *New Media, Old Media: A History and Theory Reader*, ed. Wendy Hui Kyong Chun and Thomas Keenan (New York: Routledge, 2006), 209–18.

20. Steve Jobs, "Thoughts on Flash," *Apple* (April 2010), http://www.apple.com/hotnews/thoughts-on-flash/.

21. In our work with *Project* we used the Flash decompiler software Trillix, one of dozens available. Custom decompilers exist for many programming languages and, in particular, for several other forms of electronic literature, where they are often used by authoring communities—perhaps most notably for multiple variants of command line interactive fiction. http://www.ifwiki.org/index.php/Decompiler. However, eventually Poundstone sent us his original source files (the code of which appears in Appendix D).

22. For example, I (Mark) created such a version by replacing *Project*'s story text with text from an article about another BP, the 2010 BP (British Petroleum) oil spill off the coast of Louisiana. http://tachistoscope.org/remixes/bp-oil/.

23. We discuss noise and information theory in chapter 4.

24. "Syntax highlighting" is a method of visually formatting different aspects of code (such as functions, values, and comments) in different styles. Authors commonly experience color-formatted code while working in editors such as Flash, and this helps them distinguish elements at a glance while writing and revising. Black and white reproductions of this code use bold, italics, and underlining to convey similar information. For a more authorial view, consult the online version of the code on our website: http://scalar.usc.edu/aclsworkbench/.

25. Although this acceleration behavior was occasionally noted by all three authors, separately, it bore some of the hallmarks of a bug—it vanished when the work was closed and restarted, and we could not reliably re-create the circumstances that caused it to occur (at least at first).

26. For example, *Project* may be played from the DVD edition of the *Electronic Literature Collection*, vol. 1, or it may be downloaded and then played from the desktop. In both cases the data is local but displayed in a web browser.

27. Olga Goriunova and Alexei Shulgin, "Glitch," in *Software Studies: A Lexicon*, ed. Matthew Fuller (Cambridge, MA: MIT Press, 2008), 114.

28. For more on glitches, see Iman Moradi, Ant Scott, Joe Gilmore and Christopher Murphy, *Glitch: Designing Imperfection* (New York: Mark Batty, 2009). See also Peter Krapp, *Noise Channels: Glitch and Error in Digital Culture* (Minneapolis: University of Minnesota Press, 2011).

29. Jeff Donaldson, "Glossing over Thoughts on Glitch. A Poetry of Error." *ArtPulse Magazine*, http://artpulsemagazine.com/glossing-over-thoughts-on-glitch-a-poetry-of-error.

30. Nick Dyer-Witheford and Greig de Peuter, *Games of Empire: Global Capitalism and Video Games* (Minneapolis: University of Minnesota Press, 2009): 211.

31. In certain web browsers this can be accomplished by starting *Project* in a tab, then duplicating that tab. This causes words and icons to disappear entirely in the new copy.

32. This effect can be exploited by right-clicking on the running piece and manipulating Flash's pop-up "Play and Loop" menus. When the work restarts, the entryscreen text persists in unanticipated ways.

33. Note that in the full-scale view of this montage (available on our website: http ://scalar.usc.edu/aclsworkbench/), the text in each screenshot can be read linearly.

34. A normal running length for one story cycle is 9:42; however, *Project*'s running speed may be affected by the hardware, available memory, and processor load of the specific computer where it is played.

35. Two large subfields within visualization are "information visualization" (infovis) and "scientific visualization" (scivis). Several principles have been proposed to distinguish these fields, such as their use for hypothesis confirmation (scivis) versus data exploration (infovis), or the dimensionality of representation being determined by either the original data (scivis) or by the designer (infovis). While we have no disciplinary stake, our uses of visualization here largely follow an exploratory mode most associated with infovis.

36. Lev Manovich, "What Is Visualization?" reprinted by Jaques Corby-Tuech, Data Visualization (blog), November 9, 2010, http://www.datavisualisation.org /2010/11/lev-manovich-what-is-visualization/.

37. For example, Scottish engineer and infovis pioneer William Playfair is commonly credited with publishing both the first bar chart (1786) and first pie chart (1801). Both use reduction—import/exports become rectangles; nations become wedges. In a happy coincidence, William Playfair shares a surname with *Project* geologist Nelson Playfair.

38. Although it is grammatically more jarring than flowing, this looping text enjambment in *Project* may still recall the famous concluding / beginning of *Finnegans Wake* by James Joyce: "a long the / riverrun." This connection is explored in chapter 4.

39. Moretti, *Graphs, Maps, Trees* (New York: Verso, 2005), 1.

40. Moretti, *Graphs, Maps, Trees*, 2a.

41. Moretti, *Graphs, Maps, Trees*, 4.

42. Franco Moretti, *Atlas of the European Novel 1800–1900* (1997; New York: Verso, 2007), 3.

43. Robert Poole, *Earthrise: How Man First Saw the Earth* (New Haven: Yale University Press, 2008).

44. Marshall McLuhan, Interview on *The David Frost Show* on ABC, 1972, in *Video McLuhan,* 3, written and narrated by Tom Wolfe. Acland describes *Sputnik* as a signal moment in the history of the tachistoscope as well. He describes the American public receiving news of *Sputnik* as indicating a systematic failure of

the American educational system that established the need for new, technologically mediated educational resources, such as tachistoscopic devices for speed-reading. See Acland, *Swift Viewing*, chapter 7: "From Mass Brainwashing to Rapid Mass Learning."

45. Michel de Certeau, *The Practice of Everyday Life*, trans. Steven Randall (Berkeley: University of California Press, 1984), 92.

46. De Certeau, *The Practice of Everyday Life*, 92.

47. De Certeau, *The Practice of Everyday Life*, 92.

48. De Certeau, *The Practice of Everyday Life*, 100.

49. De Certeau, *The Practice of Everyday Life*, 93.

50. De Certeau, *The Practice of Everyday Life*, 92.

CHAPTER THREE: BOTTOMLESS PIT

1. Another marker of this limit is "a magnesium flare star that fell from the sky into the Pit remaining visible up to 4 minutes." This seems to be a similar distance—at least, the common formula for free fall gives a plausible scenario in which the flare falls 22,000 feet in 4 minutes. For an example of this specific free-fall scenario as computed by the Wolfram Alpha webservice, see: http://tinyurl.com/projectflare1.

2. Note that *Project* presents distances that are incredible yet not impossible—e.g., Kellogg does not descend beyond the point at which he should have already emerged on the other side of the world. We consider the role of the impossible in this literary work and others like it, in the section titled "Genre" in this chapter.

3. The word "nidificatory" is unusual, and most commonly found in ninteenth-century natural history and science writing, as for example in Charles Darwin's "The Foundations of the Origin of Species" (1844): "the nidificatory instincts may have been acquired by the gradual selection, during thousands and thousands of generations, of the eggs and young."

4. I take the notion of "deep time" in media archaeology from Siegfried Zielinski. In *Deep Time of the Media* (2006), he performs media archaeology that is not devoted to progressive history and origin stories but is instead based on an understanding that time as more cyclical than linear. Adopting a concept of geological time that understands the earth to be a self-renewing mass, Zielinski performs media archaeology in way that makes possible the backward temporal examination of digital literature and medieval mnemonics that I pursue here.

5. Mary Carruthers, *The Book of Memory: A Study of Memory in Medieval Culture* (1990; Cambridge University Press, 2008), 42.

6. Carruthers, *The Book of Memory*, 42.

7. Carruthers, *The Book of Memory*, 43.

8. This popular paraphrase is from Friedrich Nietzsche's *Beyond Good and Evil*, Oxford World Classics 2008 edition, trans. Marion Fabor: "Anyone who fights

with monsters should take care that he does not in the process become a monster. And if you gaze for long into an abyss, the abyss gazes back into you." (Aphorism 146, p. 86). In the original, *Jenseits von Gut und Böse: Vorspiel einer Philosophie der Zukunft* (1886), Nietzsche's "abyss" is "der Abgrund", lit. "non" + "ground." (Aphorism 146, p. 98).

9. We created our volume views using the program ImageJ, an open source image processing and analysis application. ImageJ was originally funded by the U.S. National Institutes of Health, and it is now employed in both biological and astronomical science applications. Its Volume Viewer plugin was first developed in 2005 by Kai Uwe Barthel of Internationale Medieninformatik, HTW Berlin.

10. The concept of "unconscious optics" inspires later critical discourse about the "optical unconscious" and aesthetic perception, most notably in Rosalind Krauss's *The Optical Unconscious* (Cambridge, MA: MIT Press, 1996).

11. Walter Benjamin, "The Work of Art in the Age of Mechanical Reproduction," in *Illuminations: Essays and Reflections*, ed. Hannah Arendt, trans. Harry Zohn (New York: Schocken Books, 1969), 236.

12. Benjamin, "The Work of Art," 237.

13. Benjamin, "The Work of Art," 236. Friedrich Kittler makes a similar claim about audio recording technology in the "Gramophone" section in *Gramophone, Film, Typewriter*.

14. Julian Sefton-Green, "Timelines, Timeframes and Special Effects: Software and Creative Media Production," *Education, Communication & Information* 5.1 (March 2005), 109.

15. A MovieClip is an object that is comprised of a set of frames which can be placed on the stage within one or more other frames. For example, an artist might place a MovieClip of a flowing river into one or more frames on the overall timeline to avoid the need to create the same animation twice. MovieClips, which can be resized or rotated, loop through their animation.

16. The fly is captured in Jackson Pollock's *One: Number 31, 1950*, http://tiny url.com/moma-pollock-fly.

17. Poundstone, "Falling into The Void," *Project*.

18. Poundstone, "Falling into The Void."

19. Kittler describes the psychoanalyst acting like a gramophone, recording everything the patient says, including nonsense: "For that reason, it is consistent to define psychoanalytic case studies, in spite of their written, format, as media technologies" (*Gramophone, Film, Typewriter*, 89).

20. Freud, "Dream-Distortion," *The Interpretation of Dreams*, trans. Joyce Crick (1899; Oxford UP, 1999), chapter 4, p.124, italics in original.

21. Sigmund Freud, *A General Introduction to Psychoanalysis*, trans. G. Stanley Hall (1920; New York: Boni and Liveright, 1925), 160.

22. Freud, *A General Introduction*, 162., italics in original.

23. Freud, *A General Introduction*.

24. Freud, *A General Introduction*, 163.

25. See Bersani, "Is the Rectum a Grave?" *October* 43 (Winter 1987): 197–222.

26. Leo Bersani's "Is the Rectum a Grave?"

27. *The Oxford Dictionary of Literary Terms* identifies Baron Münchhausen as an early exemplar of this genre and notes its development, in nineteenth-century American fiction, with Mark Twain and George Washington Harris, within a broader folk context. The tall tale reemerges in the twentieth century in its own peculiar forms in postmodern and magic realism, which interest us here. See Chris Baldick, "tall tale." *The Oxford Dictionary of Literary Terms* (New York: Oxford University Press, 2008).

28. From "The Metamorphosis of Fiction Space: Magic Realism," in *Magic Realism: Theory, History, Community*, ed. Lois Parkinson Zamora and Wendy B. Faris (Durham, NC: Duke University Press, 1995), 210.

29. In an essay on several postmodern American writers, Melissa Stewart classifies Donald Barthelme with the authors of magical realism. She could easily be describing Poundstone when she discusses Barthelme's use of "magical beings, events, and forces to explore what we might call the "urban irrational," and how the individual and the community may accept the irrational without denying or surrendering responsibility for their actions" (479). Melissa Stewart, "Roads of 'Exquisite Mysterious Muck': The Magical Journey through the City in William Kennedy's *Ironweed*, John Cheever's 'The Enormous Radio,' and Donald Barthelme's 'City Life,'" in *Magical Realism: Theory, History, Community*, eds. Lois Parkinson Zamora and Wendy B. Faris (Durham, NC: Duke University Press, 1995), 477–95.

30. William Scott, "Donald Barthelme and the Death of Fiction" in *Critical Essays on Donald Barthelme*, ed. Richard F. Patterson (New York: Maxwell Macmillan International, 1992), 79.

31. The balloon thus acts like the eponymous jar in Wallace Stevens's poem "Anecdote of the Jar" (1919), which, when placed on a hillside in Tennessee serves to reconfigure perspective of the place around its presence: "It took dominion every where" (line 9).

32. Maurice Couturier and Régis Durand, "Donald Barthelme," *Contemporary Writers* (London: New York: Methuen, 1982), 62.

33. William Poundstone quoted in Brian Kim Stefans, "An Interview with William Poundstone," *The Iowa Review Web* (April 2002). http://web.archive.org/web/20131004173119/http://iowareview.uiowa.edu/TIRW/TIRW_Archive/tirweb/feature/poundstone/poundstone.htm.

34. Poundstone quoted in Stefans, "An Interview."

35. For more on iconology, see Erwin Panofsky's *Studies in Iconology: Humanistic Themes in the Art of the Renaissance* (New York: Oxford University Press, 1939) and W.J.T. Mitchell's *Picture Theory: Essays on Verbal and Visual Representation* (Chicago: University of Chicago Press, 1994).

36. Many more types of z-projection are possible. For example, the "maximum" projection creates a combined image of brightest value for each pixel. For *Project*, this renders as a simple white square, because every pixel on the screen

becomes bright at some point in time. This contrasts with the minimum projection, which reveals a specific pattern rather than a simple black square. Light is pervasive in the work, while dark is not.

CHAPTER FOUR: SUBLIMINAL SPAM

1. *Picnic*, directed by Joshua Logan, 1955. It is worth noting that Vicary supposedly spliced words about eating and drinking into a movie whose title and plot evokes these acts. This kind of association between overt and subliminal messages was later discovered to be key to effective semantic priming. For more on the cultural reception of Vicary's stunt, see Acland, *Swift Viewing*.

2. *The Manchurian Candidate* directed by Richard Condon, 1959, came out two years after Vicary's stunt and expresses these concerns.

3. George Horsley Smith, *Motivation Research in Advertising and Marketing* (New York: McGraw-Hill, 1954), 3, emphasis in original.

4. Smith, *Motivation Research*, 3, emphasis in original.

5. Smith, *Motivation Research*, 3.

6. Smith, *Motivation Research*, 3–4, emphasis in original.

7. Vance Packard, *The Hidden Persuaders*, 34.

8. Packard, *The Hidden Persuaders*, 35.

9. Packard, *The Hidden Persuaders*, 36.

10. Wilson Bryan Key, *Subliminal Seduction*, 10.

11. Key, *Subliminal Seduction*, 18.

12. Marshall McLuhan, *The Mechanical Bride: Folklore of Industrial Man* (Gingko Press, 1951).

13. Marshall McLuhan and Quentin Fiore, *The Medium Is the Massage: An Inventory of Effects* (London: Penguin Books, 1967), 26.

14. Poundstone, "Author's Statement," *The Electronic Literature Collection*, vol. 1.

15. The "coincidence" of this manifesto appearing in 1957 may involve a bit of poetic license. "Plano-Pilôto para Poesia Concreta" is generally cited as appearing in 1958 (*Noigandres* no. 4, São Paulo), while Augusto de Campos had previously published an earlier draft of similar text under the title "Poesía Concreta: um Manifesto" in the November/December 1956 issue of another venue (*ad - arquitetura e decoração*, no. 20, São Paulo)—respectively too late and too soon to align with the date of Vicary's hoax. More generally, a date on coining the term "concrete poetry" is now often pushed back to 1955, 1953, or earlier, with credit given to Augusto de Campus, Haroldo de Campos, Eugen Gomringer, or Öyvind Fahlström. However, for the rhetorical purposes of *Project*, what matters is not an earliest origin, but a "coeval" simultaneity. See Mary Ellen Solt's *Concrete Poetry: A World View* (1968).

16. This color reproduction of "beba coca cola" (with translation) is the one made available through the UbuWeb "Historical" collection, which documents "the trajectory of visual and concrete poetry . . . from 1516, and continuing all the way into the late 1970s." It is also the version referenced by *Project*, which links to

the UbuWeb copy but does not contain a reproduction of it. http://www.ubu.com/historical/pignatari/pignatari1.html.

17. The ice cubes of this whiskey advertisement and their (again purported) message were made famous by appearing on the cover of Wilson Bryan Key's book *Subliminal Seduction*.

18. According to the *Oxford Dictionary of Psychology*, "In a task involving recall, recognition, or some other form of cognitive performance, the provision of a contextual cue, prime, or prompt [. . .] provides information about either the identity or the time of appearance of a target stimulus and that may facilitate a response (in facilitative priming) or inhibit it (in inhibitory priming). . . . Associative priming that is dependent on verbal meaning, as when the prime bread is provided for the target butter, is called semantic priming." See Andrew M. Colman, "Priming," in *A Dictionary of Psychology*, 3rd ed. (New York: Oxford University Press, 2008), http://www.oxfordreference.com.libproxy.usc.edu/view/10.1093/acref/9780199534067.001.0001/acref-9780199534067-e-6635.

19. In math, a "variable" such as *x* is a symbolic name given to a quantity that may change. In computer programming, a variable is likewise a symbolic name—in this case, a label (e.g., "spamVar") whose name serves as a reference to some storage location in memory (e.g., a string of text loaded from the file BP.txt), with the named memory acting like a container. Variable names are seldom visible while a program runs, yet they can give insight into how the programmers conceptualized the code.

20. In fact, a decompiler is not needed to discover this variable name because it also appears in the file BP.txt.

21. Jussi Parikka and Tony Sampson, "On Anomalous Objects of Digital Culture: An Introduction," *The Spam Book: On Viruses, Porn, and Other Anomalies from the Dark Side of Digital Culture*, eds. Parikka and Sampson (Cresskill, NJ: Hampton Press, 2009) 3.

22. Brad Templeton, "Origin of the Term 'Spam' to Mean Net Abuse," Templetons.com, June 30, 2012, http://www.templetons.com/brad/spamterm.html.

23. Spam is meat torn from its history: in its industrial packaged form, it can remain edible for years. Thus, like its digital counterpart, spam is both part of and extracted from the particular historical context in which it operates.

24. A transcript from the skit reads, "Well, there's egg and bacon; egg sausage and bacon; egg and spam; egg bacon and spam; egg bacon sausage and spam; spam bacon sausage and spam; spam egg spam spam bacon and spam; spam sausage spam spam bacon spam tomato and spam." Terry Jones and Michael Palin. "Spam." Episode 25. *Monty Python's Flying Circus*, December 15, 1970, television.

25. David Henkin, *The Postal Age: The Emergence of Modern Communications in Nineteenth-Century America* (Chicago: University of Chicago Press, 2006), 157.

26. Henkin, *The Postal Age*, 157.

27. Henkin, *The Postal Age*, 157.

28. Parikka and Sampson, "On Anomalous Objects of Digital Culture, An Introduction," in *The Spam Book*, 4.

29. Alexander R. Galloway and Eugene Thacker, "On Narcolepsy," in *The Spam Book*, 251–63. The end result is a passive evolution of a poetic form. Galloway and Thacker write, "The poetics of spam, much like Surrealist automatism, obtains its uncanny quality through a strange active passivity" (263).

30. http://www.williampoundstone.net/Spam/Spam.html.

31. http://www.paulgraham.com/spam.html.

32. Poundstone paraphrases (or misquotes) Williams, for Williams writes, "No ideas but in things" in "Paterson" (*The Dial* 82.2, February 1927) and later in "A Sort of Song" (*The Wedge*, 1944) and in "Paterson: Book I" (1946).

33. Although spamVar words do not recall urban legends, the storyVar narrative bears some striking resemblances to urban legends about uncanny pits. These legends—such as "Mel's Hole" or "The Well to Hell"—still circulate endlessly via e-mail. In a reversal, the "story" resembles conventional spam more than the "spam" itself.

34. For example, Oulipo member Jean Lescure's procedure "N+7" (noun+7) transforms the nouns from a source text by shifting each seven entries forward in a dictionary or encyclopedia. However, the spam words include proper nouns not found in dictionaries, and a higher proportion of rare words than found in an encyclopedia.

35. IEEE is the Institute of Electrical and Electronics Engineers, and describes itself as "the world's largest professional organization for the advancement of technology." http://www.ieee.org/index.html

36. In *Mechanisms: New Media and the Forensic Imagination* (Cambridge, MA: MIT Press, 2007), Matthew Kirschenbaum coins the term "forensic materiality" for methods of investigating digital works in terms of their material particularities: "Forensic materiality rests upon the principle of individualization (basic to modern forensic science and criminalistics), the idea that no two things in the physical world are ever exactly alike" (10).

37. For a survey of select literary stylometric studies since the 1800s, including of Homer's Odyssey, the Bible, and Shakespeare, see Anthony Kenny, *The Computation of Style* (Oxford; New York: Pergamon Press. 1982) chapter 1.

38. We are not simply transforming poetry or prose into the form of a list, however, as the spam text already resembles a list. Instead, our method is to filter, sort, and quantify words in list form.

39. Stop word lists often eliminate articles, pronouns, conjunctions, and prepositions, which are both the most common and the least distinctive aspects of English. Although all words may be of interest in analyzing poetry, such studies (e.g. "does Shakespeare use 'the' more or less than his contemporaries?") are seldom productive unless dealing with an extremely large corpus. Our analysis used a modified SMART stop-list. Ide & Salton, *The SMART Retrieval System* (Prentice Hall, 1971).

40. WFA results were calculated using AntConc 3.2.2, a cross-platform concordance program by Lawrence Anthony. http://www.laurenceanthony.net/software/antconc/

41. Appearances of the Pit do include a few liminal cases worth noting. The Pit is once termed an "abyss" and is referenced three times as "it"—although only after "the Pit" appears in the same line. A lowercase "this pit" appears once, asserting that the Well of Conklin is not the Pit. The letters p-i-t also appear twice, when Conklin poisons the well "out of spite" and in the "pitch black" community. Neither word shares a syllable or its etymology with the word "pit," yet each still visually echoes the Pit.

42. Of the many projects that have been influenced by Joe Brainard's *I Remember*, one notable homage is *Je me souviens* (1978) by Georges Perec of the Oulipo.

43. Technically in "Howl" the top words are "the" (218) and "of" (139)—the same as in *Project*, and similar to most examples in English. Here we deal with only notable words after all "stop words" are removed. This leaves "Howl" with "who" (68) followed by "Moloch" (39), and, shortly thereafter, "Rockland" (19).

44. "Howl" is longer than *Project*, but their ratios of repetition are nearly identical: (68 / 2914) / (59 / 2483) = 98%.

45. Granted, "Howl" is certainly not the most repetitious of poems. For an extreme outlier that puts both Poundstone and Ginsberg in perspective, Tristan Tzara's "dada manifesto on feeble love and bitter love: XVI" (1920) simply repeats the word "howl" two hundred times in a row, appending only the line, "Who still considers himself very likeable."

46. Of these 223 spam words, *Project* will only display the first 200, as discussed in chapter 3. However, running our analysis on either 200 or 223 makes little difference in this case—either set contains 99 percent unique lemma.

47. The word "ah" appears twice in the spam (words 75 and 84). This exception in the design of *Project* is hard to account for, and might even be the result of an error—perhaps a double entry while typing, or an artifact of the admonition "ah ah" being written as a phrase before a list of words was scrambled in a way that separated them. Whatever the cause, "ah" is the spam's lone repetition.

48. Words that are typical of almost all English ("the," "of," "and," etc.) are removed by our stop words filter. While filtering the story dramatically changes our results, the spam is unchanged, as all words are atypical.

49. Claude Shannon, "A Mathematical Theory of Communication," *Bell System Technical Journal* 27.3 (1948): 379–423. http://cm.bell-labs.com/cm/ms/what/shannonday/shannon1948.pdf

50. William R. Paulson, *The Noise of Culture: Literature Texts in a World of Information* (Ithaca: Cornell University Press, 1988), ix.

51. Marjorie Perloff, *Radical Artifice: Writing Poetry in the Age of Media* (Chicago: University of Chicago Press, 1991), 187.

52. A fourth shared word, "distant," occurs past the two-hundredth spam source word, and so will never be loaded or displayed by *Project*. We exclude it to focus our consideration of how spam and story interact on the screen.

53. Specifically, "pitchblende" is mined uraninite, later processed into yellowcake (or urania) and further refined into uranium for nuclear applications.

Notably, such materials became notorious shortly before the publication of *Project*. In his January 2003 State of the Union address, President Bush cited Iraq's attempt to purchase yellowcake from Niger as evidence of a nuclear weapons program and, hence, as justification for a U.S. invasion of Iraq. It is particularly relevant in a work about Vicary's hoax and American paranoia that the Nigerian documents were actually forgeries. Later that year, the entire Iraq yellowcake incident was revealed to be a hoax.

54. Such a macro-cycle of playthroughs will take *Project* some thirty hours to complete.

55. We can describe this effect as follows: 2,483 mod 200 = 83. Because 83 shares no factors with 200, modulo 200 of all multiples of 83 will be unique up to 83×200. Thus the first spam cycle is offset by 0, then 83, 166, 49, 132, 15 . . . 117, then zero, in a nonrepeating sequence of two hundred different offsets. Notably, 44 other prime numbers could produce such an effect—not few enough for us to discount that such a story length might have oooccurred by chance (approximately 23 percent), but few enough that *Project*'s final design is both unusual and highly sensitive to change.

56. Such a typescript for *Project* would be roughly 4,000 manuscript pages: 4,966 words per story cycle (see Appendix B: Complete word output (first story cycle) × 200 cycles = 993,200 words. At 250 words per page, this is approximately 3,973 pages.

57. Despite their fixed order, these spam words still vary. Their display color may be black or a (more noticeable) white, and these colorations will vary unpredictably with each new playthrough.

58. When read as a cut-up, the aporetic strategy of *Project* may appear to be less a reworking of concrete poetry than a recapitulation of earlier forms, such as Tzara's "dada manifesto on feeble love and bitter love" (1920), which opens: "opening = sardanapalus / one = suitcase / woman = women / trousers = water."

59. Merriam-Webster's *Collegiate Dictionary*, 11th ed., s.v. "commode" and "commodious."

60. Steven Pinker, *The Language Instinct: How the Mind Creates Language* (New York: William Morrow, 1994; New York: Harper Perennial, 1995), 212.

61. Pinker, *The Language Instinct*, 213.

62. Pinker, *The Language Instinct*, 210.

63. Pinker, *The Language Instinct*, 214.

64. Stanley Fish, *Surprised by Sin: The Reader in Paradise Lost*, 2nd ed. (1967; Cambridge, MA: Harvard University Press, 1997), 35.

65. In the code, the spam array is advanced in this line: myStoryMovie.box2
.text=myStoryMovie.spamArray[myStoryMovie.i%spamLimit];

66. Samuel Foote's nonsense passage was performed live in 1754 as a memory challenge for his colleague, actor Charles Macklin, and later published as a poem. The original is attested in Maria Edgeworth's novel *Harry and Lucy Concluded*, vol. 2 (1825). In the novel, Harry and Lucy's father reenacts Foote's test by first

challenging his children to memorize a passage that will read out loud as quickly as possible, including the phrase "and the grand Panjandrum himself, with the little round button at top" (153). However, the word creates an aporia. The children are so surprised by being already familiar with a more recent use of "panjandrum" as a name for a flower (46–50) that they find themselves momentarily distracted and are left unable to remember anything else.

67. The Grand Panjandrum was prototyped as a huge explosive-packed wheel, making literal the nonsense phrase that ends Foote's passage: "till the gunpowder ran out at the heels of their boots." Both World War I and World War II saw a common practice of naming new weapons with previously innocuous terms (e.g., "tank") in order to obscure military communiques. The Grand Panjandrum, by contrast, commands attention, leading some military historians to speculate that the never-deployed weapon project was a hoax intended to distract the enemy from the imminent Normandy invasion. On stage, in war, and as spam, the word "panjandrum" is itself a distraction.

68. Jacques Derrida, *Aporias*, trans. Thomas Dutoit (Stanford: Stanford University Press, 1993), 12.

69. Jacques Derrida, *Paper Machine: Cultural Memory in the Present*, trans. Rachel Bowlby (2001; Stanford University Press, 2005), 91.

70. For Jameson on the symptom, see *The Political Unconscious: Narrative as a Socially Symbolic Act* (Ithaca, NY: Cornell University Press, 1981) and the recent response to it by Stephen Best and Sharon Marcus, "Surface Reading: An Introduction," in the special issue of the journal *Representations* that they coedited, titled "How We Read Now" (108, Fall 2009). There are certainly differences in the way Deconstruction and the New Criticism approach and consider the aporia. J. Douglas Kneale explains, "Unlike ambiguity, irony, or paradox" in the New Criticism, "these incompatibilities [in Deconstruction] cannot be harmonized in the service of textual 'unity' or 'integrity,'" in "Deconstruction" in *The Johns Hopkins Guide to Literary Theory & Criticism*, eds. Michael Groden and Martin Kreiswirth (Baltimore: Johns Hopkins University Press, 1994), 186.

CONCLUSION

1. For recent examples, see Burdick et al.'s *Digital_Humanities* (Cambridge, MA: MIT Press, 2012), as well as Montfort et al's *10 PRINT CHR$(205.5+RND(1)); : GOTO 10* (Cambridge, MA: MIT Press, 2012) (in which two authors of this work participated).

2. Our shared online documents platform was Google Docs, which was later incorporated into Google Drive. Over the course of the project, we also used a number of other resource-sharing methods, including hosting files on a private webserver and using the Dropbox cloud-based file synchronization service.

3. Kathleen Fitzpatrick, *Planned Obsolescence: Publishing, Technology, and the Future of the Academy* (Ithaca: New York University Press 2011), 185.

4. The American Council of Learned Societies works toward "the advancement of humanistic studies in all fields of learning in the humanities" ("Our Mission," ACLS, http://www.acls.org/mission/). The ACLS mission to advance the humanities fits well with our sense of our work not as displacing traditional approaches but helping them to evolve to include digital reading tools. Our funded proposal is titled "Transmedial Collaboration: Literary Criticism as Digital Humanities Scholarship."

5. ANVC Scalar is a powerful, free, and open source publishing platform built on a relational database. For more information see http://scalar.usc.edu/scalar/features/.

6. http://scalar.usc.edu/aclsworkbench/reading-project/.

BIBLIOGRAPHY

Aav, Marianne. *Marimekko: Fabrics, Fashion, Architecture*. New Haven: Yale University Press, 2003.

Acland, Charles. *Swift Viewing: The Popular Life of Subliminal Influence*. Durham: Duke University Press, 2011.

Arthur, Charles. "'Flash Is the New Publishing Tool of the Century'" in *The Guardian*, April 4, 2007.

Barthelme, Donald. "The Balloon." In *Unspeakable Practices, Unnatural Acts*. New York: Farrar, Straus and Giroux, 1968.

Barthes, Roland. *S/Z:* New York: Hill and Wang, 1974.

Benjamin, Walter. "The Work of Art in the Age of Mechanical Reproduction." In *Illuminations*. Ed. Hannah Arendt. Trans. by Harry Zohn. New York: Schocken Books, 1968.

Benschop, Ruth. "What Is a Tachistoscope? Historical Explorations of an Instrument." *Science in Context* 11.1 (1998): 23–50.

Bersani, Leo "Is the Rectum a Grave?" *October* 43 (Winter 1987): 197–222.

Best, Stephen and Sharon Marcus, "Surface Reading: An Introduction," *Representations* 108 (Fall 2009): 1–21.

Bogost, Ian. "MAX 2005 – Visual Programming in Macromedia Flash & SOAP Web Services." In *Ulitzer: Jim Webber*, October 17, 2005.

Bolter, Jay David and Richard Grusin. *Remediation: Understanding New Media*. Cambridge, MA: MIT Press, 1999.

Burdick, Anne, Johanna Drucker, Peter Lunenfeld, Todd Presner, and Jeffrey Schnapp. *Digital_Humanities*. Cambridge, MA: MIT Press, 2012.

Carruthers, Mary. *The Book of Memory: A Study of Memory in Medieval Culture*. Cambridge: Cambridge University Press, 1992.

Chun, Wendy Hui Kyong. "Introduction: Did Somebody Say New Media?" In *New Media, Old Media: A History and Theory Reader*. Eds. Wendy Hui Kyong Chun and Thomas Keenan. New York: Routledge, 2006. 1–10.

———. "On 'Sorcery,' or Code as Fetish." In *Configurations* 16.3 (2008): 229–324

———. *Programmed Visions: Software as Memory*. Cambridge, MA: MIT Press, 2011.

Colman, Andrew M. "Priming." In *A Dictionary of Psychology*. Oxford: Oxford University Press, 2008.

Coover, Robert. "The End of Books." *New York Times*, June 21, 1992.

Couturier, Maurice and Régis Durand, "Donald Barthelme." In *Contemporary Writers*. London, New York: Methuen, 1982.

Crary, Jonathan. *Suspensions of Perception: Attention, Spectacle, and Modern Culture*. Cambridge, MA: MIT Press, 1999.

————. *Techniques of the Observer: On Vision and Modernity in the 19th Century*. Cambridge, MA: MIT Press, 1990.

De Certeau, Michel. "Walking in the City." *The Practice of Everyday Life*. Trans. Steven Rendall. Berkeley: University of California Press, 1984.

Derrida, Jacques. *Aporias*. Trans. Thomas Dutoit. Stanford: Stanford University Press, 1993.

————. "As If It Were Possible, 'Within Such Limits'." *Paper Machine: Cultural Memory in the Present*. Trans. Rachel Bowlby. 2001. Stanford: Stanford University Press, 2005.

Donaldson, Jeff. "Glossing over Thoughts on Glitch. A Poetry of Error." *ArtPulse Magazine*. http://artpulsemagazine.com/glossing-over-thoughts-on-glitch-a -poetry-of-error.

Dyer-Witheford, Nick and Greig de Peuter. *Games of Empire: Global Capitalism and Video Games*. Minneapolis: University of Minnesota Press, 2009.

Electronic Literature Collection, Vol. 2. http://collection.eliterature.org/2/.

Estes, Adam Clark, "Adobe Quietly Surrender to Steve Jobs, Builds Flash Alternative." *Atlantic Wire*. August 1, 2011. http://www.theatlanticwire.com/technology /2011/08/adobe-quietly-surrenders-steve-jobs-builds-flash-alternative/40669/.

Fish, Stanley. *Surprised by Sin: The Reader in Paradise Lost*. 1967. 2nd ed. Cambridge, MA: Harvard University Press, 1997.

Fitzpatrick, Kathleen. *Planned Obsolescence: Publishing, Technology, and the Future of the Academy*. New York: New York University Press, 2011.

Freud, Sigmund. "Dream-Distortion." In *The Interpretation of Dreams*. Trans. Joyce Crick. Oxford: Oxford University Press, 1999. Originally published in 1899.

————. *A General Introduction to Psychoanalysis*. Trans. G. Stanley Hall. New York: Boni and Liveright, 1925.

Funkhouser, C.T. *Prehistoric Digital Poetry: An Archaeology of Forms, 1959–1995*. Tuscaloosa: University of Alabama Press, 2007.

Galloway, Alexander R. and Eugene Thacker. "On Narcolepsy." In *The Spam Book: On Viruses, Porn, and Other Anomalies from the Dark Side of Digital Culture*. Eds. Jussi Parikka and Tony D. Sampson. Cresskill, NJ: Hampton Press, 2009. 251–63.

Genette, Gerard. *Paratexts: Thresholds of Interpretation*. Trans. Jane E. Lewin. Cambridge: Cambridge University Press, 1997.

Gitelman, Lisa. *Scripts, Grooves, and Writing Machines: Representing Technology in the Edison Era*. Stanford: Stanford University Press, 1999.

Godnig, Edward C. "The Tachistoscope: Its History & Usages." *Journal of Behavioral Optometry* 14.2 (2003): 39–42.

Goriunova, Olga and Alexei Shulgin. "Glitch." In *Software Studies: A Lexicon*. Ed. Matthew Fuller. Cambridge, MA: MIT Press, 2008. 114.

Graham, Paul. "A Plan for Spam." 2002. http://www.paulgraham.com/spam.html.

Hayles, N. Katherine. "Deeper into the Machine: The Future of Electronic Literature." *Culture Machine* 5 (2003). http://www.culturemachine.net/index.php /cm/article/viewArticle/245/241.

————. "Hyper and Deep Attention: The Generational Divide in Cognitive Modes." *Profession* (2007): 187–99.

————. *Writing Machines.* Cambridge, MA: MIT Press, 2002.

Henkin, David. *The Postal Age: The Emergence of Modern Communications in Nineteenth-Century America.* Chicago: University of Chicago Press, 2006.

Huthamo, Erkki and Jussi Parikka. "Introduction: An Archaeology of Media Archaeology." In *Media Archaeology: Approaches, Applications, and Implications.* Eds. Erkki Huhtamo and Jussi Parikka. Berkeley: University of California Press, 2011.

Jameson, Fredric. *The Political Unconscious: Narrative as a Socially Symbolic Act.* Ithaca, NY: Cornell University Press, 1981.

Jobs, Steve. "Thoughts on Flash," *Apple* (April 2010). http://www.apple.com/hot news/thoughts-on-flash/.

Johnson, Steven. *Interface Culture: How New Technology Transforms the Way We Create and Communicate.* New York: Basic Books, 1997.

Kenny, Anthony. *The Computation of Style: An Introduction to Statistics for Students of Literature and Humanities.* Oxford: Pergamon Press, 1982.

Key, Wilson Bryan. *Subliminal Seduction: Ad Media's Manipulation of a Not So Innocent America.* New York: Signet, 1973.

Kirschenbaum, Matthew. *Mechanisms: New Media and the Forensic Imagination.* Cambridge, MA: MIT Press, 2008.

————. "Response: Close Reading the Digital." MLA Convention 2011. Los Angeles. January 8, 2011.

Kittler, Friedrich. *Discourse Networks 1800/1900.* Trans. Michael Metteer, with Chris Cullens. 1985. Stanford: Stanford University Press, 1990.

————. *Gramophone, Film, Typewriter.* Trans. Geoffrey Winthrop-Young and Michael Wutz. 1986. Stanford: Stanford University Press, 1999.

Kneale, J. Douglas. "Deconstruction." In *The Johns Hopkins Guide to Literary Theory & Criticism.* Eds. Michael Groden and Martin Kreiswirth. Baltimore: Johns Hopkins University Press, 1994. 185–91.

Krapp, Peter. *Noise Channels: Glitch and Error in Digital Culture.* Minneapolis: University of Minnesota Press, 2011.

Krapp, Steven and Walter Benn Michaels, "Against Theory." *Critical Inquiry* 8.4 (Summer 1982), reprinted in *Against Theory: Literary Studies and the New Pragmatism.* Ed. W.J.T. Mitchell. Chicago: University of Chicago Press, 1985. 11–30.

Krauss, Rosalind. *The Optical Unconscious.* Cambridge, MA: MIT Press, 1996.

Landow, George. *Hypertext: The Convergence of Contemporary Critical Theory and Technology.* Baltimore: Johns Hopkins University Press, 1991.

Macromedia. *Macromedia Flash 5: Using Flash.* San Francisco: Macromedia, 2000.

Manovich, Lev. "Generation Flash." In *New Media, Old Media: A History and Theory Reader.* Eds. Wendy Hui Kyong Chun and Thomas Keenan. New York: Routledge, 2006. 209–18.

————. "What Is Visualization?" Reprinted by Jaques. Data Visualization (blog),

November 9, 2010. http://www.datavisualisation.org/2010/11/lev-manovich
-what-is-visualization/.

Marino, Mark C. "Critical Code Studies." *Electronic Book Review*, December 4,
2006. http://www.electronicbookreview.com/thread/electropoetics/codology.

Márquez, Gabriel García. "A Very Old Man with Enormous Wings." In *Leaf Storm
and Other Stories*. New York: Harper Perennial, 1972.

McLuhan, Marshall. *The Mechanical Bride: Folklore of Industrial Man*. Berkeley:
Gingko Press, 1951.

———. *Understanding Media: The Extensions of Man*. 1964. Cambridge, MA: MIT
Press, 2001.

———. *The Video McLuhan: 1972–1979*. Videorecording. Narrated by Tom Wolfe.
Directed by Matthew Vibert. Toronto, Ont.: McLuhan Productions, 1996.

McLuhan, Marshall and Quentin Fiore. *The Medium Is the Message: An Inventory of
Effects*. London: Penguin Books, 1967.

Mitchell, W.J.T. *Picture Theory: Essays on Verbal and Visual Representation*. Chicago:
University of Chicago Press, 1994.

Montfort, Nick. "Continuous Paper: The Early Materiality and Workings of Electronic Literature." MLA Convention 2004. Philadelphia. December 23, 2004.
http://nickm.com/writing/essays/continuous_paper_mla.html.

Montfort, Nick and Patsy Baudoin, John Bell, Ian Bogost, Jeremy Douglass,
Mark C. Marino, Michael Mateas, Casey Reas, Mark Sample, and Noah Vawter.
10 PRINT CHR$(205.5+RND(1)); : GOTO 10. Cambridge, MA: MIT Press,
2012.

Moradi, Iman with Ant Scott, Joe Gilmore, and Christopher Murphy. *Designing Imperfection*. Mark Batty, 2009.

Moretti, Franco. *Atlas of the European Novel 1800–1900*. 1997. New York: Verso,
2007.

———. *Graphs, Maps, Trees: Abstract Models for a Literary History*. New York: Verso, 2005.

Nietzsche, Friedrich. *Beyond Good and Evil*. New York: Oxford University Press,
2008.

Packard, Vance. *The Hidden Persuaders*. 1957. New York: Ig Publishing. 2007.

Panofsky, Erwin. *Studies in Iconology: Humanistic Themes in the Art of the Renaissance*. Oxford University Press, 1939.

Parikka, Jussi and Tony D. Sampson, eds. *The Spam Book: On Viruses, Porn, and
Other Anomalies from the Dark Side of Digital Culture*. Cresskill, NJ: Hampton
Press, 2009.

———. "On Anomalous Objects of Digital Culture: An Introduction." In *The
Spam Book: On Viruses, Porn, and Other Anomalies from the Dark Side of Digital
Culture*. Cresskill, NJ: Hampton Press, 2009. 1–18.

Paulson, William R. *The Noise of Culture: Literature Texts in a World of Information*.
Ithaca, NY: Cornell University Press, 1988.

Perloff, Marjorie. *Radical Artifice: Writing Poetry in the Age of Media*. Chicago: University of Chicago Press, 1991.

Pinker, Steven. *The Language Instinct: How the Mind Creates Language*. New York: Harper Perennial, 1995. First published in 1994 by William Morrow.

Poole, Robert. *Earthrise: How Man First Saw the Earth*. New Haven: Yale University Press, 2008.

Poundstone, William. *Digital Emblems*. 2001. http://collection.eliterature.org/2/works/poundstone_newdigitalemblems.html.

———. *Priceless: The Myth of Fair Value (and How to Take Advantage of It)*. New York: Hill and Wang, 2010.

———. "Project for Tachistoscope [Bottomless Pit]." 2005. Web. http://collection.eliterature.org/1/works/poundstone_project_for_tachistoscope_bottomless_pit.html.

———. "Spam Poem for Paul Graham." 2005. http://www.williampoundstone.net/Spam/Spam.html.

Pressman, Jessica. *Digital Modernism: Making It New in New Media*. New York: Oxford University Press, 2014.

Salter, Anastasia, and John Murray. *Flash: Building the Interactive Web*. Cambridge, MA: MIT Press, 2014.

Sefton-Green, Julian. "Timelines, Timeframes and Special Effects: Software and Creative Media Production." *Education, Communication & Information* 5.1 (March 2005): 99–110.

Scott, William. "Donald Barthelme and the Death of Fiction." In *Critical Essays on Donald Barthelme*. Ed. Richard F. Patterson. New York: Maxwell Macmillan International, 1992.

Shannon, Claude. "A Mathematical Theory of Communication." *Bell System Technical Journal* 27.3 (1948): 376–423.

Smith, George Horsley. *Motivation Research in Advertising and Marketing*. New York: McGraw-Hill, 1954.

Solt, Mary Ellen. *Concrete Poetry: A World View*. Bloomington, IN: Indiana University Press, 1968.

Stefans, Brian Kim. Interview. "An Interview with William Poundstone." *The Iowa Review Web* 9.1 (2002). http://web.archive.org/web/20131004181052/http://iowareview.uiowa.edu/TIRW/TIRW_Archive/tirweb/feature/poundstone/interview.html.

Stewart, Melissa. "Roads of 'Exquisite Mysterious Muck': The Magical Journey through the City in William Kennedy's Ironweed, John Cheever's 'The Enormous Radio,' and Donald Barthelme's 'City Life.'" In *Magical Realism: Theory, History, Community*. Eds. Lois Parkinson Zamora and Wendy B. Faris. Durham, NC: Duke University Press, 1995.

Templeton, Brad. "Origin of the Term 'Spam' to Mean Net Abuse." Templetons.com. June 30, 2012. http://www.templetons.com/brad/spamterm.html.

Vismann, Cornelia. *Files: Law and Media Technology*. Trans. Geoffrey Winthrop-Young. Stanford: Stanford University Press, 2008.

Waldron, Rick. "How It Began." *Flash Magazine*. November 20, 2000. http://www.flashmagazine.com/news/detail/the_flash_history/.

Whipple, Guy Montrose. *Manual of Mental and Physical Tests*. Baltimore: Warwick & York, 1914.

Wilson, Rawdon. "The Metamorphosis of Fiction Space: Magic Realism." In *Magic Realism: Theory, History, Community*. Eds. Lois Parkinson Zamora and Wendy B. Faris. Durham, NC: Duke University Press, 1995.

Zielinski, Siegfried. *Deep Time of the Media: Toward an Archaeology of Hearing and Seeing by Technical Means*. Trans. Gloria Custance. Cambridge, MA: MIT Press, 2008.

INDEX

absence, 14, 29, 50, 58, 67, 71, 78, 83, 89, 95, 103, 105, 113, 115; of ground sense, 58; of history, 67; of image, 25, 71, 78, 95, 103, 105; of repetition, 113, 115; of source comments, 29; of text, 29, 50, 89, 115; of the Pit, 50, 67, 71, 83. *See also* aporia

abyss. *See* Pit, The Bottomless

academia: in crisis, 74; knowledge work, 140

accidents, 39, 41–42, 73, 119, 129, 142; during collaboration, 142; glitches, 39, 41–42; word conjunctions, 73, 119, 129. *See also* glitch

Acland, Charles, 24–25

ACLS (American Council of Learned Societies), 143, 145

Adobe Systems, 28

advertising, 7, 8, 9–10, 11, 21, 27, 66, 87–89, 98–104, 108, 110, 114, 133, 139; ARF, 98; depth marketing, 98–99; drink Coca-Cola, 10, 98, 102; marketing, 88, 103; motivation research (MR), 98–99, 103; promotions, 66, 110, 114; sloganeering, 9, 58, 102

allegory. *See* literature

animals, 56; blind midge, 53; feral cats, 3, 80; fly, 80; horned lizards, 86; horses, 124; locusts, 86. *See also* birds, bodies

animation, 1, 2, 5, 7, 16, 18–19, 26–28, 31, 32, 37, 40, 43–44, 48, 49, 64, 65, 68, 74–78, 95, 125, 136, 145; key-frames, 16, 27, 64, 76–78

Ankerson, Ingrid, 5

annotation, 33, 80, 142, 143

aporia, 7, 8, 104, 111–115, 118, 120, 132–134, 135; etymology, 111

Apple Computers, 28

archaeology. *See* media archaeology

architecture, 12, 29; ballroom, glass-bottomed, 66–67; casino, 3–4, 6, 65–67, 71, 89; concrete, 119; dams and levees, 43–44; floor, 66–67; homes, 3, 58–59, 82, 94, 130; houses, 3, 11, 54, 55, 58, 67; shantytown, 3; skyscrapers, 51, 58, 85; walls, 6, 82, 115, 118, 125. *See also* construction

ARF (Advertising Research Foundation), 98

art, 5, 6, 8, 10, 11, 14, 15, 19, 25, 26, 40–41, 51, 68, 71, 74, 78, 79, 80–81, 83, 84, 88, 101, 136, 143; assemblage, 14, 58–59, 68, 129; avant-garde, 80–81, 84; biomorphism, 87; born-digital, 6, 8, 135, 136–137, 142, 143; gallery, 81; palimpsests, 12, 15, 33, 44; ready-mades, 14; Unikko (design), 14. *See also* color

astronomy, 3, 72; nebulae, 72; planet, 50; star (flare), 86

audio, 16, 32, 34–36, 47, 116, 117, 131, 142; echoes, 8, 39, 82, 87, 119–120, 123, 126; hearing, 131; inaudible, 78; sonic effects, 33, 35–36, 85; sound, 5, 16, 18, 29, 32–35, 48, 64, 78, 108, 118, 119, 131, 136. *See also* music

avant-garde. *See* art

Barthelme, Donald, 85–87

Bayes, Thomas, 109, 116

Benjamin, Walter, 74–75

Benschop, Ruth, 22

Bersani, Leo, 82

birds, 53, 58–60, 123, 139; cloaca, 115,

collaboration, 1, 21, 61, 74, 92, 134, 135–140, 142–146; comments, 53–54, 141, 142; conversations and intellectual exchanges, 1, 21, 53, 97, 138–141; cowriting and revision, 139–141; epiphanies, 138; sharing, 15, 80, 82, 97, 140–143, 145; voices (individual), 140; vulnerability, 140

computers, 28, 125. *See also* technology

concrete poetry. *See* poetry

construction, 2–4, 29, 49, 54, 58, 59, 60, 63, 64, 65, 66, 67, 69, 70, 71, 87, 89, 94, 119, 123, 124, 125, 126, 130, 131, 132, 146

Conway, Adelia, 79

counterplay. *See* games

Couturier, Maurice, 85

Crary, Jonathan, 24, 43

Critical Code Studies. *See* code

cultural analytics, 135, 136

culture, 7, 9, 10, 11, 23–25, 28, 50, 67, 87–88, 98, 101, 104, 107–109, 114, 136–137

cycles. *See* repetition

de Campos, Augusto and Haraldo, 102

de Certeau, Michel, 51–52

de Peuter, Greig, 41

de Queiroz, Maria José, 102

death, 2, 14, 73, 82, 94, 100, 130; grave, 82; killInterval code, 128; mausoleum, 130; suicide, 73

depth marketing. *See* advertising

Derrida, Jacques, 133–134

Dichter, Ernest, 98

Dietrich, Craig, 143

digital humanities, 37. *See* Critical Code Studies, forensics, humanities, media archaeology, visualization

dimensions, 14, 67–68; axes (x, y), 17, 19; z-axis, 19, 35, 37, 62, 69, 92

disciplines. *See* art, architecture, astronomy, economics, geography, geology, history, humanities, literature, media studies, philosophy, psychology, science

distraction. *See* cognition

drugs, 9, 110; poppy as opiate, 14

Durand, Régis, 85

Dyer-Witheford, Nick, 41

economics, 3, 86, 88–89; businesses, 88–89, 98, 100; capitalism, 6, 11, 28, 65, 87, 88–89, 103–104, 114; casino, 3–4, 65–67, 71, 89; Chamber of Commerce, 50; commodities, 9, 11, 14, 15, 108, 114; consumers, 9, 11, 30, 87–88, 98–99, 100, 103–104; financing, 2, 3, 66; labor, 23, 76–77, 135; markets, 3, 14, 24, 68, 77, 87–88; money, 2, 100, 107, 110; price tags, 88; prices and fees, 3, 6, 88; products, 27, 87, 88–89, 103, 107, 114; property, 50; sales, 3, 4, 10, 88, 103, 114; stock market, 68; trademarks, 89, 107

electronic literature, 1, 5–6, 9, 19, 28, 84, 101, 145; collection (ELC), 6, 101. *See also* literature

ELO (Electronic Literature Organization), 6

endings, 4, 16, 46, 65–66, 76, 80, 86, 89, 115, 122–123, 124, 132, 146; conclusions, 129, 134, 135, 145, 146; stopping, 40, 42, 44, 62, 79, 123, 125, 128

entryscreens. *See* Project for Tachistoscope {Bottomless Pit}

environment, 2, 25, 51, 55, 123; canyons, 53; cliffs, 83; cloudless, 2; Earth, 50–51, 58, 70, 72; ground, 2, 4, 50, 55, 61, 66–67, 70, 89, 100, 113, 119, 123–124; mountains, 54, 56, 58; ocean, 58; river, 43–44, 55, 123; sky, 68, 71–73, 85–86; weather, 3, 56; wind, 86. *See also* nature

errors, 40–41, 94, 109; bugs (code), 28, 40–42, 61; glitch, 41–42, 117

etymologies: aporia, 111; commodius, 123; pigeon-holes, 59; pit, 119; tachistoscope, 22

film, 5, 15–16, 18, 68, 75, 76–77, 88, 103; filmstrip, 16, 64, 68, 92, 103; Monty Python (TV), 107; movies, 10, 35, 68, 98; *Picnic*, 98; reel, 18, 68. *See also* video

Fish, Stanley, 126

Fitzpatrick, Kathleen, 142

Flash, 5, 9, 15–19, 25, 26–31, 32–38, 39–40, 49, 62–65, 75, 76–80, 87, 98, 105, 129, 132–133, 135, 143, 145; as stage, 16, 18–19, 29, 32, 63–64, 86, 132, 141; files (.fla .swf), 15, 18, 28–31, 38, 39, 62–64, 76–78, 129, 143, 145; temporal tactics, 40; tween, 16, 75–78, 133. *See also* code, software

food, 80, 100, 107; beverage, 80, 103; hunger, 103; martini, 11, 88; menus, 88, 107; milk, 99; popcorn, 10, 98; spam (as spiced ham), 107–108. *See also* drugs, spam

forensics, 79, 112, 136; digital forensics, 136; forensic linguistics, 112; lemmatization, 112–113, 115, 119; stylometry, 112; word frequency analysis, 112–113, 118, 138

Foucault, Michel, 25

Freud, Sigmund, 14, 80–83, 98–99

Galloway, Alexander, 109

games, 6, 8, 27, 28, 41, 122; counterplay, 41–42; game studies, 41; in Poundstone's books, 6; surrealist games, 8, 122

garden path sentences. *See* language

Genette, Gerard, 8

geography, 55, 67, 119, 140; America, 10, 23, 25, 53, 55, 85, 87–88, 98–102, 108, 114; Beale Pike, 2, 54–55, 69–70, 94, 122–124, 130; Bluefields, 2, 54–55, 123–124, 130; Brazil, 9; Breezewood, 2, 54, 123–124, 130; Carbondale, 3, 55, 58; cartography, 54, 62; cities, 51–52, 79, 84–85; compass, 3, 37, 54–55, 56, 80, 86; directions, 54–55, 58, 61, 69, 73, 105, 113, 115–116, 124, 139; Latin America, 85; Manhattan, 85; maps, 11, 19, 43–44, 49, 51–55, 56, 58, 60–62, 64, 67, 73, 95, 133, 138–139; Miltown, 54–55; New Lebanon, 3, 54–55, 61; regions, 54–55, 56; roads, 2, 3, 54–55, 88, 131, 132; Roanoke Park, 2, 54, 123–124, 130; streets, 51–52; surveying, 3–4

geology, 2, 3, 50, 54, 56, 61, 69, 79, 86, 123; calcite spars, 88; core samples, 48, 69–70; cracks and deformations, 4, 50, 83, 89; crystalline formations, 119; geologists, 60–61, 66, 71; ground, 2, 4, 50, 55, 61, 67, 70–72, 89, 113, 119; kaolin silica and gabbro, 2; karstland, 2, 55, 123–124, 130; radon, 110–111, 130; sinkholes, 2, 18, 46, 50, 61, 79, 121, 123–124, 127, 130, 132, 134, 146; soil, 2, 55, 70, 119, 123–124, 130; stones, 55, 80; subsidence, 3, 4, 55, 67, 113, 119; subterranean, 80, 99; uranium ore (yellowcake), 119. *See also* Pit

Ginsberg, Allen, 114

glitch, 41–42, 117. *See also* errors, remix

Goriunova, Olga, 41

Graham, Paul, 109

Grusin, Richard, 25–26

Hayles, N. Katherine, 5

hearing. *See* audio

Henkin, David, 108

Heraclitus, 43

history, 2–4, 5–10, 21–27, 29, 37, 41, 49, 54, 59–61, 67, 69, 70, 71, 84, 87, 95,

99, 101, 104, 107–109, 128–129, 136, 141; dates, 5, 55, 101; first-century, 59; medieval, 59, 60, 139; modernism 24, 43, 74, 99, 110; nineteen fifty-seven (coincidence), 101; nineteenth century, 2, 24, 61, 108; Renaissance painting, 51; twentieth century, 22–23, 25; twenty-first century 23–24. *See also* advertising, media history

Hormel Foods, 107

Horsley Smith, George, 98–99

humanities, 74, 137, 143, 146; digital, 137

humor, 123; comedy sketch, 107; euphemism, 122; foolish authority, 131; mockery, 107, 130; nonsense term, 131; parody, 102; puns, 9, 89; scatological, 123

images, 1, 5, 7, 9, 11–14, 16, 18, 22, 25–26, 29, 39, 42–46, 48–50, 59, 61, 62, 63, 64, 65, 67, 68, 69, 70, 71, 74, 75, 87, 90, 91, 92, 93, 94, 95, 97, 103, 110, 116, 126, 136, 138, 141, 142, 145; emblems, 14, 15; icons, 7, 8, 9, 10, 11, 12, 13, 14, 32, 33, 34, 36, 39, 43, 46, 64, 72, 87, 88, 90, 91, 93, 94, 103; illustrations, 11, 14, 18, 44, 53, 59; image-texts, 9, 11, 19, 46, 87, 93–94. *See also* screens, vision, visualization

information theory, 116–118

interactivity, 5, 8, 12, 27, 40, 76, 84, 136, 143, 145; interactors, 31; noninteractive, 40

interpretation, 2–3, 8, 13–14, 18, 31, 42, 44–45, 48–54, 60, 62–63, 70–73, 75, 78, 82–83, 84–86, 90, 92–93, 95, 100, 104, 108, 110, 112, 118–119, 125–126, 130, 133–134, 135–139, 143, 145; criticism, 5, 25, 28, 41, 48–49, 54, 60, 61–62, 74, 76, 80, 83, 100, 103, 108, 131–134, 135–138, 140–146; hermeneutics, 83, 85, 89, 136, 137;

theory, 6, 26, 31, 70, 76, 82–83, 98, 109, 116. *See also* reading

Iowa Review Web, The, 87–88

Jameson, Fredric, 133

Jobs, Steve, 28

Joyce, James, 123

Key, Wilson Bryan, 99–100, 103

Kirschenbaum, Matthew, 17

Kittler, Friedrich, 24–25

Klein, Yves, 81

Kowalski, Evans, 79

language, 11, 26–29, 100, 102, 104, 110, 121, 128, 131, 133; garden path sentences, 123–127, 133; grammar, 46, 109–110, 124; metaphor, 10–11, 15–19, 27, 32, 59–69, 71, 73, 76–77, 89, 98, 104–105, 117, 121; metonymy, 136; nomenclature, 106; noun, 2, 7; paragraphs, 8, 30, 42, 44, 141; rhetoric, 50–51, 103, 111; semantics, 8, 107, 111, 119, 131, 132; semiotics, 2, 4, 11, 88, 100, 115; sentences, 2, 4, 46, 54, 62, 111, 123–126, 127, 130–131, 133, 138; signifiers, 78, 109, 131; speech, 131; synonym, 81; syntax, 110, 124–125; tropes, 13, 18, 83, 133; verb, 7, 126. *See also* humor, literature, poetry, words

languages: English, 102, 113, 115, 131; Greek, 3, 22, 66, 111; Latin, 86, 119, 122; Portuguese, 102

Lanham, Richard, 117

layers. *See* screens

literature, 1, 4, 5–6, 9, 19, 21, 25–26, 28–29, 31, 39, 42, 49, 52, 59, 60–61, 66, 73, 74, 76, 79, 80–81, 84–85, 101, 104, 105, 109, 111, 112, 117, 125, 126, 132–134, 135–138, 143, 145; *A Very Old Man With Enormous Wings*, 85–86; allegory, 4, 59–62, 73, 83, 85–86, 88,

95, 135, 139; deconstruction, 66, 82; defamiliarization, 59, 92, 103; fantasy, 2, 51, 56, 66, 73, 81, 84–85; fiction, 49, 51, 53, 85; *Finnegans Wake*, 123; folk tales, 84–85, 100; foregrounding, 104; genre, 9, 49–50, 59, 83–87, 104, 106, 109, 143; magical realism, 84–85; nonfiction, 6, 88; novels, 5, 137; paratexts, 8–9, 39, 81, 101, 104–105, 109, 111–112; postmodern fiction, 85; prose, 2, 68, 84–85, 110, 114, 126, 140–141; symbolism, 2, 4, 9, 11–14, 16, 19, 24, 29, 50, 73, 80–83, 86, 95, 99–100, 139; *The Balloon*, 85–87; tragedy, 86. *See also* electronic literature, myth, narrative, poetry, text

loops. *See* cycles

Loyer, Erik, 143

Manovich, Lev, 28, 45

marketing. *See* advertising

Márquez, Gabriel García, 85–86

Martial (Marcus Valerius Martialis), 59

McLuhan, Marshall, 25–26, 50–51, 100

meaning: affective, 25; figurative, 11; in code, 80, 106; in crisis (disruption), 59, 84, 87, 118–120; in juxtaposition (alignment), 33, 113, 119–122, 138; meaning-making, 58–59, 81, 118, 125, 138; meaningless, 117, 131; word-by-word, 124–125

media, 4, 6, 9, 10, 21–22, 24–26, 31, 39, 41, 45, 50, 59–60, 73–74, 81, 83, 88, 92, 95, 100, 102–104, 116–118, 135–140, 143; acetate, 16; books, 6, 59–60, 69, 74, 135, 143, 145; CD-ROM, 27; celluloid film, 68, 103; e-mail (inbox), 1, 97, 107–110, 116, 140–141, 142; materiality, 41; microscope, 74; multimedia, 6, 145; multimodal, 31, 32, 61, 100, 124, 136, 142–143, 145; pages, 27–28, 44–45, 48, 60, 64, 67–69, 81, 102–103, 116, 121; paper,

21, 66, 86; telephone, 8; telescope, 72; television, 41, 59, 72, 116. *See also* remediation, technology

media archaeology, 22, 25–26, 43, 62, 88, 135, 136, 139

media ecology, 4, 25, 60, 62, 73–74

media history, 6, 21–22, 24–26, 59, 95

media studies, 25, 41, 50, 100

media-specific analysis (MSA), 18, 21, 45, 48, 60, 62

media visualization. *See* visualization

mediation, 15, 21, 32, 41, 67, 75, 103–104, 116–118, 126, 133, 135

military, 22, 131, 139; Army and Navy, 23; bomb, 6, 11; Cold War, 98–99, 101, 131;

panjandrum (siege-cart), 110, 130–131

Miller, Lucas, 143

Milton, John, 126

mind. *See* cognition

modernism, 24, 43, 74, 99, 110

montage view. *See* visualization

Monty Python, 107

Moretti, Franco, 49, 51

music, 2, 32–36, 39, 47, 81, 100, 107; instruments, notes, and chords (cello, flute, organ) 34–36; jazz, 35. *See also* audio

myth, 6, 72, 84–85, 88; Icarus, 52; legends, 72, 110; spirits, 72, 122; supernatural, 73, 85, 89; tall tales, 10, 84–87. *See also* religion

narrative, 2–4, 6, 9–10, 11, 15, 18, 30, 32, 45, 49–50, 54–56, 58, 60–62, 65–67, 71–73, 80–83, 84–85, 87–89, 90–91, 94, 105–106, 114, 116, 123, 126, 129–130, 132, 134, 138–139, 145–146; diegesis, 3, 18, 60, 67, 71, 84, 126, 138; nonnarrative, 129. *See also* literature, myth

nature, 19, 28, 41, 43, 46, 48, 50–51, 66,

99, 106, 118, 120, 123, 137; biohazard, 12–14, 44, 93; biomorphism,
87; flowers, 12–13; native, 119; trees,
69, 82, 125; vineyard, 82. *See also*
environment

Neumann. *See* von Neumann, John

new media, 26, 136. *See also* electronic
literature, media

nidificatory limit, 53–54, 58–59, 60, 62,
64, 82, 123, 138. *See also* birds

Noigandres, 102

noise, 33, 36, 105, 111, 115, 116–118,
132; static, 115, 116, 118–119. *See also*
audio, vision

Oulipo (Ouvroir de littérature potenti-
elle), 8, 111

Packard, Vance, 99–101

Paik, Nam June, 41

paradox, 61; aporia as, 111, 133; of
word-image containment, 14; of
modernity, 24; of pre-failure, 67; of
non-repetition, 120; of spam mail,
108; of stasis and mobility, 43–44

Parikka, Jussi, 109

Paulson, William, 117

Perloff, Marjorie, 117–118

Peuter. *See* de Peuter, Greig

philosophy, 3, 4, 111; epistemology, 2–3,
24; ontology, 3, 138

photography, 18, 50–51, 77, 88, 90, 92,
103, 141; long-exposure, 90, 92

Pignatari, Décio, 9, 102–103, 114–115,
123

Pinker, Steven, 124–126

Pit, The Bottomless, 2–4, 7–8, 10, 13,
18–19, 30–31, 43, 49, 50–67, 70–74,
78–91, 93–95, 98, 101, 106, 107,
113–115, 119–120, 123, 126, 130–135,
138, 146; abyss, 2, 54, 66, 71, 81;
agency of, 55; as enigma, 2, 56,
73–74, 84–85; as void, 81, 103; attrac-

tion of, 56, 83, 88–89; bottomlessness, 66–67; chasm, 2, 48, 94, 119;
consuming, 93; edgeless, 90; edges,
3, 56, 65, 89, 91, 94–95; etymology,
119; fragments, 3; rim, 3–4, 11, 13, 61,
70, 72, 80, 86, 89–95, 109, 133; Well
of Conklin, 72. *See also* geology

platform studies, 39, 136, 145–146;
platforms, 18, 28, 40, 77, 79, 87, 136,
140, 143, 145. *See also* Flash

poetry, 2, 7–10, 42, 45–46, 48, 49, 78,
81, 85, 89, 101–104, 106, 109–110,
111, 114, 116–118, 120, 123, 126, 131,
133, 137; concrete poetry, 7–9, 81,
101–104, 110, 118, 120, 133; couplets,
45; Dada, 122; enjambment, 46;
Howl, 114; *I Remember*, 114; Oulipo,
8, 111; PoemsThatGo, 5; poetics, 2,
5–10, 13, 15, 18, 19, 21, 25–26, 31, 33,
36, 38–39, 44, 48, 52, 53, 56, 60–61,
72–74, 77–78, 80–81, 84, 87–89, 95,
101, 103–104, 106–107, 109, 110, 114,
116–118, 121–122, 125–126, 129–130,
132–136, 138, 139, 146; prose poetry,
114; rhyme, 118–119, 131; rhythm, 2,
12, 32, 34, 46–47, 131; stanzas, 44–48,
68; surrealism, 110, 122; techno-
poetics, 25, 132, 135; tension, 2, 9, 48,
56, 61, 65, 70. *See also* literature

Pollock, Jackson, 80

Poundstone, William: author statement
and entryscreens, 9–10, 30, 39, 80,
101, 104, 132; authorial code, 21, 31,
32–37, 77, 78, 80, 105–106, 129, 132;
books, 6; coinage of 'nidificatory,' 58;
comments, 33, 34, 36–37; electronic
literature, 5, 9, 109; interview, 87–88;
Spam Poem, 109–110, 116; writing
style, 2, 6, 86, 88, 111, 133

priming. *See* semantic priming

programming, 15–19, 27–29, 62, 64–65,
76–77, 80, 105–106, 129; programmer-artist, 76, 105–106

141; radio, 116; satellites (*Sputnik*), 50–51; satellite dish, 58, 59; winch, 53; X-ray, 79, 93. *See also* computers, media, Tachistoscope

Templeton, Brad, 107

text, fonts, 14; illegible, 39, 81, 130; notes (records), 60, 78, 141; typescript, 121; typography, 87. *See also* literature

Thacker, Eugene, 109

threshold volume view. *See* visualization

tween. *See* code

Vicary, James M., 10, 25, 98–99, 101–103, 114, 131

video, 40, 43–45, 68–69, 97, 116, 140, 143; movie clips (Project), 31, 33–35, 37, 63–64, 78. *See also* animation, film

vision, 3–5, 9, 10–19, 22–24, 26, 27, 36, 37, 38, 42, 43, 44, 45, 46, 47, 48, 49, 50, 51, 52, 56, 58, 59, 60, 63, 64, 65, 66, 67, 68, 69, 70, 71, 72, 73, 74, 75, 76, 77, 78, 81, 83, 85, 86, 87, 90, 91, 93, 94, 95, 99, 101, 117, 118, 121, 126, 129, 130, 133, 138, 142, 146; gaze, 25, 38, 66, 71, 72, 73, 86, 94; illusions, 3, 27, 56, 73, 77, 100; invisible, 12, 19, 64, 81, 99, 104–105, 141; ocular devices, 26; optics, 22, 36, 37, 54, 66, 72–77; perspective, 2, 21, 48, 49, 51–53, 61, 65, 66, 71, 73, 85, 95, 129, 137; seeing, 1, 3, 9, 24, 28, 39, 41, 44, 46, 47, 49–51, 55, 58, 64, 65, 70, 72–75, 77, 82, 97, 98, 104, 133; thresholds of perception, 22, 52, 133; training, 22–24, 32, 59, 139

visualization, 1, 12, 44–47, 48–52, 65, 67–71, 74–76, 78, 89–93, 120, 134, 135, 137, 138, 143, 145; media visualizations, 45; montage, 1, 43–48, 51, 52, 67–70, 74, 90, 93, 120, 136, 143; proto-graphic, 53; slice, 62, 68, 90–91, 93–94; threshold volume, 70–71, 91; volume view, 65, 67–71, 73, 74, 90–94; z-projection, 89–93

Volkmann, Alfred W., 22–23

volume view. *See* visualization

von Neumann, John, 6

Weaver, Warren, 116

web, 24, 26–28, 38, 40, 64, 87–88, 106, 109, 142–145

Whipple, Guy Montrose, 23

Williams, William Carlos, 110, 115

Wilson, Rawdon, 84

word frequency analysis. *See* forensics

words, 1, 2, 7, 9–15, 19, 22–24, 26, 30, 31, 35–39, 41, 43–49, 51, 59, 61, 64, 66, 68, 70, 72, 76, 79–80, 87, 89, 95, 97–115, 117–125, 127–133, 135, 138, 142; acronyms, 111, 130; alphabetical, 110; capitals, 7, 12, 27; etymology, 22, 59, 111, 119, 123; letters, 7, 13, 23, 38, 110, 120, 137; panjandrum, 110, 130, 131; portmanteau, 27, 107; stems (roots), 115, 119; syllables, 23, 45, 130

Workbench (ACLS), 142–145

YHCHI (Young-Hae Chang Heavy Industries), 5

z-projection. *See* visualization

CONTEMPORARY NORTH AMERICAN POETRY SERIES

Racial Things, Racial Forms: Objecthood in Avant-Garde Asian American Poetry
BY JOSEPH JONGHYUN JEON

We Saw the Light: Conversations between the New American Cinema and Poetry
BY DANIEL KANE

History, Memory, and the Literary Left: Modern American Poetry, 1935–1968
BY JOHN LOWNEY

Paracritical Hinge: Essays, Talks, Notes, Interviews
BY NATHANIEL MACKEY
UNIVERSITY OF WISCONSIN PRESS, 2004

Behind the Lines: War Resistance Poetry on the American Homefront
BY PHILIP METRES

Hold-Outs: The Los Angeles Poetry Renaissance, 1948–1992
BY BILL MOHR

In Visible Movement: Nuyorican Poetry from the Sixties to Slam
BY URAYOÁN NOEL

Frank O'Hara: The Poetics of Coterie
BY LYTLE SHAW

*Renegade Poetics: Black Aesthetics and Formal Innovation
in African American Poetry*
BY EVIE SHOCKLEY

Radical Vernacular: Lorine Niedecker and the Poetics of Place
EDITED BY ELIZABETH WILLIS